PRAISE FOR THE PRICE OF FORGIVENESS

"Passionately advocates for individuals in need while highlighting that bankruptcy is far from a black and white process."

— *BOOKLIFE* BY *PUBLISHER'S WEEKLY*

"A deeply personal account of a life led in service of the law as well as a forcefully presented and thoughtfully written account of debt in modern America."

— *KIRKUS REVIEWS*

"Humanizes the bankruptcy experience in a way that's accessible and clear."

— NANCY B. RAPOPORT, JD, UNLV DISTINGUISHED PROFESSOR, SPEAKER ON BANKRUPTCY ETHICS

"Informative, humorous, and compassionate."

— *FOREWORD* CLARION REVIEWS

"A pleasurable read."

— BARBARA H. MURPHY, AWARD-WINNING CERTIFIED PROFESSIONAL GEOLOGIST AND FORMER NATIONAL PRESIDENT OF AIPG

THE PRICE OF FORGIVENESS

THE PRICE OF FORGIVENESS

DEBT, BANKRUPTCY, AND THE FUTURE OF FAIRNESS IN AMERICA

SARAH SHARER CURLEY

INTREPID
PUBLISHING

INTREPID PUBLISHING
A Division of Intrepid Literary, Inc.
New York, NY
intrepidpublishinggroup.com
intrepidliterary.com

Cover Design by Lauren Harms

First Edition

Hardcover ISBN: 978-1-972992-06-7
Paperback ISBN: 978-1-972992-05-0
Ebook ISBN: 978-1-972992-00-5

For Kiernan, Rachael, and Sheridan

CONTENTS

"Capitalism without bankruptcy is like Christianity without hell."

Frank Borman, CEO of Eastern Air Lines

AUTHOR'S NOTE

Drawing on my experiences as an attorney, the cases I've presided over as a judge, and my current work as a legal commentator, I've sought to shed light on the many people and companies who find themselves navigating bankruptcy.

In some chapters, I share my own connection to certain cases—whether I represented a client as their lawyer or oversaw the matter from the bench. All information described is drawn from the public record; no confidential or non-public details have been disclosed. Wherever possible, I've included footnotes and references to court decisions and governmental records. My recollections of hearings I attended or presided over are based on official decisions and docket entries. In some instances, to protect privacy or maintain anonymity, I've used pseudonyms or slightly modified identifying characteristics and facts.

In other chapters, I step back to explore the broader history and current landscape of bankruptcy law, offering commentary and my opinion on how the system operates today—and how I believe it could evolve for the better. These perspectives are grounded in my professional experience, as well as in statutes and well-known public cases that have recently shaped the field.

Some of the terminology may feel antiquated or unfamiliar. Where that's the case, I've added footnotes to explain key concepts and a bibliography at the end for readers who wish to dig deeper into the cases and articles that inform this work in greater depth.

PROLOGUE

Bankruptcy affects every stratum of society—from the very wealthy and politically savvy to the impoverished who depend on kidney dialysis to stay alive. The bankruptcy system does work, but the inequities in the system are not easily solved. Lobbying efforts by powerful groups, such as landlords, credit card companies, or financial institutions, who want higher rates of return regardless of consequences, have dictated a shift in the bankruptcy law from focusing on debt-free fresh starts for debtors to favoring creditors' control of the bankruptcy system.

Recent high-profile bankruptcies reflect the unfairness or fraud in the system. LTL Management (the Johnson & Johnson subsidiary that manufactured baby products with talc, a carcinogen), Purdue Pharma (the Sackler family's company that sold opiates), Alex Jones's InfoWars (Jones's attacks on the Sandy Hook Elementary School families), and Boy Scouts of America (allegations that over 7,800 leaders were involved in sexually abusing children in their care for over 78 years) have used different techniques to allow individuals who control entities to have not only their companies' debts forgiven, but also to get a pass on any responsibility they may have to their victims. Although in a recent decision, the United States Supreme Court justices concluded that any forgiveness of an individual's responsibility for egregious conduct must be with the consent of the victims, it is unclear how the victims will be treated fairly and compassionately in the future.

In this book, I outline lessons to be learned from the cases that were assigned to me as well as cases that are in the news. In the final part of the book, I discuss how you can be proactive, advocating for changes in the bankruptcy system to make it more equitable for you and the average American.

PART ONE
LISTENING AND LEARNING

CHAPTER ONE

THE BANKRUPT THAT COULDN'T

From the time I was a child, my father railed against the legal profession. An accomplished surgeon at a Chicago hospital, he never forgot a railroad worker he tried to treat in the mid-sixties. The worker had been injured while uncoupling a railroad car and had fallen under the wheels of the train. Both of his legs were cleanly amputated around his knees; the worker's legs had been found and preserved by a medical team. My father advised the patient that complete recovery was possible but that the surgery needed to be done immediately. Otherwise, the worker's preserved legs would atrophy and could not be surgically attached. The patient would never walk again.

The railroad worker consulted a lawyer who advised the worker to wait for the court case to wind its way to trial. If the worker were wheeled into the courtroom with just his stumps for legs, the jury would be more sympathetic and award more money in damages. Dad was livid when he learned of the lawyer's advice. "Think of your quality of life," he begged his patient. He described what he thought could be achieved through surgery and what the patient would enjoy, over the long term, if he had two functional legs. The patient did not listen.

After many delays, the trial was finally held a year and a half after the accident. The patient was wheeled into the courtroom and was ultimately awarded a modest amount of money. He never walked again. My father filed a complaint against the lawyer with the disciplinary commission of the Illinois Supreme Court, but nothing ever came of his complaint.

I had the same drive as my father, and I was determined to make a difference. By the summer of 1973, I had graduated from college and was working for a not-for-profit company in New York that was providing knowledge and expertise to business executives around the world. As an administrative assistant, I was trapped in a no-woman's land. The monotony of my day numbed my mind—I was getting coffee, being deferential, preparing letters, and arranging schedules for the male executives who got to travel the world.

I was destroying myself from the inside out. I developed severe stomach pains. When I could no longer stand it, I visited an internist in Manhattan, who recommended that I eat bland food.

"A bland food diet will never resolve any underlying issues," my father told me when I repeated the internist's advice over the phone. "What do you want to do with your life?"

I paused. "I want to make a difference," I told him.

"Figure out what you want to do long-term—not what others want you to do. Then take that direction."

I had toyed with getting an MBA, but if I went to law school, I could combine my interests in law and business. Of course, when I advised him that I wanted to attend law school, he was adamant that I try some other—any other—profession. I refused.

"I'm not going to pay for law school," he warned me.

"I'll pay for it myself," I said.

"Why won't you listen to me on this one, Sarah?"

"Because you encouraged me to think for myself," I said. We were both stubborn, independent people.

MY HUSBAND, Roger, was in his third year at NYU Law, and I matriculated at New York Law School as one of its older students. Although in some graduate programs at the time, the female enrollment was close to 50 percent, the law schools lagged far behind. Only 25 percent of my law school class was female.

In my first-year torts class, I was presented with a textbook that included a helpful cartoon at the top of a little man holding a package who looked like he had wandered off the board of a Monopoly game. He was jumping onto a moving train just as the train workers on the train and platform, respectively, were pulling and pushing him on board. The caption explained that as the little man was finally getting his footing on board, he dropped his package, which exploded on the tracks. The explosion caused a clock on the opposite side of the platform to fall off the wall, hitting a waiting passenger on the head.

"Was the railroad liable because of the conduct of its employees in pushing the little man on a moving train?"[1] the professor asked us. "No," he continued, before we could answer. "How could the railroad have foreseen that the little man would be jumping on a train with explosives in a package that would knock a woman silly on the opposite side of the tracks?"

Really? I thought. *I paid a third of my yearly salary as a secretary*

1. Palsgraf v. Long Island R. Co., 248 N.Y. 399 (Ct of Appeals 1928).

to listen to this nonsense? I needed an immediate course correction.

In my first year, I also took required courses in property, contracts, and criminal law. We explored the Anglo-Saxon tradition of the father transferring his real property or estate to his oldest son, how contracts always had to have a meeting of the minds, and the difficulty of convicting a murderer if all of the suspects were on a lifeboat together. I did not want to spend a lifetime considering such issues.

In high school and college, I had always done well in math and courses based on logic. By my second year in law school, I had taken courses in income tax and securities regulation. Both the internal revenue code and the security laws have rules associated with them that explain the statutes—most law students find this very boring. To me, it was very logical. But I had a fear I would end up in an eight-foot by eight-foot cubicle with no windows and only a small door to let me out.

Thinking that business issues might add some spice to the law, I signed up for a summer school course in bankruptcy law. That same summer, I was also selected to be in a judicial clerkship program based on my grade-point average and academic standing. I knew of no women in the bankruptcy field, at the law school or among any of the acquaintances I had in the legal community. Perhaps bankruptcy offered an opportunity to advance my career at a more rapid rate given the male dominance in the field.

In the summer of 1976, I felt as if the stars had aligned. At last, I was taking a course that didn't put me to sleep every time I read a few pages after dinner, and I was a student law clerk to bankruptcy judge Edward J. Ryan. The World Trade Center Towers, near the tip of Manhattan, were under construction.

At the time, the bankruptcy court was located within walking distance of the Towers, just south of Little Italy. The bankruptcy court was on the first floor of the venerable but utilitarian-looking federal courthouse at Foley Square, next door to the classically stylish state court building. On Tuesday afternoons or Friday mornings, I would stroll from the law school a few blocks east to the federal courthouse. I had found my niche.

One day, while I was in chambers, Judge Ryan told me and the other law clerks the story of a well-known criminal who had decided to seek relief from all of his enemies by filing a bankruptcy petition in this court decades earlier. Of course, the criminal had to attend the meeting with his creditors, which would take place in the courthouse and was open to the public. The criminal was concerned about facing his creditors. The public meeting meant his enemies might be there.

"Yet," the judge advised, "he still wanted forgiveness of his debts, just like anybody else."

The fatal day arrived. The man arrived at his appointed time and waited patiently in the courtroom for his case to be called. When it was, he walked forward toward the witness stand to be sworn in and looked his creditors in the eye. As he glanced at the crowd, he saw a few familiar faces. Fear suddenly took hold of him, and he visibly shook. Several men ran forward, firing handguns. He hightailed it from the witness stand, right behind the judge and court staff, into the judge's chambers. He quickly dismissed his bankruptcy case, and no one saw him again.

We were incredulous until Judge Ryan led us into his courtroom and showed us the bullet holes from long ago that were still in the wall. There was no security in those days. The judge said he was a young man at the time and still remembered the incident. A shoot-out in a courtroom. Law was filled with surprises.

THE WEALTHY HAD a different approach to bankruptcy. One example was the case of Adela Holzer, known as the Angel of Broadway, where dreams were born and, sometimes, died an early death. She had produced a string of hits, including *Hair*, *Sleuth*, and *The Ritz*. She claimed to be an international entrepreneur and threw lavish dinner parties and elegant soirees at her townhouse in Manhattan. In fact, she was engaged in a Ponzi scheme, using the funds of new investors to pay off those investors who had demanded an immediate return of their money.

In the summer of 1977, Ms. Holzer's creditors filed an involuntary petition against her, trying to force her into a bankruptcy proceeding, alleging fraud. Judge Ryan, while I was still serving as his law clerk, was assigned to her case. Holzer was accused of defrauding investors of $2,300,000 (about $11 million in 2022). The creditors wanted an independent bankruptcy trustee to take control and sort things out.

Ms. Holzer denied engaging in any fraud. She was vague about what she owned and where it was located. She also could not recall the names of, or pertinent information about, her creditors. Of particular importance was a potentially valuable painting that seemed to have disappeared. Ms. Holzer was directed to appear before the court and her creditors. Would she be forced into bankruptcy, or would she simply breeze in and out, returning to her glamorous lifestyle?

Although I was not there because, to my utter regret, I had to attend some law school classes, the reports from lawyers and staff on the scene were that her courtroom appearance was high drama. The courtroom was packed, standing room only. Lawyers and the curious public flowed into the surrounding hallways. She was reportedly dressed to the nines, a nod to her love of haute couture. The creditors crowded the table near Judge Ryan's bench and the witness stand where Ms. Holzer was perfectly poised. The creditors pressed her to reveal the location of the painting. The lady remained vague.

The creditors asked Judge Ryan to direct her to answer the question.

"We're here on a serious matter," Judge Ryan told Holzer. "You need to answer the reasonable questions of your creditors."

The lady was unmoved.

"If you do not answer," the judge said, "there will be repercussions." Holzer refused to answer. More stern admonitions from the judge followed. Silence from the witness stand. The courtroom became tense. The exchange seemed to indicate that there would be no resolution as to the mystery of the disappearing painting, or anything else for that matter.

Judge Ryan gave a final warning. "Ms. Holzer, if you do not answer the question as to the location of the painting, I will certify you in civil contempt of court. You will be arrested and remain in federal custody until you do answer the question. Do you understand?"

"I understand," she said, "but I choose not to answer the question."

Then Judge Ryan's voice reverberated throughout the courtroom: "Ms. Holzer, you are certified in civil contempt of this court. You are under arrest." She was led by the court security officers out of the courtroom, down the packed corridors, to the nearest elevator, where she was taken to the courthouse holding cell for the recalcitrant.

The afternoon newspapers were saddened to report that the angel was in custody. Who would finance Broadway shows? Who would have ever thought that a bankruptcy judge would hold her in contempt of court and have her arrested?

In August, Judge Ryan found that the creditors had cause to force Ms. Holzer into bankruptcy because of her fraudulent acts. The bankruptcy trustee assembled her assets—including her brownstone where she resided—and sold them to pay creditors. Ms. Holzer was later convicted in state court of grand larceny of her investors and other crimes involving immigrants and her promises to provide them with green cards. She ultimately served fourteen years in prison. She had lost her empire, but she maintained her innocence and was a hot topic in the lifestyle section.

On the streets of Manhattan, Roger and I walked to the small market nearby, our metal grocery cart in tow. We purchased one-day-old bread and the makings of spaghetti. From our living room, we had a view of the Empire State Building only because the building directly across the street from us had burned down in a fire. Only the charred remains of the foundation remained, protruding from the rocky earth. I wore jeans and sweatshirts to law school. For my student clerkship, I purchased an emerald-green shirtwaist dress, a pale orange shirt and matching skirt, and a green-and-white striped top that I layered over a matching mid-calf-length skirt. I washed my three work outfits in the basement laundromat where I lived.

During my student clerkship, I attended court hearings or read court documents that allowed me to understand all types of consumer and business cases. We used to say that every day brought us the $1.98 problem as well as the $10 million problem. And every problem, no matter how small in monetary value, required our full attention.

I thought about the many who filed bankruptcy petitions who were worse off than I. Perhaps they had medical issues and couldn't keep up with their payments for medication and their mortgage. Perhaps they had graduated from college or law school, had incurred debts, but had not yet found a job. Perhaps their building in Brooklyn or the Bronx had burned down, and they were living on the street. Who would help those individuals? Everyone deserves to be treated with dignity and respect. I was determined to help if given the chance.

I thought of my father who had become a general surgeon rather than taking on the sophisticated, more remunerative practice of a specialist. My father loved being a general surgeon, even though he spent 90 percent of his time on routine matters. It was the unexpected, the surprises, in 10 percent of his cases that kept him going. It was going to a hospital at 2:00 a.m. for emergency surgery, not knowing the severity of the injury until the surgery was well underway.

I thought of bankruptcy as being the emergency room of the law. A lot of what I would see would be routine, but it was the other 10 percent that would show up occasionally that would keep me engaged for a lifetime.

THE CONCEPT of debt has always been a part of our lives. Five thousand years ago, ancient civilizations relied on the existence of debt, whether it was a personal obligation owed by one family member or friend to another, or a sum that one party owed another, recorded in one of the formal ledgers created in Mesopotamia (circa 3500 BC) or pharaonic Egypt.

Bankruptcy is a more recent system of settling one's debts, but it existed in our colonies before the United States was ever formed. In colonial times, the moral shame of not paying one's debts led to individuals being placed in stocks or being marked in some manner with a mark to the hand or an ear nailed to a post. The bankruptcy laws depended somewhat on the foreign country that settled the colony. For instance, England enacted a law concerning the transfer of property as a fraudulent conveyance, which could be unwound if the person became insolvent or bankrupt, as early as 1571 under the reign of Elizabeth I.[2]

2. A classic case that law students learn about in a basic bankruptcy class in the United States is In re Twyne's Case (1601), 3 Coke 80b, 76 ER 809, in which an individual being pursued by creditors pretended to transfer all of his property (including his sheep) to another party. However, when the wily creditors viewed his pasture and environs, they found that Twyne was a scoundrel and had retained possession and control of his property. The scheme was

Bankruptcy was such an important part of our culture that on June 21, 1788, when the Constitution was ratified, the United States Congress was charged with enacting uniform laws on bankruptcy.[3] From the founding of the US, bankruptcy has always involved forgiving debt; distributing the bankrupt's assets, in a fair manner, to all creditors; stopping individual creditors from seizing the bankrupt's assets for themselves; forcing certain creditors to accept what the debtor was proposing to pay creditors in a plan; and selling assets if that seems the best way to benefit everyone.

Over the next 110 years, Congress enacted bankruptcy laws—usually when there was some type of financial crisis—only to repeal them. The crisis had passed, or Congress thought the law was too generous to creditors, bankruptcy had become too expensive, or the system needed to be abolished because of rampant corruption.[4] When the Bankruptcy Act of 1898 was enacted, it finally provided stability to those commencing bankruptcy cases and to their creditors. It remained in place, with some amendments over the years, [5]

---

presented to the court, and the court ruled against Twyne, his fraudulent transfers undone!

3. See Article I, Section 8 of the US Constitution. The Bill of Rights, or the first ten amendments to the US Constitution, were not ratified until December 15, 1791.

4. The first bankruptcy law, the Bankruptcy Act of 1800, resulted from the financial panic from 1792–1797. The Bankruptcy Act of 1867 was enacted following the financial crisis of 1857. The Bankruptcy Act of 1800 was deemed too pro-creditor, as was the Bankruptcy Act of 1867, which only provided a "discharge," or forgiveness of debt, to one-third of the debtors that commenced bankruptcy cases. The Bankruptcy Act of 1841 was repealed because of the expenses incurred by the parties and the corruption that was rampant in the system.

5. For instance, the Chandler Act of 1934 resulted from the Great Depression and the inability of municipalities to pay their debts as they came due. This led to the inclusion of Chapter IX in the Bankruptcy Act, which allowed municipalities to commence bankruptcy proceedings. The Chandler Act, however, was ruled unconstitutional by the US Supreme Court because it violated the Tenth Amendment to the US Constitution, allowing judges too

until the 1970s when, at the request of Congress, a commission was formed of judges, scholars, and practitioners to overhaul the system.

I became a law clerk at a turning point in bankruptcy law, which meant I had to learn the existing system as well as what was being proposed. The language and procedures in the bankruptcy system were different from most of what I had learned so far in law school.

The idea of creating an estate from which creditors would be paid reminded me of what happened when someone died and the assets were gathered to pay creditors, with the balance going to family members. I had learned quite a bit about how to pass assets on to family members and what happened when someone died without a will. Roger, my husband, had become an estate planning lawyer at a Wall Street law firm, so I had been regaled with stories that now made sense to me as I studied bankruptcy law.

There was also a bankruptcy trustee, whose duties seemed similar to those of a trustee who was appointed to take control of the assets of a wealthy or deceased individual. In bankruptcy, unusual documents were filed with the court, but it reminded me of how one handled a decedent's estate. Bankruptcy proceedings had the feeling of being in the land of the living dead.

Once the individual or corporation decided to file a bankruptcy case, they had to decide what relief they wanted and how long they wanted to be under the supervision of the bankruptcy court. The chapters outlined what to expect and when they would finally, if appropriate, be forgiven of their debts.

---

much discretion in the operations of the municipality, a power solely reserved to the States.

Later amendments to the bankruptcy law taking away some of the judicial discretion and, quite frankly, a change in the makeup of the US Supreme Court allowed municipalities to commence their bankruptcy cases.

The new bankruptcy law simplified the ability of individuals, companies, or partnerships to have a "fresh start," which was the phrase used for forgiveness of debt. The liquidation proceedings under the old law, the Bankruptcy Act, and the proposed new law, the Bankruptcy Code, were very similar. Gather the assets, pay creditors, and if anything was left, turn it over to the company or the individual.

However, under the new law, there was a simplification of the bankruptcy process. The Bankruptcy Code combined the reorganization chapters of public companies, smaller companies, and real estate partnerships or entities into one chapter, chapter 11. Wealthy individuals who seemed to have the ability to deal with the complexities of bankruptcy were also placed in chapter 11.

Individuals who were employed and had the financial ability to pay their creditors something had their own separate chapter, chapter 13. Given the unique needs of family farmers and fishermen, who had dramatic cyclical changes in their incomes, they were placed in their own chapter 12. Finally, municipalities, which were required to provide public services no matter how dire their financial circumstances, were placed in chapter 9.

What I loved about any reorganization proceeding was the eternal optimism of those in control. They would argue that if they just had a few dollars, they could dig themselves out of any problem. The businesses were endlessly fascinating. From 1870–1894, roughly six hundred railroads filed bankruptcy cases. Bankruptcy allowed the railroads to continue to operate and quickly transport consumer goods, commodities, and cargo to a honeycomb of cities and towns in a growing economy. However, on June 21, 1970, the bankruptcy system was tested to the breaking point. Penn Central, the country's largest railroad, filed the largest bankruptcy case at the time, shocking the financial markets. In 1968, the nation's two rival railroads, the New York Central and the Pennsylvania Railroad, had merged. Penn Central, the newly created behemoth, became the sixth largest US company. It had an extensive real estate portfolio and controlled more than twenty thousand miles of track. It carried one-eighth of the nation's freight, and its network spread from St. Louis to Chicago, Montreal, and Boston. The merger did not create a nimble company. Freight cars were lost, and switchyards were backed up with passenger and freight traffic. Management failed at many levels. Losses soared, and stock prices headed for the basement. The government tried to save the company, but the concept of "too big to fail" had not yet been invented. Bankruptcy awaited. A little over a decade later, Penn Central was transformed into the Consolidated Rail Corporation, with the US Department of Transportation selecting investment bankers to sell $1.6 billion, or 85 percent, of the new company's stock in a public offering that pulled the railroad from an inglorious defeat. When the new bankruptcy law took effect, railroad reorganization proceedings were included, reflecting the importance of keeping the railroads operating.[6]

There were local grocery stores that needed some help because mammoth grocery chains were coming on the scene, dramatically dropping prices that smaller stores or chains could not match. And then there was the fashion district! A top designer who had many chic fashions and New York runway shows found that his clothing manufacturer had encountered financial difficulties and had filed a bankruptcy petition. It was a way to see the latest fashions without leaving the bankruptcy court.

I began to see a difference in how the wealthy seemed to breeze through bankruptcy. One winter's day while I was a student law clerk, I overheard elevated voices through the

---

6. The railroads filed under Section 77 of the Bankruptcy Act, with receivers rather than trustees controlling their operations. The Bankruptcy Code has a special section of chapter 11 for railroads.

chamber's doors. I went through the hallway and headed into the back of the courtroom. At the front of the courtroom was a woman on the witness stand wearing a mid-calf length mink coat. She clutched a custom Gucci handbag in her gloved hands. At the podium was the bankruptcy trustee asking the woman some questions about her assets, including the coat and purse that she had brought to court that day. The trustee asked the judge if he might approach the woman so that he could more closely examine the coat and purse. The request was granted. The trustee asked the woman to remove her coat. He looked at the label and stroked the luxurious pelts. He also examined the purse's Gucci trademark, looked at the label, and patted the leather. He took the coat and the purse back to the table near the podium.

"Judge, I want the debtor to turn over her coat and purse to me today. These are luxury assets which should be sold immediately to help pay her creditors."

The courtroom was silent. The judge seemed to be pondering next steps. He couldn't send her out on a cold, snowy day with no coat and no purse. The woman must have read his thoughts. She protested the indignity of being undressed in a courtroom.

The judge turned to the woman, who had reseated herself on the witness stand. He explained to her that under bankruptcy law, a debtor was allowed to keep certain items to clothe and feed herself. A warm winter coat or a utilitarian handbag to carry the essentials of life were certainly permissible. The mink coat and Gucci bag were not. He ordered the trustee to follow the debtor home to her Manhattan town home, at which point, she was to surrender the mink coat and Gucci bag to the trustee. The judge then decided to take a short break while the trustee closely followed the woman, her mink coat, and Gucci bag out of the courtroom.

The wealthy owned many homes, but their explanation for filing bankruptcy was that their investments were not performing as anticipated. The value of their assets far exceeded the amount of their liabilities. But for *some quirk of fate*, as they described it, they had insufficient funds on hand to pay their staffs, taxes, mortgages, pilots, or lease payments on the corporate jets.

They sighed. They needed a break from their creditors—a chance to collect their breath—before creditors seized their assets. Bankruptcy was just the ticket. Many filed bankruptcy petitions for what they described as "technical difficulties."

In contrast, the average consumer was just trying to pay the rent, gas or electric bill, and stay employed. There were stories of those who had medical expenses or had lost their jobs and just needed a chance to restart their lives, yet creditors seemed suspicious of consumer debtors' motives as to why they filed. The creditors set up more hearings to question the consumer debtors under oath or requested that the creditors or the trustee be able to explore, in a more detailed manner, the individual's finances.

It seemed that the creditors were more willing to work with the wealthy to have a plan confirmed. The individuals at the lower economic levels usually liquidated certain assets to get relief, or it took them longer to get the requisite financing to have a plan approved in a reorganization case.

UPLIFTING IMMIGRANTS WAS A NOT-FOR-PROFIT company that provided assistance to immigrants in Manhattan. I have used a fictitious name for the corporation since it still provides services in the New York area today and only reluctantly filed a bankruptcy petition.

In 1936, the principals had established the company as a means of advocating for, and raising money to facilitate, the independence of their Caribbean nation from Britain. When the nation won independence in 1962, the principals refocused their efforts on the immigrants that had journeyed to New York.

The company owned a twelve-story building in a desirable Manhattan location near Central Park and the Plaza Hotel. There was just one problem: It had entered into an agreement to obtain a substantial loan from a bank that secured itself with an interest, or lien, in the company's property.

Almost immediately, the company began having money troubles. As so frequently happens, the staff focused on the needs of the community they served, not necessarily on whether the building was being kept up to local fire code standards or whether the interest payments on the loan were being made in a timely manner or were even affordable.

The principals wondered: *Wasn't it more important to pay its employees, keep the lights on, and keep the building warm during the winter months*? They had accomplished so much for their island home and for their fellow countrymen who had chosen to settle in New York. Notices from the bank, indicating that payments had been missed for far too long, could be resolved. The company just needed a little more time. As is true of so many in financial trouble, they were optimists.

Then it happened. The bank demanded payment in full. A thirty-year loan suddenly had to be paid immediately. A judgment was entered against the company, quantifying just how much they owed the bank. The company's home, the place of refuge, where all the services were being provided to those in need, was about to be sold to the highest bidder.

At such sales, auctioneers stood in front of the courthouse with clipboards listing the properties to be auctioned off that day. If it appeared that a particular property was about to be sold for far below its fair-market value, a crowd of eager bidders might gather around the auctioneer.

Such a property might have been in a well-established neighborhood of rising property values, but the owner, for medical or other reasons, had not paid the lender in time to prevent the sale on the courthouse steps. The bidders had done their research and knew that the lender would start the bidding process far below the true value of the property.

Excitement would build as eager bidders shouted over each other, trying to have their bids acknowledged by the auctioneer. Finally, the auctioneer would announce the winner. The unlucky bidders would wander off or join another auctioneer with another promising sale.

Off to the side, an auctioneer might also quietly auction a property that was "underwater," meaning the lender was owed far more than the property was worth. This auction would go to the lender's own agent, who would bid a debt amount sufficient to have the property transferred to the lender. There was no crowd. Usually, the indebted owner of the property would not even be there.

Dreams were lost in the quiet bid of the lender's agent in the auctioneer's ear. Uplifting Immigrants wanted to prevent such a public sale. It retained the firm where I was an entry-level attorney, and the bankruptcy case commenced on the eve of the building's sale on the courthouse steps. Unfortunately, as is common for many in financial trouble, such a last-ditch effort limited what any bankruptcy counsel could do.

However, in our case, a buyer miraculously appeared who wanted to acquire the building at a fair market price. If the sale went through, there would be sufficient funds to pay the bank in full and allow the company to rent a smaller space where it could still operate its nonprofit. It seemed the company would be saved.

The bankruptcy court was notified of the third-party offer for the building, and Judge Ryan, the bankruptcy judge for whom I had been a student law clerk, set the building's potential purchase for a hearing, along with a request that the building not be sold in a forced-sale process on the courthouse steps.

On the day of the hearing, we were all there: the principals of the company, the potential purchaser of the building, the partners at my law firm, and me. When the judge called our case, we moved to the front of the courtroom feeling cautiously optimistic, ready to present our arguments.

"Judge, this is a unique case," my firm's senior partner began. "One of the few that I have seen recently that will allow a company to emerge stronger from bankruptcy. We have a buyer ready to purchase the company's building on short notice. We just need a brief period to finalize the purchase documents and close. The debtor will remain open, a valuable asset to the community. We don't want the bank to profit by forcing a sale at which only it may bid."

The bank presented its counterargument, which focused on the rule that once a creditor had a judgment for an unpaid loan secured by a lien on real property, it should be allowed to sell the property on the courthouse steps.

I had researched the cases. Granted, it was a gray area of the law—some courts agreed with our position; others agreed with the bank. But I knew Judge Ryan. After all, I had been his student law clerk. He had been my mentor. I was convinced he could help the company. We waited for his decision.

"I can't approve this sale," he said simply. "I wish I could. But to me, New York law is clear. The lender has a judgment and may sell the property on the courthouse steps. I can't delay the sale. I'm sorry."

How could this happen? He was a careful reader with an analytical mind. I was sure that he had read our memorandum of law and the applicable cases.[7] Nevertheless, we had lost. I was crushed.

7. Recent decisions indicate that the ability to unwind the judgment of foreclosure and sale existed at the time, even under the old bankruptcy law that the bankruptcy judge had applied to the corporation's legal issues. (See Hallenback v. Penn Mutual Life Ins. Co., 323 F.2d 566 (4th Cir. 1963); In re

The company was unable to convince the third-party purchaser to wait for the results of an appeal of the bankruptcy judge's order. With no basis to appeal, our case was over. The company closed its business operations in Manhattan.

Who would have been hurt if the sale to the third-party purchaser had occurred and the bank had been paid in full? The bank would have had the benefit of its bargain. The company would have been able to continue to operate. It was just a two-party dispute. The company had no other unpaid creditors. At times, the law did not provide a solution that was fair. I learned that if the client sought legal assistance at an early stage as to financial issues, bankruptcy could be the solution. I had not given up on my desire to be a bankruptcy practitioner. I loved the financial aspects of any case that was presented to me, and I thought the law could give companies and individuals the relief that they desired.

My father had thought that I had made the biggest mistake in the world in attending law school. But when he attended my law school graduation ceremony, he told me that he was proud of me. "After all," he said, "how will the legal profession ever change, if honest, ethical people don't join it? I think you can make a difference." I was overwhelmed; grateful that he had changed his mind. Unfortunately, he died only a few years after that graduation ceremony. He would never see me sworn in as a bankruptcy judge.

Freed Co., 534 f.2d 1235, 1239 (6th Cir. 1976)). The enactment of the Bankruptcy Reform Act of 1978 ("Bankruptcy Code") also helped to change the legal result. (See Elfriede Di Pierro v. Taddeo (In re Taddeo), 685 F.2d 24 (2d Cir. 1982) (A judgment of foreclosure and sale may be unwound to afford a debtor in bankruptcy the ability to pay it over time, and prevent the forced sale of the property. Also see Sections 1124(2) and 1322(b) of the Bankruptcy Code.)

CHAPTER TWO

SOME DREAMS DO COME TRUE

In the winter of 1979, I was offered a position as an associate attorney with Otterbourg, Steindler, Houston & Rosen, a New York firm that had a well-known practice representing debtors, creditors, and other bankruptcy stakeholders. The firm had a bankruptcy department consisting of fourteen attorneys and was mentioned in a Second Circuit Court of Appeals decision as the "champagne of bankruptcy firms."

Conrad Duberstein, known to everyone as "Connie" and one of the senior partners at the law firm, decided to visit Judge Ed Ryan at the courthouse after finishing up a trial before another bankruptcy judge. Ed and Connie had known each other for many years and had become friends. Judge Ryan invited the lawyer to sit in a nearby armchair as Connie began his request.

"Ed, I got a problem . . . My senior associate has left me to form his own firm." Connie paused. "What am I going to do? We have a lot of cases coming in. I can't take someone just out of law school. I need someone with experience."

Ed was ready. "Connie, I know of someone who would be great. She doesn't have four or more years of experience . . .

But she started out as my student law clerk. She has about a year of experience with a boutique firm, she learns quickly, and she drafted the best opinion I ever put my name to."

Connie sighed. "A year of experience . . . I don't know if that's enough."

"Connie, trust me . . . you won't regret it."[1]

The next day, I received a call from Connie advising me that he had just talked with Judge Ryan. Could I come in later that day for an interview? He was going to convince me to change firms. I exhaled. I could not pass up his request. I agreed to meet him around six.

At the end of a snowy day, I took a cab to the Helmsley Building, a thirty-five-story building at 230 Park Avenue, a classic building that you still see in many photos of New York to this day. Between Forty-Fifth and Forty-Sixth Streets, the building blocks Park Avenue, forcing traffic going north or south to enter tunnels cut through the structure. At the time, Pan Am, flying high, had its insignia on the skyscraper that loomed over Helmsley's glowing golden cupola as the traffic circled in and out of the portals like fireflies.

Coming in from the darkness, the ornate lobby, with its polished gold and chinoiserie, overwhelmed me. No expense was spared, no decorative item was too bold. I gathered my thoughts as I took the elevator to the twenty-ninth floor. The door opened to a softly lit hallway, with just the light of a single lamp visible in the dark.

Had I come to the wrong floor? Just as I was about to retreat, I saw Connie walking toward the door. He unlocked the front door and beckoned me in with a smile. Once inside, I took a tour of the bankruptcy department, which was on the floor just above the rest of the law firm, with no connecting

1. Both Conrad "Connie" Duberstein and Judge Ryan separately confirmed how I came to be offered a position at the firm.

staircase. It was as if the department existed in its own world. No one else was there other than a female associate attorney.

However, I was able to chat with her, and she and Connie both seemed welcoming. Later that evening, as I was leaving the office, Connie made an offer for me to become an associate attorney with the firm. I told him I would think about it.

I was reluctant to leave the boutique law firm where the partners had treated me as if I were a family member. Although I had been with the firm for only a year, I had attended the wedding of one of the partners at the then-elegant Tavern on the Green restaurant in Central Park. I genuinely enjoyed working with and learning from them. However, ultimately, I decided to move on to explore what a larger firm might have to offer.

When I joined Otterbourg, Steindler, Houston & Rosen the firm did offer many complex issues to be resolved but in what had been described as a "highly pressurized environment." Everything was done on a short deadline or an emergency basis.

I was constantly dictating on a desktop Dictaphone machine that was connected to a large continuously looped tape concealed in the wall, from which one or more secretaries could simultaneously type what was being dictated.

When I was not dictating, I was appearing in bankruptcy court on various cases. Because I then resided outside of Manhattan, I not only appeared at the Manhattan Bankruptcy Court, but I was also the designated attorney to appear at the various bankruptcy court hearing sites in New York State's Westchester and Suffolk Counties and, occasionally, Newark, New Jersey.

There were interesting cases. I paid attention when Beck Industries, which owned Joseph Salon Shoes that made the fashionable heels I wore to court, went bankrupt. Mr. Joseph, the original proprietor, had started his shoe salon in a Chicago suburb in 1927. Like the French salons that catered to wealthy women who wished to purchase a couture gown, Mr. Joseph created a salon for shoes that had the opulence of a living room, where his customers were treated like welcome guests. He had a limited supply of shoes on hand to create an air of exclusivity and elegance. My mother had purchased a pair of high-heeled pumps for me when I was in college, and I treasured and still wore those well-made shoes.

In 1969, Beck Industries acquired Mr. Joseph's company. In 1976 or shortly thereafter, Beck, as a large public company, was trying to restructure its debt. Unfortunately, it would later be liquidated. Joseph Salon Shoes was about to have an ignominious ending.

At the time, I was one of the attorneys helping a group of Tennessee businessmen purchase the shoe salon at a bankruptcy court auction. Unlike the Uplifting Immigrants case, I now had a different up-close view of the auction process: not as the attorney for the company trying to reorganize but for a third party. Honoring the Joseph Salon Shoes brand, I was hoping that my clients would be the successful bidders of an insolvent company's division and make it a profitable company.

Unfortunately, the bid of the Tennessee businessmen was not accepted, and they moved on to other opportunities. I realized that if Beck Industries, a large public company, had to seek bankruptcy relief, any company or individual would need a little help from time to time. From an economic standpoint, bankruptcy could provide a benefit.

Being an attorney in Manhattan also had its grittier moments. I commuted into Manhattan each workday on the Hudson River commuter rail line. On one occasion when the New York subways were not operating but the commuter rail, or feeder, lines outside of the city were, I arrived at work to find a desperate partner seeking attorneys to cover hearings that were to take place in a few hours.

Another associate attorney and I took all the files for the matters that were on the calendar that day. He walked 3.2 miles to the bankruptcy court in lower Manhattan from our midtown office. I walked 1.3 miles to Penn Central, dragging my wheeled litigation bag behind me, and rode the commuter line to the bankruptcy court that was then located in Westbury, Long Island. At one of the hearings, the judge remarked that I looked a bit "harried."

"No, Your Honor," I said. "I just walked a bit more than usual."

On another occasion, I was handed a file early one morning when I arrived at the firm. I was asked to leave immediately for the commuter line that would take me to Newark, New Jersey. It was an emergency hearing. I was to read the file on the train ride over. I arrived in Newark, took a taxi to the courthouse, and arrived at a packed courtroom. Most bankruptcy matters were set on a "calendar basis," meaning that many matters were set for 10:00 a.m. I whispered to a woman in the back of the courtroom where the record company case was on the judge's calendar. She looked at me with a mixture of concern and pity and said, "The only matter on the calendar today is the record company case, and the hearing has already started." I thanked her, then looked at the packed courtroom and noticed about twenty male lawyers at the front of the courtroom arguing their positions to the judge. I was late for the hearing, but I was there to represent the firm's client.

As I walked toward the front of the courtroom, my high heels tapped lightly on the floor. Some heads turned to regard me, then followed me as I walked by as quietly as I could to the front of the courtroom. I felt the stares at my back as I approached the other lawyers and the judge.

Apologizing profusely as I neared the bench, I stated my name for the record, the name of my client, and the fact that my client and firm had just learned of the hearing, hence the reason for my being tardy. The bankruptcy judge paused, looked at me, then welcomed me to the hearing. I took my place at the end of the row of assembled male attorneys.

The attorneys continued with their arguments. I soon realized that the record company wanted to use funds to continue with its business operations. Unfortunately, my client also had an interest in those funds.

As soon as one of the lawyers paused, I immediately interjected: "Your Honor, I need to alert the court that my client has an interest in the funds that we are now discussing and cannot consent to the record company's use of the funds. We just learned of this hearing. We just need a little time to discuss the matter to work out a resolution to allow the company to continue operating." I hesitated. Would I be reprimanded for interrupting? No, as it turned out, other attorneys voiced similar concerns, so the bankruptcy judge continued the hearing to another day.

When I returned to the office after the hearing, I heard one of the firm's partners discussing the hearing with another attorney on the phone. As I waited for the partner to finish his telephone conversation, I heard the partner say, "Who was that woman who appeared for the firm in the record company case, you ask?" He looked at me and then said, "That's the tigress. I am sure she will be able to help in similar matters."

I had acquired a moniker.

I began representing a company that had filed a bankruptcy case before another judge in Westbury, New York. Counsel for the other critical party in the case, a secured creditor, was an associate attorney with a well-known New York City bankruptcy law firm. She had made the mistake of telling a group of male attorneys that she had been a beauty queen when she lived in Teaneck, New Jersey. The male attorneys did not forget the tale. She soon became known as the "Beauty Queen."

When she filed the documentation to appear on behalf of

a creditor in a matter in which I was the attorney for the company trying to reorganize, the male partners at my firm joked that it was the Tigress up against the Beauty Queen, and the smart money was on the Tigress.

We had a pretrial conference in the chambers of the bankruptcy judge assigned to hear the case in Westbury, New York. He sat at the end of the conference table, with each of us sitting near him on opposite sides of the table. The Beauty Queen sat to his right; I was to his left. We each had a neat pile of pleadings on the conference table. Our hands rested on the table as the conference began. The judge looked to his right and to his left, then made a remark that made both of us uncomfortable. We said nothing. We only looked at each other across the table. Comments on a woman's appearance was a part of life.

After the conference, our clients worked toward an amicable settlement. We never had a clear winner in the contest. But from time to time, there were wistful references as to whether there would be another matchup between the Beauty Queen and the Tigress. There never was.

The firm also gave me the opportunity to argue an appeal before the Second Circuit Court of Appeals at the ripe old age of thirty-two. I had been representing a creditor at the trial court level against an individual who had filed a bankruptcy case without counsel.

After I won at the trial court level, the individual chose to appeal the matter to the federal district court, the intermediate appellate court. He thought that the appellate might agree with his position. However, he lost once again. Now he moved to the next level, the Second Circuit, one of the busiest appellate courts in the country.

The partner handling the case decided to let me draft the appellate brief and present the argument to the Circuit Court Judges. There was one problem. I was not yet admitted to the Circuit Court of Appeals. Admission to the bar of the court was not a pro forma matter of simply filling out a form. I needed to show the circuit that I had the requisite experience. I had drafted and argued a number of complex matters, and I had handled a certain number of appeals at the federal district court level.

A partner from the firm also had to submit an affidavit vouching for my character and ethics, requesting that I be permitted to present the appellate matter to the Second Circuit. The Second Circuit granted the motion for me to be admitted to its bar. With a partner's oversight and consent, I finalized my arguments.

I vividly remember my argument to the court that day. All matters on the calendar were argued in an ancillary hearing room for the Second Circuit that was in a nondescript building annex. I was early that day, finding my way to the courtroom and sitting in the back. About one-third of the attorneys in the courtroom were female. One woman walked in, saying in a loud voice, "What is this? Ladies' Day at the Court of Appeals?" No one said a word. I later learned that the female attorney was a government lawyer who frequently argued before the circuit court. She was apparently surprised at the number of women who were there that day.

My matter was heard by three judges who were sitting on a panel to hear any matter that was on the calendar. One of the judges was Amalya Lyle Kearse, who was relatively new to the Second Circuit, having been confirmed to her position in 1979. Another panel member was Judge Price, who was a federal district court judge from Brooklyn, had bankruptcy expertise, and had agreed to assist the Circuit Court Judges with their workload. I don't remember the third member of the panel.

I had carefully prepared what I was going to say that day, but once I stated my name for the official record of the hearing, we were off and running. I was peppered with questions from the bench. I liked the give-and-take of the oral argument that day. I wanted more of it. I also won the case for the client.

Bankruptcy was a rough-and-tumble world in the early 1980s. Hearings were set with a few hours' notice, clients were rounded up and sent by taxis to the courthouse, and cigar-smoking men brokered deals in a nearby restaurant. Not many women were interested in such a chaotic world. I liked the challenge.

I remember appearing in the Brooklyn bankruptcy court; it was a busy bankruptcy court, with many cases heard daily. In one matter, I successfully presented my position to the court for my client. One month later, I returned to the same courtroom, same judge, but on a different case. The court reporter greeted me by name when I arrived in the courtroom prior to the hearing. I was amazed that he remembered my name, so I quizzed him on his excellent memory.

He laughed and said his memory was not that great. Although I had done well at the last hearing, he had remembered me because I was the only female attorney who had appeared in the Brooklyn Bankruptcy Court over the last month.

At times, clients were not receptive to having a female attorney as their counsel. The case of Schatz Federal seemed to amplify the issue for me.

In 1895, Adolf and Herrman Schatz, father and son, founded a metal specialties company. In 1910, they acquired a ball bearing company, which became Schatz Federal Bearing Company. At its peak, Schatz employed about 1,200 people. It was one of the largest manufacturers in Poughkeepsie, New York, a city that hugged the Hudson River and was a long way from Manhattan. In 1979, the company lost valuable contracts with the automotive industry, and layoffs resulted. It was a union shop, and within a year, it ran short of funds to pay its employees, its suppliers, and its creditors.

The creditors refused to provide any more funding to the

company until new management was installed. An expert in out-of-court arrangements or restructurings (known as a "turnaround manager") was installed, along with his team, as the new management of the manufacturer. My firm was retained to represent the company when it filed its bankruptcy case. Since my home was midway between the Manhattan bankruptcy courthouse and the courthouses in Poughkeepsie and White Plains, New York, where the hearings most likely would be held, I became the associate attorney assigned to the case.

I was representing the company during one difficult, contested hearing at which the turnaround manager was an important witness. I carefully prepared him for the hearing, reviewing the documents that he intended to rely on, then asking him proposed questions to make sure he was ready for the hearing. The next day, we prevailed at the hearing, and the company was able to obtain the funding that it needed.

After the hearing, as the turnaround manager and I were walking to our cars in the parking lot, my client suddenly commented that we had won because of the dress that I was wearing that day. I paused in the sun on the hot asphalt.

I had chosen that day to wear a short-sleeved, knee-length red dress with white polka-dots, over which I had layered a white linen jacket that was wilting on me. Most female lawyers at the time wanted to be taken seriously. One way to accomplish that was to wear "serious purpose" clothing: jackets and skirts in muted colors accompanied by starched shirts, with velvet or silk ties, usually in black, strung as ribbons around the collared shirts. I had resisted that trend. I favored dresses, particularly in the summer heat.

I looked at him and said that we had been successful at the hearing because he had been well prepared and he had been persuasive in his testimony. We had convinced the judge to grant the relief that the company was requesting. I had complimented him, and I had been clear as to my role in that success. He looked at me as he reflected on what I had said. He then said he still liked my dress. We left it at that.

I remember one telephone conversation that I heard although my office was half a New York City block away. I never heard what the client was saying, but I did hear the partner whose voice became louder and louder during the conversation. The call ended with the partner yelling, "She will continue to work on this case with you, and if you don't like it, you can eff off and take your file somewhere else."

The case also had a great deal of drama. One day, angry Schatz employees stormed the gates of the Poughkeepsie plant, demanding entry so that they could be paid for the work that they had performed. The fear was that they would tear down the fence, destroy property, and not return to work.

The company had focused on keeping the plant open at any cost. It had gone to its lender, obtaining loans at high interest rates that it would never be able to repay. In turn, the lender demanded that if the company did not make its loan payments on time, the lender would start taking equipment out of the plant, piece by piece, to repay the debt. The company was losing its source of income. The automotive industry had become an unreliable, demanding partner. Our strategy was to keep the plant in operation until we received funding from a financial institution or some other third party. To keep the plant operating, we had to pay the employees.

We had an emergency. The judge who was handling the case just happened to be at a reception at the Manhattan bankruptcy court, thirty-five miles from White Plains, New York, where he usually held court. The judge agreed to leave the reception, grab one of his colleague's courtrooms, and immediately conduct a hearing.

I quickly drafted some pleadings and headed for the courthouse. At the reception, I spotted and rounded up the attorneys who represented various critical parties in the case, handed them their pleadings, and we all headed for the courtroom where the judge was waiting.

"Judge, the employees are at the gate," I stated. "They are highly skilled. They have to be to make ball bearings that are nearly perfect for the exacting standards of the automotive industry. Our employees are essential to us. It would take a long time to hire and train employees to take their places. If they walk out on us, we will need to close our operations. Judge, just give us a little more time."

The judge listened to the views of opposing counsel, who stressed that the company could not survive. Better to close the facility immediately and put everyone out of work. Fortunately, an attorney for the workers was also present and supported my position. The plant was the major employer in Poughkeepsie at the time. Closing the plant on short notice would have an immediate deleterious impact on the city's social services. The judge agreed with my argument that day. He reviewed the budget I presented and signed the order. By the end of the day, Schatz was paying the wages it owed its employees, and operations were up and running.

Connie and I spent many an hour after that dramatic hearing working with the businesspeople to put together some type of plan to pay creditors over time that would win their approval. Yet, even after trimming operations to the bare minimum, the business was not profitable. It seemed unthinkable to shut the company down. Too many people in Poughkeepsie relied on an operating business.

The only solution was to sell the company at a bankruptcy auction and hope that the purchaser would continue the operations. Business brokers were retained, and we used formal and informal networks to provide information to suppliers, creditors, and competitors to analyze the assets and the business operations and make a bid.

Because the company had retained professionals to market the business operations to a select group of competitors or others that wanted to enter the automotive market, we soon had a solid offer for the operating business, which would become part of our plan to pay creditors. The hearing was held at the bankruptcy court, the highest offer for the company's operations was approved, and the company was sold in an orderly manner.

A few years later, the purchaser encountered its own financial problems and had to sell the company to one of its former suppliers based in Canada. The supplier acquired almost all the assets, including the Schatz name, and reinvented the business model to take full advantage of all the skilled workers who still resided in Poughkeepsie, New York.

The *In re Schatz Federal* case is an example of how bankruptcy can work. Today, the company still exists in a plant near the old manufacturing facility, still under the ownership of the former Canadian supplier who saw possibilities where no one else did, selling ball bearings to the defense and aerospace industry.

After three years at the Otterbourg, Steindler, Houston & Rosen firm, it was time for me to leave New York. I had learned a great deal and had been accorded a great deal of responsibility within a relatively short period of time, handling many complex cases. I was a senior associate doing work that I genuinely enjoyed, but it was a pressurized environment. Living in New York was emotionally draining. It was an hour commute each way, each day, to the office. There was little or no time for lunch. I was returning late to my home, then working into the early hours of the morning. And there was no such thing as a vacation.

I was also pregnant with my first child, and I had developed pneumonia in my ninth month of pregnancy. I discussed my next step with my husband, Roger. If we remained where we lived in New York, we would leave the sleeping baby with a nanny in the morning and return home to a sleeping baby at night. We decided to head to the Midwest, hoping for a more low-key lifestyle.

CHAPTER THREE

BAD GIRL IN THE BOARDROOM

I started looking in financial publications and newspapers for companies looking for an attorney with a specialty in the bankruptcy area. I wanted to try the Midwest, but not the Chicago area where I grew up, or Detroit, my husband's hometown.

I would find a job first, then my husband, also an attorney, would look for a job in his area of expertise—trusts and estates. I dealt with the living who had money problems. He dealt with the dead who had amassed a great deal of money and moved beyond all problems.

Two ends of a spectrum. We thought our respective areas of the law promised that no matter what happened to the economy, we would be able to survive.

I was immediately intrigued by an ad from a bank holding company in Milwaukee, Wisconsin, that was looking for an attorney who could advise "the entire system" on bankruptcy issues. I would also be the attorney for one or more lending groups that needed advice on financial issues. For the first time in my career, I would advise a lender on whether to make a loan to a particular borrower. Could I help structure a loan at the beginning so that the borrower would be less likely to file a bankruptcy petition? I was excited to find out. Of course, if the borrower made unwise business decisions or the economy collapsed, I would be there at the end to handle any bankruptcy issues that might arise.

I applied for the job and was advised that I should come in as soon as possible for the interview. Although I had never been to Milwaukee before, having grown up in the Chicago area, I was familiar with Geneva Lake since a few of my parents' friends had homes in the area. I had surprised them with one of my responses. They had asked what size loans I had worked on as a New York bankruptcy attorney. I replied that I usually worked on cases involving loans in the amount of $16 million. They smiled. I didn't realize that $16 million was a great deal of money for the bank holding company.

I accepted the position as a senior-level counsel for the then largest bank holding company in Wisconsin and a major financial player in the region. I was to provide bankruptcy advice to the officers in the bank holding company and to any individual with a bankruptcy question in the far-flung branches across the system. I was based at the largest branch in the system, the mothership.

Roger soon followed, accepting an associate attorney's position with a well-respected Milwaukee law firm. We established ourselves, with our baby son, in a home on a street that ran along a bluff above Lake Michigan. In the summer, we would open the windows and listen to the sound of the waves gently caressing the shore below. In a storm, the wind would rattle the windows, and we could hear the waves exploding and hissing on the beach beneath the bluff.

Having grown up in the Chicago area, I never minded the Milwaukee winters. I jogged by the lake until the accumulated snow made my steps unsure. Then I would retreat to an indoor track that was monotonous in its symmetry. On other days, I bundled up my toddler son, with only his eyes showing above his woolen scarf, placed him on a sled, and off we would go in the blue-filtered winter light to explore shadowed snow mountains and mysterious tire tracks in the snow. My son would shout and laugh at this magical world, wondering what was behind each snowy wave or in each shadow. And then we would return home to warmth and cocoa.

My duties for the bank holding company were varied. Many of the small banks in the system were in rural areas far from the mothership, and they were run by men who were familiar with duck decoys and hunting prints. They had known their local customers since kindergarten.

At times, the commercial lending team in Milwaukee would ask the presidents of these smaller banks to participate in a commercial loan (or a "syndicated loan"); that is, the smaller banks would provide funding for a large loan to a commercial lending borrower of the main branch, for which the smaller banks received an appropriate percentage of the risk and reward of the loan. Of course, the risk would be that the borrower would not repay the loan and none of the banks would be repaid—a loss to be absorbed by all the participating banks. The reward was the access to fees and higher interest rates that the smaller banks would not normally receive since most of their customers only wanted loans in a lower dollar amount, meaning less of a return for the smaller banks.

Another benefit for the smaller banks was they had access to the resources of the mothership, which meant that they had access to the lawyers with the bank holding company who were familiar with the latest laws and legal decisions as to consumers, commercial lending, securities transactions, and, my area, bankruptcy.

If their loan went bad, which usually meant no payments were being made on the loan, I became the small banks' attorney to assist the borrower to become current in payments over time (a "workout") or, worst case scenario, to represent the small banks in bankruptcy court.

Of course, trying to resolve the issues with a commercial

loan meant that the group of small bank presidents, a loan officer from the main branch, and me, as their attorney, would take road trips to Chicago to work on modifying the terms of a commercial loan.

Five of us would pile into a car and head for Chicago. Since I had grown up in the Chicago area, I became the guide and was allowed to sit in the front passenger seat. The three presidents were squeezed into the backseat, knee-to-knee, usually discussing the latest events in their lives or the hunting conditions in their respective areas.

Many became close friends over the years, and they simply referred to themselves as members of the "presidents' club." I always alerted the loan officer, who was the designated driver, of land changes or when to exit the crowded expressways. However, some drivers were more responsive than others, some preferring to wait until the last possible moment to cross four or more lanes of traffic on the expressway. Such trips were not for the faint of heart.

On one memorable trip, we arrived at a well-known private club in Chicago, near the frozen wonderland of the Lake Michigan shore. White waves, arcing and reaching for the shore, had become frozen in place. Next to the shore was the calm, gray facade of the club. The club appeared to welcome us to a place that the regional bankruptcy community favored to work out deals.

In the front reception area, there was a coat check requiring everyone to hand over their coats. It was winter, and we all were wearing heavy overcoats of one sort or the other. Of course, my group went immediately to the woman handling the coat check, placing their coats on the counter near her.

I also placed my coat on the counter with the others. The woman grabbed my coat and handed it back to me, directing me to take my coat down a long hallway and check it in the ladies' room. I thanked the woman for the information but advised her that I was with a group, that they had all checked their coats with her, and that I did not need to go to the ladies' room for any reason.

She told me that women could not check their coats with her, that they were required by club rules to check their coats in the ladies' room. My bankers protested, saying we were all in a hurry and there was no need for me to go down the hall and hold them up. The woman refused to pick up my coat. It simply lay there, alone.

The bankers then suggested that she place my coat over one of theirs. Problem solved—my coat was not being checked; it was simply, like a scarf, floating over one of their coats.

The woman was unmoved and unfriendly with a fixed expression of displeasure on her face. It was a standoff. And we needed to get to our meeting.

I grabbed my coat from the counter and headed off at a fast clip for the ladies' room, telling the bankers over my shoulder that they could go to the meeting room. I would join them shortly. I hung up the coat in the ladies' room on a metal rack inserted into the area where chairs or loungers were usually placed. There was no security for the coat. I grabbed a tag from the hanger and left.

I headed for the reception area, where the bankers were still protesting to the coat-check woman the absurdity of the situation—I was their lawyer, they were in a hurry, and I should not be sent down some long hall. I said nothing, just heading for the elevators. The bankers followed.

As we got on the elevator, we noticed that our host for the meeting, a lawyer and the club member who had arranged the meeting, was on the elevator with us. We rode the elevator to the third floor, exchanging a few initial pleasantries. When the elevator doors opened at the grill floor, the bankers all got off the elevator. The lawyer member called them back, telling them that we were headed for the top floor.

The bankers got back on and immediately demanded to know why we were not meeting at the grill as they had always done before.

The lawyer member responded, "Because Sarah is here."

There was silence.

"Why does that make a difference?" they asked.

He responded, "We are going to a private room on the top floor. The view is great. The food is much better than in the grill." Finally, he added, "Women are not allowed in the grill."

That started a cacophony of complaints: "You are a member of this club, why do you allow such a policy? Why can't women negotiate in the grill like everyone else? Sarah had to check her coat in the ladies' room—she couldn't use the coat-check room at the reception area."

The lawyer responded that he did not agree with the policies and had voted against them. No effort to change the policies worked. He was always in the minority. The bankers then asked, "Why are you still a member of this club?" The lawyer responded that the only way to change things was to remain a member of the club and that all the bankruptcy deals were negotiated in the grill. The bankers said, "Exactly. Why are you still a member of this club?"

We arrived at the top floor, the elevator doors opened, and we stepped into a private room with a large table and seating for twenty-four. Outside, the lake was dark and uninviting.

The lawyer's client was already in the room waiting for us. Lunch was set up on a side buffet. No one said anything. We simply collected our lunches and sat down at the table. The bankers moved to my side of the table. The lawyer and his client faced us. After a few minutes, we commenced the negotiations for the working out of the client's loan then in default.

At the end of the meeting, the bankers pulled the lawyer to the side and told him they had no intention of returning to the club again. They told him to resign.

Within a few years of our meeting, the club was sued by a

group of female bankruptcy professionals who stated that they could not effectively practice in their chosen area because all the critical negotiations in any regional bankruptcy matter took place in that club's grill, a place they were denied access to.

Given the importance of the club in regional practice, the fact that the club was a private club was irrelevant. I did not follow the lawsuit, but I do know that within a few years, the club's rules were changed.

Women were admitted as full members of the club. That's not to say that Wisconsin did not have its own issues at the time. While on vacation around Thanksgiving, I received an urgent call from one of my colleagues at work. It was unusual. Wisconsin did not work on a 24/7 schedule like New York.

My colleague advised me that while I was away, one of the banking groups I had consistently represented had revolted and requested that a new attorney from the in-house law department be assigned to them. The colleague said that upon my return, I had to sort out my issues with the group.

When I returned, I immediately requested that the head of the rebellious banking group and everyone on his team meet with me. We set a date and time, and I said nothing more. When we assembled in the meeting room at the appointed date and time, there was palpable tension in the room. I looked at every member of the team.

I said, "Et tu, Brute?" A pause. Then I asked, "Why didn't you notify me of any problems you had? Whatever issues we have between us, we can resolve them."

To their credit, they voiced their concerns. At the end of the meeting, I felt real progress had been made. I was correct. We continued with our meetings, putting in place changes to business forms or procedures that made their jobs easier but still kept them in compliance with applicable law. That group became my strongest supporter. When I left Wisconsin, they all arrived at my going-away party to thank me and wish me well.

Although that group came over to my side, another group did not. Returning from another vacation, I learned that a work-out group had been created in my absence. The group was to handle commercial borrowers whose business operations were unprofitable ("troubled loans"), who were unable or unlikely to make payments on time ("nonperforming"), or who were in default, having failed to make payments for at least ninety days or more. At the bank holding company, the executives needed a lawyer to head the group. Senior management had simply called a male colleague who worked with me in the law department and stated that he was the new head. Nonplussed, he told them that loan work-outs were not his area of expertise. He was my supervisor and had no knowledge of bankruptcy law. He urged senior management to reconsider. They would not. Finally, he said he would not manage the group without my assistance.

And so I became second in command. I met with the group and provided legal advice. My supervisor found inventive ways to be unavailable whenever I had group meetings. Over time, the members of the division called me for advice and no longer requested that my supervisor be present at any meeting. However, I was never officially promoted to lead the group.

I was also asked to attend various meetings of the senior management of the bank holding company. My years as a New York lawyer helped me. Having presented arguments before various appellate courts, I argued my case to the gentlemen in a similar fashion. They listened attentively and followed my recommendations.

Female commercial lending officers struggled. Their supervisors tended not to listen to their ideas, and the male borrowers wanted to discuss their business problems with men. Over time, I became an advocate for the women, suggesting various approaches that they might utilize to persuade their supervisors. The women always seemed grateful for my help.

Although I enjoyed my home by Lake Michigan and my position with the bank holding company, Roger was looking for a position that was advantageous for him—trusts and estates and probate litigation. We needed new opportunities in a new part of the country, and we wanted to move when our almost four-year-old son would be able to adjust readily to a new home. I could always obtain a position in the bankruptcy area almost anywhere.

Roger found a position with a bank in Phoenix, Arizona, and so I encouraged him to take it. He and our son, in a fully packed car, began the long drive to Arizona. Roger would start the Tuesday after Labor Day weekend, and our son would be in preschool daycare. I would remain behind to sell our home, joining them when I could.

Within a month of arriving in Arizona, our son caught chicken pox—a rather severe case for someone his age. We knew no one in Arizona, and no qualified services would provide a sitter for a contagious child. Roger had to stay home and take care of our son, and I flew to Arizona whenever I could to help.

Our son would laugh when he first saw me. Then he'd promptly sit in my lap or next to me and not move until we ate or he had to go to bed. On Sunday or Monday, I would take the long flight back to Wisconsin, arriving at night with the increasing cold of fall greeting me. Months passed, and our Wisconsin home had not been sold, and I did not yet have a job in Arizona.

When we sold our home, Roger and our son flew back to help me pack up and move. At one point, our son was watching the movers start to pack his remaining toys. As one of his trucks was being placed in a box, he started to cry. At some level, he knew he was leaving the only home that he had known. Although we tried to reassure him that the truck was simply being packed, and he would soon see it in Arizona, he was inconsolable. I took the truck out of the box and handed it back to him. We would have to figure out some way to get it into his suitcase so he could take it back to Arizona with him.

The next day, they flew back to Arizona, and I remained in Wisconsin. I didn't have a job in Arizona yet, and we had agreed that I would remain in Wisconsin until I received a job offer that I could accept. Since I no longer had a home, I lived with friends for a week until my realtor found a condominium that I could rent on a temporary basis.

There were no cell phones, no email. The only way to contact me was at my work or on the landline at the condominium at night. We sent letters to each other, and I received a few drawings from my son. Several months later, I finally had a job offer, which I accepted. I gave my colleagues at the bank holding company one month's notice, and I set my date of departure for mid-January. I would ship all that I had left—a few boxes and my car. And I would fly to Arizona with two suitcases.

I was soon to be an associate attorney with a boutique law firm newly installed in a renovated building in downtown Phoenix. The law firm was on the top floor, with views of the mountains that surrounded Phoenix. I attended the holiday party. It was a celebration and a chance to meet everyone at the firm before I started in mid-January.

The soft sunset light of an Arizona evening welcomed me to the event. The panoramic windows that surrounded us reflected the valley of rose, crimson, orange, and deep blue light enfolded by the purple mountains. How could I be so lucky?

I returned to Wisconsin, only to learn that the firm had dissolved. Like a mirage, it had shimmered in the heat then disappeared. I was offered an attorney position with a spin-off of the boutique firm at less than half the salary that I was originally offered. I accepted the position.

My friends in Wisconsin provided a going-away party, retelling pleasant memories and giving recommendations of places in Arizona that Wisconsinites assured me I had to visit or experience, such as the Grand Canyon and the Pink Jeep Tour in Sedona. And then it was over. A place that I had hoped to make my forever home faded away in my airplane window.

Even now when I am sleeping, I dream of our home by Lake Michigan. It is a hot summer day, and we walk with our young son down the path near our home to the shore of the lake. I step into the dark, cold, translucent waters. At times, I can see my toes in the shallow water and pebbly sand. I swim a few strokes in the cold water, ignoring the pain, then turn around and swim back to the shore. I am unable to reach the shore. I wake up in my Arizona home.

PART TWO
CORPORATE BANKRUPTCY

CHAPTER FOUR

A STRANGER COMES TO TOWN

In the late '80s, there were not that many Arizona federal judges. They could all sit around a large conference table. There were two main courthouses: one in Phoenix, one in Tucson. Arizona continued the tradition begun during colonial times of having judges "ride the circuit," referring to a time when judges and lawyers would ride horseback or in carriages from town to town to hear civil and criminal cases.

Arizona was still a rugged country, consisting of deserts, mountainous regions, and remote areas accessible by dirt roads only. As a result, the federal judges held court in small cities in many parts of the state to provide access to those who lived far from the metropolitan areas.

The appointment process for bankruptcy judges had changed dramatically since 1978, when a new comprehensive bankruptcy law had been passed. Under the old law, in effect with some modifications since 1898, federal district court judges selected what were known as "referees" in bankruptcy. Referee was an apt title for what they did.

They acted as neutral parties who handled disputes and administrative tasks, making sure that all bankruptcy cases moved along in a timely manner. Documents needed to be filed on time; trustees needed to be appointed to make sure all assets of the bankrupts were found, assembled, and sold for creditors; fraud needed to be discovered and penalties meted out; creditors received payments on their debts in an organized manner; and the bankrupts hopefully received fresh starts, or the forgiveness of their debts, at the end of their cases.

The 1978 law upended prior practice. Of critical importance was the change in how bankruptcy judges were appointed. There were widespread rumors as well as evidence to show that federal judges had appointed their friends, former business partners, or people to whom they owed a moral or legal obligation to referee positions. The courts of appeals, the federal appellate courts just beneath the US Supreme Court in power and authority, would objectively appoint bankruptcy judges based on merit. The title "referee" had been changed to "judge" to reflect the more professional nature of individuals who would be presiding over bankruptcy matters. The US Congress had also authorized a number of new positions for those federal districts that had seen a dramatic growth in cases and needed more judges to handle the workload. New judges would need to be appointed to these positions as well.

Although Arizona had experienced exponential growth after World War II, it retained the same allotment of only four judges. One of the referees was not reappointed. The other three referees became bankruptcy judges, opening up a position that needed to be filled in Phoenix. The new judge would also have to travel to Yuma, Arizona, at least once a month. That Yuma duty station would remain with the newly appointed judge until a new Arizona bankruptcy judge position was included in federal legislation, passed by the US Congress and signed by the president, or a fellow Arizona bankruptcy judge agreed to take over.

When I learned that Arizona sought a new bankruptcy

judge, I decided to take a chance on the new appointment process and applied for the position. The application was eighty pages, asking for the addresses of every place that I had lived as an adult, any current neighbors who would vouch for me, personal references, professional references from clients and opposing counsel in cases that I had handled, the names of bankruptcy judges in the jurisdictions in which I had practiced, the college and law school from which I had graduated, and a detailed description of why I was qualified to be a bankruptcy judge.

After several months had passed, I learned that I was one of three finalists for the position. The next step? A final interview with the Ninth Circuit appointment committee in Phoenix. The committee was composed of twelve members: a Ninth Circuit judge as the committee chair, representatives from the local law schools, an Arizona District Court judge, the chief judge of the Arizona Bankruptcy Court, a representative from the state bar, and six federal litigators and bankruptcy lawyers.

The day of the interview before the committee was a blur. I had read over my application once again, read a few court decisions that had recently come down, and arrived early. When I was led into the room, I was struck by the fact that there were no women at the conference table. Twelve men would judge me.

In my favor were a number of factors. My bankruptcy experience had been before trial and appellate courts. I had handled trials and motion practice in the New York and Wisconsin bankruptcy courts and had argued appeals before the federal district courts in the Southern and Eastern Districts of New York and an appeal before the Second Circuit Court of Appeals based in Manhattan. Although I had also represented a commercial lending group in Wisconsin, I continued to represent a number of banks on loan workouts and bankruptcy issues. Over time, I had represented all of the key players in any bankruptcy matter. The other applicants had not devoted their practices to bankruptcy law. They had been litigators or had specialized in the real estate or commercial lending areas. The appointment committee was also chaired by an Asian American Ninth Circuit judge who was known for his thoughtful consideration of any issue presented to him.

I later learned that although the committee thought I was the most qualified applicant, they wanted to make sure. They contacted the Wisconsin and New York bankruptcy judges, opposing counsel on the cases that I had listed on my application, and all my references, including the clients. They called members of the Wisconsin and New York Bars and asked for their opinions. The thorough investigation took several months.

In June 1986, many months after the interview, a Ninth Circuit executive contacted me. Was I still interested in the position? If so, I would start in October 1986. I was honored to be selected for the position.

In June 1986, I was also scheduled to take the Arizona bar exam at the end of July. Since I was already admitted to practice in the courts of Wisconsin and New York, it was not essential that I be admitted to the Arizona courts. A bankruptcy judge was appointed under federal law and only needed to be admitted to practice in the courts of one state or the District of Columbia. However, I didn't want anyone to wonder whether I knew Arizona law, so I decided to be admitted to the Arizona courts. I subsequently passed the bar exam and was sworn in as a federal judge before I was admitted to practice in Arizona.

In a bit of serendipity, the clerk of court, who was one of the individuals that executed my certificate to practice before the Arizona District Court, had also signed my certificate to practice in the Eastern District of New York so many years before. The clerk had moved from Brooklyn, New York, to Phoenix, Arizona.

A week before I was officially sworn in as a judge, I appeared at the Phoenix courthouse. I wanted to meet everyone: the other judges, court staff, my chambers' staff, and lawyers. I was asked whether I wished to have a formal investiture ceremony in the federal district court's ceremonial courtroom or have a private ceremony in the chambers of a district court judge.

What was the best way to introduce myself? One bankruptcy judge advised that if I chose a more formal ceremony, it was unclear how many would attend. In my mind's eye, I saw a few people gathered at the front of the courtroom, with the remainder of the benches empty. Perhaps it was best to be low-key until I became more familiar with my duties and responsibilities as a judge and became acquainted with Arizona lawyers. I chose to take the oath of office in the chambers of a federal district court judge with my husband and toddler son in attendance. I became the first woman ever to be appointed to the Arizona bankruptcy court. I began a new chapter in my life, moving from lawyer to judge.

Although many in Arizona felt that some type of celebration should be held to introduce me to the bankruptcy community, it was the Arizona Women Lawyers Association that took control and planned the event. I had a wonderful time. At the celebration, the women lawyers presented me with a wooden gavel and a judicial robe that was embroidered with my name on the inside yoke. I wore that robe from my first day on the bench to the day that I retired. After almost twenty-eight years, it was a bit shiny and worn at the ends. At times, I contemplated retiring the robe. I just couldn't do it. I still have the robe today. It has an honored place in one of my closets at home.

Over the years, I became a sponsoring member of the organization. I can remember attending meetings at one of the local country clubs where we met in the women's bathroom/locker room. Over the years, we progressed to much better locations, a sign that we were being taken seriously. I later received an award from the county chapter of the Women Lawyers for my professionalism and for serving as a mentor to the next generation of women lawyers.

One day, I was seated at my desk when I was suddenly greeted with a cheerful, "Hi, I'm Mary Schroeder from upstairs." She was carrying a heather plant as she breezed past my desk, adding, "I've brought you a little welcome present." Mary, a Ninth Circuit Court of Appeals judge based in Phoenix, would become my mentor, friend, and invaluable guide for many years to come. Her heather plant was always proudly displayed on my windowsill.

After many years of enjoying the Arizona sun, one day the plant no longer seemed to need water. I investigated. In the intense light and heat from the window, the plant had dried in place—still a beautiful purple, still in the same leafy shape. I kept the plant. Fortunately, no one ever took a close look.

When I was first appointed, there were few women on the federal or state bench in Arizona. Mary and I were in Phoenix; Nancy Fiora had recently been appointed a magistrate judge in Tucson. Nancy came up with the brilliant idea that the women judges needed to have some type of social gathering. Didn't the male judges play golf, after all?

Our gathering would be yearly, always over a weekend, at a resort midway between Phoenix and Tucson and at our personal expense. But we did not play golf. It was an intimate weekend of talking and laughing and emotionally connecting.

We wanted to be able to discuss freely what we were experiencing, including the comments of colleagues, staff, and the lawyers who appeared before us. We talked about the joys and burdens in our personal lives. No topic was off the table. By discussing difficult issues, we built a sense of community. After each conference, we felt a sense of renewal.

However, as the years passed and more women became members of the judiciary, they started to get pushback from male colleagues about our yearly conferences. A few of the male judges wanted to know why they weren't invited. It also became more difficult with the increase in the number of women judges to coordinate a successful conference that would be of interest to state and federal trial and appellate judges. In a sense, we became victims of our success.

Some of the women who had recently become judges felt they no longer needed to be part of such a social gathering. They had female colleagues at work that they felt they could trust, and many felt that their professional achievements were the result of their hard work. To my regret, the conferences stopped. Yet some of the male judges continued with their golf outings.

As a final hoorah, when I was an officer of a national organization, I planned a weekend of substantive issues and social gatherings at a pink-hued resort that had a picture of John Wayne in the bar and was midway between Phoenix and Tucson. The national organization had male and female members, but events were mixed or female only. Since one of the purposes of my weekend gathering was to encourage women to join the national organization, our invitations primarily focused on women judges as the attendees. However, although male judges were encouraged to attend, none did. None of us played a single round of golf. We had a wonderful time.

During the same period, I remember attending a business luncheon at which discussions were held on the finer points of lunching at a Hooters restaurant. When I pointed out that such discussions were not appropriate at a business meeting, the individual regaling us turned to me and pointed out that a man on my staff was the one who had been at the restaurant recently and was discussing his adventure with everyone. I said that I would have a private conversation with the staff member, but the current discussion was still not appropriate at a business luncheon. Then there was a chorus of *We were just kidding around. Why are you so concerned? Couldn't we have a little fun?* It was a no-win situation. Whether I felt uncomfortable or not was irrelevant.

Arizona remained a puzzle. I had practiced law in Wisconsin and New York, which had more formal court proceedings. Deference was given to federal judges. Differences of opinion and background were welcomed. No one called a woman a bitch on the record.

I had only been called a disparaging name on the record once before. It was when I was practicing law in New York. I was representing the trustee, and another lawyer was representing a creditor in the case. I needed information from the lawyer and his client about a potentially valuable asset. The lawyer stonewalled me at every turn. Finally, after trying to resolve the dispute, I filed a pleading with the court asking the bankruptcy judge to assess a penalty (my attorneys' fees) for the other side's recalcitrant behavior. At the hearing, the lawyer called me a bitch on the record.

At that statement, the bankruptcy judge became visibly angry, pointed at my opposing counsel, and stated on the record, "You will not speak that way, ever, in my courtroom. Your last statement is expunged from the record. I want to see you and Ms. Curley in my chambers *now*." In chambers, I sat and listened as the judge berated the opposing counsel for his lack of professionalism, including foul language. Any further bad behavior, including not turning over documents that I had reasonably requested, would result in the judge filing a complaint against the attorney with the New York State Bar.

In Arizona, since I was a woman, not from the old boys' bankruptcy network, and probably the youngest person appointed to the position, there were many who did not welcome me and were quick to let me know that. To be clear, I was not alone in receiving disparaging comments. Women at state or regional conferences would buttonhole me and describe the behavior that they had endured. I started with simple changes in my courtroom. No woman would be addressed by her first name at any of my hearings. No attorney would speak for any female attorney, even though in the past they had done so as a matter of convenience for the woman. No foul language would be used in my courtroom. One attorney, who became one of my colleagues and a friend, described my courtroom at the time this way: It was clear changes were happening, and the attorneys needed to get used to it.

One of the hardest attorney habits to break was their desire to have a discussion with me in my chambers as to how a case would progress. Over the years, a number of the Arizona bankruptcy judges had welcomed such informal, off-the-record conversations in their chambers. No court reporter was present to document what was said. Not all of the parties affected in a case were invited to participate in the conversations. One colleague later told me that the attorneys would put their feet up on a nearby table or desk and discuss how the case would progress. In New York and Wisconsin, such conversations were not permitted. They were *ex parte* communications, or interactions with a judge without the knowledge or presence of all parties involved. I was firm on how conferences were to be handled. All parties were to be present in the courtroom, and a record of the proceeding would be recorded.

Over the course of almost twenty-eight years, I did on two occasions require the principal attorneys to come to my chambers. On each occasion, two attorneys had been at the podium arguing over a legal issue. However, the oral argument had devolved into name-calling and foul language. When my warnings on the record did not stop the bad behavior, I stopped the hearing and advised the offending attorneys that I needed to see them immediately in my chambers without their clients. On each occasion, I made my position clear. I would not tolerate such unprofessional conduct in my courtroom. To their credit, I never had a problem with any of the four attorneys at any hearings from that point on.

A major part of my job turned out to be listening—to partners, associates, clients, and to the court's stakeholders. As a judge, it was an even more critical skill. Many wanted to tell their stories, whether through family letters or photographic albums or legal documents. At one settlement conference, the owner of a bar and restaurant in Northern Arizona had a photograph album with her. She described her family's purchase of the land in the 1800s, the building of the initial business, and how the business had been forced into bankruptcy because of wild dreams funded by excessive debt and internecine warfare.

The work I did depended on what was happening on the ground. Arizona had always had a cyclical, boom-or-bust economy. It centered around a stubborn reliance on and even a celebration of real estate. Arizona had always been the place of the five C's: copper, cattle, citrus, cotton, and climate. And lurking in the background was the persistent uncertainty of the water supply. Would we continue to develop into the surrounding mountains until we had no more water?

On many occasions, I traveled to the Los Angeles area for various court conferences. If one were heading west, Quartzsite was the last stop to get cheap gas before crossing into California, where the landscape looked pretty much the same, but everything else was more expensive.

Quartzsite was the land of the rugged individualists and recreational vehicle aficionados. Since the 1960s, Quartzsite was also an open-air flea market with purveyors of rocks, gems, minerals, and fossils that has since morphed into the Desert Gardens Rock, Gem and Mineral Show and seven other shows, drawing a million visitors a year.

In 2023, during the summer months when temperatures

ranged from 110 to 120 degrees Fahrenheit, the city had only seven thousand permanent residents. In the winter months, 250,000 people showed up for the shows and sun, paying about $40 per month to camp on federal land.

In Quartzsite, I also switched from the interstate to state highway. I often struggled to stay awake as I traveled through mile after mile of desert.

As the newest bankruptcy judge, I covered Yuma, a city along the Colorado River. In 1986, Yuma was about three hours away by car. I drove on the interstate, through the desert, past nuclear power plants, and into Gila Bend, which was the home of the Space Age Lodge. In 1965, the owner of the lodge decided to display his friends' connections with the military and the federal government in a tangible way. He acquired autographed photos of the astronauts, and he owned a plastics factory, which allowed him to manufacture space-age artifacts as his décor. The owner died, and the astronaut photographs and other valuable memorabilia were returned to family members. Then the lodge's restaurant burned down. A banner placed in the burned-out ruins claimed that aliens from outer space were responsible. At some point in the 1990s, a flying saucer, or dome, was placed above the lodge's lobby, and in 1999, the restaurant was rebuilt.

Because I only went to Yuma once a month, it was hard to drive the distance, hold court for three hours, get something to eat, then travel home. Flying was an alternative. Subsidiaries of major airlines or smaller regional carriers provided commercial service, but the prop planes only held about eighteen passengers, and the seats looked like card table chairs that a passenger folded down when being seated. Since I had to be in court and ready to go by 10:00 a.m., I needed a flight out at 6:00 a.m. from Phoenix.

Flying to Yuma was about forty minutes from wheels up. However, I needed to factor in delays at the airport as well as wind and dust from passing storms. Moreover, Yuma did not have that much passenger traffic at the time, so flights were few and far between. My return flight also had to be timed based on how long I thought I would be in court. The court was usually three hours, but it could go longer. I added an hour for lunch at a local restaurant, booking a flight for around three or four in the afternoon.

Unfortunately, three or four in the afternoon was when the haboobs rolled in. Yes, haboobs exist in Arizona and in Sudan and other parts of Arabia. A haboob is not a dust storm. The haboob is a roiling wall or cloud of dust reaching above skyscrapers and mountains. As with things that are dangerous, it is thrilling to watch. In 1972, the American Meteorological Society categorized 50 percent of the dust storms in Phoenix as haboobs.

Jet engines do not do well in haboobs. Since Yuma was a civilian as well as a military airport, if any US Marine jets were out on maneuvers when a haboob was approaching, they had priority to land before any commercial aircraft could take off or land. There were a number of times when my aircraft would be ready to take off but was held in a queue until the jets landed. We would sit there as the dust swirled around us on the taxiway. Sometimes we were in for a long day. Even after taking off from Yuma, we could be placed in a holding pattern around Phoenix as another haboob blew through.

I got the bright idea to learn how to fly so I could rent a single engine plane and fly to Yuma for court hearings. I would no longer be tied to the commercial airline schedule. If a storm came in, I could wait it out. There was a slight problem. I was afraid to fly.

My first flight was when I was five years old. My dad took a two-week family vacation every summer in Florida (of all places). He said he didn't like crowds on his vacations, but I always thought there must have been some wooded retreats in Wisconsin, near a lake, that would have been better choices. We went to Cordray's, a mom-and-pop motel on the ocean in

Jacksonville Beach, Florida, year after year until I was ten. It was always hot and humid. When I was two, my family of five drove from Chicago to Cordray's. Along the way, I developed a heat rash, which made me so miserable that I cried or screamed for hours on end. After that adventure, Dad decided to implement Plan B—fly.

I remember one memorable flight to Florida when I was five. It was 1954, when flying was for the wealthy or the desperate (like my dad). The planes were sleek and stylish, known as Lockheed Constellations, with four, propeller-driven engines and a beautiful *T* tail. We usually flew with Eastern Air Lines, which ceased operations in January 1991. Since there were six in my family by 1954, we sat in a large area directly behind the pilot on one side of the aisle.

During takeoffs and landings, the curtain between the pilots was open as well as the curtain to our compartment. As a result, I could watch the pilots as they approached Atlanta, where we would change planes. In the 1950s, Atlanta was notorious for delays because of foreign and domestic travel. I remember one pilot saying to another on approach, "Head on a swivel."

There was that much traffic, and radar and aircraft instruments were not as sophisticated. Was it the hard landing? Something else? I just remember that the landing in Atlanta in 1954 was memorable to me. I cried and didn't like flying after that.

I continued to fly over the years. I flew back and forth from Chicago to an airport near my college in Massachusetts, I flew on various vacations when I lived in New York, I flew to several meetings on behalf of the Wisconsin bank, and now I was traveling back and forth to Yuma with a small regional carrier. I would even trade in my points to fly some more. But I didn't like it one bit. I thought that if I learned to fly, I would solve all my problems as far as getting to Yuma and getting over my fear.

I decided to take flying lessons at an airport near my home. Since I was working, I had to take a course that was structured to allow me to learn at night and/or early in the morning. At night, I took a ground course that talked about the basics of navigation, including night flying with the stars as a guide. I enjoyed that part of the course and easily passed the exam.

In the next stage of training, I learned to fly in a Cessna single-engine aircraft. I had to fly either at 6:00 a.m. before court started or late in the evening after work.

As luck would have it—or maybe it was karma or that this man had the same work schedule as me—I was assigned to a marine pilot who had been based in Yuma, left the service to fly as a corporate pilot for one of the local banks, and became a flight instructor. I had no intention of telling him that I was afraid to fly.

I managed to do well as a pilot. I would go out for the day and report back various adventures to my new friends also learning to fly. It seemed as if I was getting a different type of license from them. We all learned the basics, but I also learned, during night flying, to keep my plane at a certain altitude, do a 360-degree turn, and fly by instruments. My friends wondered if I was somehow blending a private pilot's license with a certification to be a commercial pilot.

I was just getting the basic license. However, the marine had a strong sense of duty. If he was going to teach someone to fly, he wanted to make sure the person was ready to fly under all circumstances. It was also a sense of pride. The marines did things to the point of perfection. Anything less than that reflected negatively on the marine.

Although I flew to Yuma for business, I also rented a plane just to have fun and get a different view of the Arizona landscape. I would fly over new developments being carved out of the desert, watch dirigibles or airships from a distance as they lazily circled over stadiums, fly to Eloy and watch the aerobatic pilots perform stunts, fly midfield over Luke Air Force Base, view the Palo Verde nuclear power plants giving off plumes of white steam over cultivated fields, and a fly over an auxiliary air base used in World War II near the town of Dateland. What I experienced is no longer possible after 9/11. A pilot who doesn't have the appropriate clearance may no longer fly over Luke Air Force Base or near the Palo Verde nuclear power plants.

In the end, I decided that the amount of concentration it took to fly to and from Yuma, hold hearings, and render decisions on pending matters was not sustainable. There was also the problem that I was renting a single-engine plane that did not have air-conditioning when I held hearings in Yuma on 120-degree days. The plane was uncomfortably hot until I got to around eight thousand feet, and the extreme heat tended to cause turbulence and a rougher ride.

The older plane also had a transponder that only provided my position to air traffic control, not my altitude, which led to frequent requests as to my altitude to make sure I was not on a collision course with a military or commercial aircraft. More commercial flights in air-conditioned planes were also being offered, so I gave up flying on business.

I did continue to fly for fun, switching to gliders, which had few instruments and were flown in more remote areas far from any restricted airspace. A series of events, such as breaking my ankle skiing and having a second child, eventually ended my flying career.

CHAPTER FIVE

WAIT, WHICH COURT ARE WE GOING TO?

In the '80s, the bankruptcy world was turned upside down when, in two key rulings, the United States Supreme Court determined that the new bankruptcy law was unconstitutional and the bankruptcy courts were unable to hold jury trials.

The decision of *Northern Pipeline v. Marathon Pipeline*, 458 U.S. 50 (1982), holding the bankruptcy law unconstitutional, had an immediate and deleterious impact on Americans. The bankruptcy courts had to stop conducting all hearings or trials until further notice. Since millions of Americans had relied on the bankruptcy courts to stop creditor harassment, prevent families from being wrongfully removed from their homes, and even to keep the electricity on in the middle of a heat wave, the decision left the vulnerable with no access to relief.

To keep the bankruptcy courts open, the courts' administrative office worked with all federal district court judges to enact local emergency rules allowing bankruptcy judges to hear core matters until the US Congress acted.

It was an uncertain time. Bankruptcy courts entered orders and judgments, which were then separately reviewed by federal district court judges who entered separate orders or judgments as necessary to make sure bankrupts, creditors, or other parties had something on which to rely.

As to the US Supreme Court decision, there was no majority opinion. Rather, several justices forming a majority had agreed on a result that was based on several theories, which left many experts confused as to how to proceed. The justices held that the power to hear a matter, or jurisdiction, given to the bankruptcy courts in the new law was too broad.

Their reasoning was that a bankruptcy court, an Article I court created under the US Constitution and federal law, was deciding matters that had been previously reserved for only US Constitutional Article III federal district court judges.

Their resolution was to return to what had been done under the old bankruptcy law permanently enacted in 1898. Bankruptcy had always focused on giving bankrupts or debtors a fresh start, allowing them to have their debts forgiven if they turned over almost all their assets to help pay creditors. Hearings on such key issues would still be heard in bankruptcy courts.

Since 1934, bankruptcy courts had also handled plans to reorganize the debt or payment structure of public and major corporations. That decision-making process would also continue in the bankruptcy courts.

However, contract disputes between parties that had not filed bankruptcy cases, disputes between individuals involved in wrongful death actions, international trade, government contracts, patents, trademarks, disputes between individuals living in different states, disputes between states, controversies between the US government and foreign governments, and federal criminal law cases would be heard in the federal district courts. Other matters, such as divorce and child custody, trust and probate matters, state consumer protection laws, and state criminal law proceedings would be heard in state trial courts.

The US Congress amended the new bankruptcy law to

return to the bankruptcy courts what had previously been their core jurisdiction. However, the congressional fix, cobbling together the past and present bankruptcy laws, created many gray areas of the law where there were no clear answers.

The question of what the bankruptcy courts would be able to hear and decide was never resolved. As a result, in 1989, the US Supreme Court revisited the issue. In the decision of *In re Granfinanciera, S.A. v. Nordberg*, 492 U.S. 33 (1989), a bankruptcy trustee sought to recover assets that had been fraudulently transferred by the bankrupt to a Colombian company. The trustee filed the lawsuit in the bankruptcy court, and the Colombian company promptly requested a jury trial. Could a bankruptcy court which had traditionally never conducted jury trials be able to do so under the amended law?

Under the old bankruptcy law, a trustee appointed in a bankruptcy case always had to consider who was entitled to a jury trial under the Seventh Amendment to the US Constitution. If a jury trial was required, the trustee requested that the matter be transferred to the federal district or state trial court. In *Granfinanciera*, the trustee was testing the limits of the new law.

From a historical context, after the Norman Conquest of England in 1066, the kings began to consolidate their authority and provide "specific remedies for a specific wrong." This practice, which became known as the common law, became too rigid, so individuals began to appeal to the king for relief. A new court of equity was created, which became known as the court of chancery, named for the king's chancellor who generally presided.

A court of equity could rely on Roman law or other law in determining the result in a particular case. Fraud was considered a common law matter. During the reign of Elizabeth I, queen of England and Ireland from 1158–1603, a statute was enacted as to what constituted fraud and the remedy for it.

Fraud continued to be considered a common law action, and a party accused of fraud was entitled to a jury trial.

However, pundits believed that the new bankruptcy law gave the bankruptcy judges the necessary authority, or jurisdiction, to preside over jury trials. Unfortunately, the US Supreme Court justices came up with a plurality that prohibited bankruptcy court jury trials. The justices relied on English and American legal history in their analysis, concluding that the US Constitution ensured a jury trial for common law matters, and fraud remained part of the common law.

Fortunately, since I had practiced under the old as well as the new bankruptcy law, I had an easier time than most bankruptcy judges determining what I could resolve and what was a bridge too far. Nevertheless, it slowed me down. I had to do a report and recommendation to the federal district court if I decided that my ability to hear a matter might be questioned.

The report was a detailed document that outlined my analysis of factual matters and the legal conclusions that I had drawn from the facts. The federal district court judge would then review my report and decide whether he or she would enter a final order or judgment on the matter or retry it. I don't remember a case where my report was not accepted by a federal judge. The US Congress also continued to amend the bankruptcy law, hoping to resolve all constitutional issues.

The 1982 and 1989 US Supreme Court decisions and further amendments to the bankruptcy law did not end the controversy as to what the bankruptcy court could hear. In the bankruptcy case involving Vicki Lynn Marshall, known as Anna Nicole Smith and a former Playboy bunny, and J. Howard Marshall II, her deceased elderly Texas billionaire husband, the bankruptcy court once again tested the limits of what could be heard and bedeviled the bankruptcy community. Even Justice Roberts began the majority opinion comparing the tragedy of Vicki and Howard Marshall and their families to the legal cases that were fictionalized and satirized by Charles Dickens in his novel *Bleak House*, written between 1852 and 1853.[1]

Vicki had anticipated inheriting Howard's estate even though they had only been married for a short period of time. After Howard died, his son, E. Pierce Marshall ("Pierce"), filed a probate proceeding in Texas, which was the appropriate place to fight out who got what and why under Howard's will.

However, Howard had not included Vicki in his will. Vicki filed a lawsuit in Texas stating that Pierce had fraudulently induced Howard not to include her in any trust or estate documents. Vicki lived in California at the time and believed that she might get a more receptive review of her plight there. She was also having financial problems, so she decided to file a bankruptcy case in California to sort everything out.

Pierce filed a complaint in the California bankruptcy court, stating that Vicki had defamed him, and he didn't want his damage claim against her ever forgiven. Pierce also made the mistake of filing a claim (known as a "proof of claim") with the bankruptcy court, asking that it be approved and that he be paid as any other creditor.

Of course, since Pierce had arguably consented to the jurisdiction of the California bankruptcy court by filing pleadings with the court, Vicki filed a counterclaim (or claim against Pierce) in Pierce's defamation lawsuit, stating that she had not maligned him (What she said about him was true!) and Pierce had defrauded her. Vicki argued that Pierce had

1. Justice Roberts' opinion began, "This 'suit has, in the course of time, become so complicated, that...no two lawyers...can talk about it for five minutes without coming to a total disagreement as to all the premises. Innumerable children have been born into the cause: innumerable young people have married into it,' and sadly the original parties 'have died out of it.' A 'long procession of [judges] has come and gone out' during that time, and still the suit 'drags its weary length before the Court'" (Stern v. Marshall, 564 U.S. 462, 131 S.Ct. 2594, 180 L.Ed.2d 475 [2011]).

willfully denied her an expected gift, an inheritance from her husband. She wanted substantial damages because of Pierce's actions. Vicki had inserted matters that were already before the Texas probate court into her bankruptcy proceedings.

The bankruptcy court plunged ahead, deciding that Pierce had willfully denied Vicki's inheritance claim and that she should receive millions of dollars in damages. However, the Texas probate court had already denied her claim to an inheritance.

The usual rule when courts have ruled on the same issues was to give preference or deference to the court which first entered its ruling by judgment or order. It was clear that the Texas court had ruled first on whether Vicki was entitled to a gift or inheritance from her husband. Pierce had not defrauded her.

The appellate courts, including the US Supreme Court, could have simply honored the Texas court decision and allowed the bankruptcy court to set a trial on Pierce's separate claim that Vicki had defamed him. Unfortunately, the US Supreme Court waded into deep water and created an unnecessary layer of nuance. The justices wondered how to handle Vicki's claim about a denial of her inheritance that she had inserted in her answer to the complaint filed by Pierce in the California bankruptcy court.

Vicki's claim against Pierce should not have been heard by the bankruptcy court. Certain matters were creatures of state law, such as divorces, custody of children, and criminal actions. A bankruptcy court couldn't enter a divorce decree, decide which parent had custody of a child, or try a murderer. One more item was added to the list—a bankruptcy court was not to resolve a state law claim asserted by a debtor/defendant as a claim against the creditor/plaintiff (a "counterclaim"), which was not resolved in ruling on the creditor's claim even though a counterclaim was statutorily a matter that bankruptcy courts decided. The Supreme Court analysis was confusing. Bankruptcy courts were charged with resolving disputes where claims and counterclaims were asserted by the parties. The bankruptcy law allowed the courts to resolve issues between the parties and enter a judgment that netted out the damages on the various claims asserted by both sides.

The *Stern v. Marshall* decision dramatically changed what the bankruptcy courts could resolve. It required bankruptcy courts to analyze issues brought before it and throw out matters that didn't belong there even if one or more parties had initially asked the bankruptcy court to decide the issues.

The bankruptcy courts wanted clarification. What if the parties had a unique claim that was related to the outcome of a bankruptcy case and consented (for the convenience of everyone) that the bankruptcy court hear everything? Finally, in *Wellness International Network, Limited v. Sharif*, 575 U.S. 665 (2015), the bankruptcy community received an answer.

Wellness International Network, a manufacturer of health and nutrition products, had entered into a contract with Richard Sharif, who would distribute the products. Contract disputes led Sharif to sue Wellness International in the federal district court in Texas. Sharif did not comply with court orders, so a judgment was entered against him, with Sharif to pay Wellness International's attorneys' fees.

In February 2009, Sharif filed a bankruptcy case in Illinois. During the bankruptcy proceedings, Sharif advised Wellness and the trustee that he had lied on a 2002 loan application, stating that he had $5 million in assets. The assets he had listed were owned by family members, and he was only the administrator.

Wellness then filed a complaint in the bankruptcy court, alleging that Sharif should not receive forgiveness of his debts as to all his creditors (known as a discharge) because Sharif had concealed property from his creditors by claiming that assets he owned were owned by family members. Wellness, however, had also requested the bankruptcy court to conclude that the assets that Sharif asserted belonged to his family members should become a part of the bankruptcy estate since Sharif had engaged in fraud and treated the assets as his own.

On appeal, even though Sharif had not raised the issue, the Seventh Circuit Court of Appeals held that the bankruptcy court did not have the power to bring third-party assets into the bankruptcy estate.

Based on early bankruptcy law, the US Supreme Court concluded that the bankruptcy court could determine which assets were a part of the bankruptcy estate to be distributed to creditors if the parties consented. In 1789, bankruptcy was added to the US Constitution as a matter that would be determined by federal courts.

Under the 1898 bankruptcy law, district court judges referred or asked individuals known as referees, masters, or arbitrators to hear bankruptcy disputes and file a report with the federal district court as to how to resolve the disputes if the parties to the dispute consented.

As a result, the justices stated that a constitutional right to have an "impartial and independent" determination by a federal district court judge was a "personal right subject to waiver, just as are other personal constitutional rights." Sharif had not asked for a federal district court judge to resolve what assets were part of the bankruptcy estate, so he had waived a personal constitutional right; in essence, he consented to the bankruptcy court resolving the issue.

However, in reaching their decision, the majority engrafted another condition. The consent of the parties could never be used to resolve "an actual violation of Article III" of the US Constitution or where a "structural principle protected by Article III" was implicated. Presumably a contract dispute between third parties that have not filed bankruptcy petitions, as in the *Northern Pipeline v. Marathon Pipeline* decision, or a contract claim against the United States government would be the types of matters that could not be decided by the bankruptcy court even with the consent of the parties.

Revisiting earlier decisions, the justices determined that if a party did not want the bankruptcy court to hear a matter, the party had to let the court know that it "did not truly consent to" having the bankruptcy court enter a judgment or order in the case. The justices' advice to the bankruptcy court was it would be a "good practice" for the bankruptcy court "to seek express statements of consent or nonconsent" at the beginning of a matter.

Even before the US Supreme Court decided *Wellness International*, I began asking parties in lawsuits before me whether they consented to my hearing all issues. I usually posed the question at the first administrative hearing and asked all the lawyers to file their consents with the court. If one or more lawyers did not consent, I usually set a hearing to decide what to do next.

CHAPTER SIX

WALL STREET WAS WATCHING

One day, while I was still working in Wisconsin, I wandered into the office of the bank's stock traders to learn more about what they were doing. For companies that didn't qualify for traditional loans, the trading group was consummating transactions based on a new idea that allowed securities to be purchased and sold between willing parties according to what they thought the market would do. Essentially, they were placing bets on which way the financial markets would trend. This was a new way for a bank to finance a company without doing its due diligence.

From a practical standpoint, what were the securities traders doing? Let's say Person A wants to place a bet that the stock of G corporation will go down five points, and Person B, sometimes a financial institution, takes the other side of the bet, believing that the stock will do the reverse, going up five points.

Person A, who owns one hundred shares of G corporation stock, agrees to sell the shares to Person B for $55 per share, or $5,500. Person A electronically transfers the shares to Person B, who gives Person A the sum of $5,500. The problem?

Person A has just given away $5,500 on a speculative bet that could have been used to help with business operating costs.

Person A has also agreed to repurchase the G corporation stock from Person B at a specific time or date in the future. Since the parties are setting up the transaction, they can agree that the stock will be repurchased two minutes, two days, or two weeks from when they sign the agreement. The repurchase price will be at whatever the market price is at the future agreed upon date or time. Since it is a stock sale, Person B may then sell the shares to Person C, who then sells the shares to Person D, and on into infinity until the music stops at some date and time in the future. Do all the contracts have to match? No. Person B may agree to sell the shares to Person C for a time period less than what has been agreed between A and B.

What if Person A is wrong and the G corporation stock has a market price that has gone up five points to $60 per share? On the day that Person A has agreed to repurchase the shares from Person B, Person A must repurchase the G corporation shares for $6,000 from Person B. Funds desperately needed for Person A's business operations now must be turned over to Person B. Person B, in turn, hopes that Person C, Person D, etc., are able to unwind their bets so that Person B receives the G Corporations shares in time to present them to Person A.

What if Person A is unable to turn over $6,000 on the agreed-upon date? Person A may decide to file a bankruptcy petition. However, because of lobbying efforts by Wall Street financial institutions and broker-dealers, Person A will gain little in bankruptcy. The bankruptcy court must enforce these contracts. These speculative bets being placed are known as repurchase and reverse repurchase agreements, which are similar to derivative contracts. A repurchase agreement is Party A's agreement to sell its stock with a concomitant agreement to repurchase it from a third party on a set date and time. A reverse repurchase agreement is Party A's purchase of the third party's stock with the concomitant agreement to resell it to the third party on a set date and time.

In 1989, one of my cases allowed me to understand how this unregulated market for speculative contracts had grown, become more complicated, and could result in disastrous consequences. Residential Resources was a company of creative people who relied solely on the purchase of various mortgage assets for their business operations. Any net income received from their investments was distributed directly to the shareholders. They also decided to enlist a New York brokerage firm to help them with what they thought would be a profitable new market.

The company and the broker entered into repurchase and reverse repurchase agreements. Each side was basically placing bets on what would happen in the market. These agreements could be entered into over and over again and were timed to last only a day or two. On a given day, it was unclear who really had the securities and how many agreements had to be unwound to return the securities to the original company.

The company thought that by selling its securities and purchasing some of the broker's securities it was hedging its bets while getting cash to operate without going through the rigors of obtaining a loan from a financial institution. In any event, the company was a start-up, with little or no cash flow and no tangible assets. It never would have qualified for a traditional loan.

These agreements only work if a company has substantial capital that will allow the company to continue with its everyday operations while absorbing losses on all its market bets. Residential Resources saw its losses from the agreements exponentially rise. It literally ran out of cash. It had no recourse other than to file a bankruptcy petition.

Normally the filing of a bankruptcy petition creates an

injunction, known as the "automatic stay," that stops all activity of a creditor. The creditor can't demand payment of a bill, and it can't seize assets even if it has a lien on the company's car, stock, or some other asset. However, with the changes to the Bankruptcy Code, thanks to the lobbying efforts of the financial industry, the repurchase and reverse repurchase agreements were not subject to an automatic stay. At the time, the financial market leaders believed that the market for these agreements was so substantial that any attempt to regulate them would be catastrophic.

The issue, in any given case, was whether the agreement met the statutory requirements to be considered exempt from any interference from the bankruptcy court or creditors. If a creditor believed it had such an agreement but turned out to be wrong, the debtor would argue that the automatic stay had been violated and would request damages for any monetary loss that it suffered, plus punitive damages. Punitive damages were tied to what a judge thought was a sufficient penalty to deter abhorrent behavior. As a result, creditors proceeded cautiously and asked the bankruptcy court to confirm their analysis.

The creditor in Residential Resources asked me to determine the nature of their agreements. As a result, Residential Resources had a brief respite to sort through its agreements and see whether it was a winner or a loser. The issue that I had to resolve was relatively simple: Had the company entered into repurchase and reverse repurchase agreements, free from regulation, or had it entered into a secured transaction where the broker only had a lien on the securities? If the broker only had a lien on the securities, it would have to wait, like other creditors, to give the company additional time to try to propose a plan to pay creditors.

Wall Street was watching my case. I ruled in favor of Thomson McKinnon, the New York broker. However, Residential Resources appealed my decision. Unfortunately, the appellate courts did not rule quickly enough. Thomson McKinnon, one of the oldest brokerage houses on Wall Street, was unable to liquidate the securities in time to continue its operations. Both Residential Resources and Thomson McKinnon went out of business.

In the decades since, speculative trading has increased exponentially. Some estimate that $1 trillion dollars or more are now invested in these agreements. They are no longer the sale and repurchase of securities. They can be a bet on anything in the market. In the *Delphi* bankruptcy case, filed in 2005, agreements were entered into as to whether the public company's stock would rise or fall in market price.

In some cases, the parties to the agreements said they would transfer the stock of Delphi to the party that had won the bet. Unfortunately, there were so many bets placed that there was insufficient issued and outstanding stock of Delphi available once the music stopped and required certain parties to perform under their derivative agreements.

The losing parties to the bets were required to deliver the stock electronically, but they could not purchase the stock on any market. They defaulted on their agreements, causing cascading events of default that forced many parties to file their own bankruptcy petitions.

Because these types of agreements still exist in unregulated markets, it is impossible to grasp the universe of creditors of any bankrupt company. These parties, to infinity, are out there. And no one really knows what will happen if the market collapses and all these transactions are unwound. These types of agreements may be in your own retirement portfolio.

CHAPTER SEVEN

THE BILLIONAIRE'S GAMBIT

Like an overly strong cup of coffee that caused the jitters, he was there every morning on the radio on my drive to work. In a folksy voice, he invited us to see a new development, thirty miles west of Phoenix, in the desolate, desert foothills of the Estrella Mountains: "You gotta buy now! My new model homes are in a community dominated by family values! Close to nature, yet such a convenient commute to Phoenix." Or he implored us to stay at his new luxury hotel, the Phoenician, in the shadow of Camelback Mountain, the tony area of Phoenix, where no request from a guest was too large, too small, or unreasonable.

Sometimes, he advised the listener that not only was he a successful businessman, but he personally knew Mother Theresa. Newspapers featured photos of him leaning over as Mother Theresa whispered in his ear. Later he would advise us that he had made substantial donations to her many worthy causes and charities. Other times, he would berate federal regulators for any fine levied against a savings bank. "These banks are essential to the homeownership of the many," he argued. "Aren't the people who run those savings and loans today knowledgeable and caring and able to run a bank without federal interference?"

Then one morning in April 1989, instead of his radio ad, there was a breaking story: Charlie Keating, the businessman with the folksy voice, had placed his company, American Continental Corporation, in bankruptcy. In 1989, there were not very many mega-cases—cases exceeding $100 million in assets or liabilities—but American Continental was one of them.

The bankruptcy judge randomly appointed to the case was forty years old and had only been a judge for three years. She was the first woman in Arizona history to hold the position. The local newspaper tried to get her to comment, but her phone number was unlisted. The reporters contacted her next-door neighbor, who was listed. Would the neighbor mind going next door and asking the judge to call the reporters back? The neighbor soon returned to advise the reporters on the telephone that the judge had no comment.

The judge was relatively new to Arizona, and reporters contacted local attorneys for their opinion and called the bank in Wisconsin where she had previously worked. In the press, the local lawyers thought she would probably do a good job, although a few demurred, stating that it was unlawyerly to comment on any sitting judge.

The lawyers in Wisconsin stated that she would be fantastic as the judge presiding over the case. She had started out as a lawyer in New York and had always been in the bankruptcy field. In Arizona, the newspapers knew little about the judge. They hungered for more; who was this judge, and what was she about to do?

In the spring of 1989, I was randomly assigned to the American Continental bankruptcy case, a mega-case, with liabilities exceeding $100 million. Because American Continental had spun off many diverse companies in many locations, sorting out the issues would be complex and time-consuming. Charlie Keating was the charismatic head of the company. American Continental would be unforgettable, a challenge from the beginning.

Charles H. Keating was born December 4, 1923, and was enrolled at the University of Cincinnati at the beginning of World War II. He enlisted in the US Naval Air Corps, trained as a pilot, and was discharged in 1945 without engaging in combat. He became a lawyer and practiced law in Cincinnati, founding his own firm in 1952.

In 1972, Charlie Keating became executive vice president of American Financial Corporation, an insurance company. By 1979, Charlie and Carl H. Lindner Jr., then head of the company, would be charged with defrauding stockholders by the Securities and Exchange Commission (SEC). The SEC alleged that they had improperly made loans in the amount of $14 million to themselves and other officers of the company.

Although the SEC fined Keating, he maintained his innocence. In 1980, he resurfaced in Phoenix, Arizona, as a prominent real estate developer. American Continental, the shell corporation he created in Arizona, would eventually hold stock or ownership interests in entities connected with his real estate empire. Keating was particularly interested in the savings and loan industry. His deregulation lobbying efforts and his willingness to use savings and loan assets to fuel his real estate empire would ruin the financial institution he controlled and eventually destroy the industry.

Savings and loan associations were begun in the 1800s to finance housing for those who lacked sufficient savings to purchase a home. They began as member-only associations that allowed individuals to pool their funds and then provide a member with funds to build or purchase a home.

As funds were repaid, new loans were provided to

members. Any funds held by the savings and loan were conservatively invested to ensure that there were always sufficient funds on hand to operate. Over time, savings and loan associations, later also known as thrifts, provided financing to an important part of the mortgage market. In 1980, there were almost four thousand savings and loans, with assets of $480 billion in mortgage loans and total assets of $600 billion.

But trouble was brewing. In the late 1970s and early 1980s, inflation and interest rates on loans rose dramatically. In 1979, because of inflation, the Federal Reserve of the United States raised the discount rate, or the rate that member banks had to pay to get cash to make loans, from 9.5 to 12 percent. As a result, the average rate of interest on a thirty-year fixed-rate mortgage rose to 12.9 percent or higher for consumers.

Market interest rates on short-term United States Treasury securities guaranteed by the federal government rose to over 12 percent. Conversely, the savings and loans, because of government regulations, could only pay 5.25 percent on depositors' accounts. Depositors, squeezed by inflation, withdrew their money from savings and loans, seeking investments with higher rates of return. The savings and loans were hemorrhaging cash.

Another problem was that because of an acute shortage of affordable housing for veterans returning home after World War II, savings and loans had provided low-interest, long-term, fixed-rate mortgages to veterans and their families. Counterintuitively, savings and loans held these mortgage loans as their assets, and the depositors' funds were listed as liabilities.

Any interest paid by a borrower on a mortgage loan would be booked as income to the savings and loan. As the borrower repaid the loan principal, the asset value of the loan on the savings and loan's balance sheet would be reduced.

In the 1970s and early 1980s, as mortgage loan interest

rates began to rise, savings and loans found they were trapped with assets rapidly decreasing in value. The mortgage loans would not mature for another twenty-five to thirty years, and the mortgage loans' interest rates were far below the market rate. They could try to sell their portfolio of mortgage loans, but who would buy them? Long-term mortgages at a lower interest rate would generate less profit to any buyer over time. The savings and loans saw their assets plummet in value, and there was nothing they could do about it.

The savings and loans were on the verge of becoming insolvent. The government regulators did not have congressional funding to solve the industry's problems, so they began industry deregulation. However, the regulators' actions had unintended consequences. By 1983, many savings and loans had insufficient cash to operate.

Rather than close the businesses, which required congressional funding to wind up operations and pay depositors and other creditors, the regulators allowed the savings and loans to keep their doors open. Like a house with lights on but no one at home, the savings and loans were open, but no business could be conducted. There was no cash on hand. They became known as "zombie banks." The federal government estimated that it would cost $25 billion to pay the insured depositors if they closed all the zombies, but the insurance fund held by the Federal Savings and Loan Insurance Corporation only had $6 billion on hand.

In the crisis, Keating and other wealthy individuals saw an opportune way to make a lot of money in a short period of time. In 1984, Keating acquired Lincoln Savings & Loan, based in Irvine, California, as one of American Continental's wholly owned subsidiaries. Lincoln would finance Keating's empire.

Once Lincoln Savings & Loan was acquired, American Continental subsidiaries that owned real estate began exchanging properties among themselves. They were described as "purchases and sales," but they were simply book entries. Lincoln Savings & Loan was listed as the financial institution that allowed one subsidiary to finance the purchase of real estate from another subsidiary.

For instance, Subsidiary A might sell property to Subsidiary B for $1 million, and Subsidiary B might sell the same property to Subsidiary C for $1.5 million. Lincoln Savings provided the funding for the sales to take place. The paper transactions greatly inflated the aggregate value of Keating's residential and commercial properties. Within a short period of time, huge profits appeared to be generated on real estate transactions that were manufactured by those in control.

It was also alleged that Keating was pressuring appraisers to come up with his desired values for his companies' properties. Before Keating came to the Valley of the Sun, appraising real estate property had always been an art as much as a science. He was creating financial statements that reflected a huge increase in his companies' net worth over a short period of time.

In California, Lincoln Savings & Loan began selling American Continental's uninsured bonds to retirees who were seeking a safe investment. The retirees had ventured into the bank to open a savings account or acquire government-insured bonds and ended up purchasing "junk bonds," or worthless debt, in American Continental, which held overinflated assets and little cash. American Continental had insufficient assets to make any of the bond payments. Depositors soon learned that they had been had.

After depositors filed complaints with the Federal Home Loan Bank Board, which regulated the savings and loan industry, Keating allegedly pressured five US senators to force the board to expedite its review and approve what Lincoln Savings & Loan had been doing. In May 1988, M. Danny Wall, chair of the board, transferred the financial review of

Lincoln from the San Francisco office, which recommended seizure, to the bank board's home office in Washington, DC.

Meanwhile, Keating celebrated in Phoenix. The transfer of the financial review to Washington meant that seizure of his savings and loan was not imminent. Later William Black and Michael Patriarca would testify before the House Banking Committee that Keating's pull with senators was sufficient to delay the takeover of Lincoln by at least two years.

The senators' apparent actions triggered a separate investigation by the Senate's Ethics Committee. During its fourteen-month investigation, the committee found that more than $1 million had been donated by Keating to the senators for their campaigns, for four trips by the senators to the Bahamas, or for all-expense-paid stays by the senators at resort hotels. The $1 million had come from Keating's Lincoln Savings & Loan, money paid by retired persons to Lincoln with the hope of purchasing safe investments.

Another part of Keating's empire was the acquisition, along with the Kuwait Investment Office, of an ownership interest in vacant land at Camelback Road and Sixty-First Street, a wealthy area of Phoenix. A local artist who had originally owned the land gave it to her son and daughter-in-law in 1926 for construction of a residence.

Initially the residence, an adobe-style home, was known as "jokake," or "mud house," and was used to host guests. The Jokake residence, once a fashionable getaway frequented by the Astors and Rockefellers, fell into disrepair and eventually closed in 1979.

In 1985, Charlie Keating saw the potential in locating a luxury resort on 254 acres of the original land owned by the artist, which had commanding views of the nearby mountains and the Phoenix skyline. In 1988, the resort, named the Phoenician Hotel, opened. On the grounds of the resort was the old Jokake residence, which later became known as the Jokake Inn.

Keating spared no expense in constructing his luxury resort, with marble for the lobby imported from Carrera, Italy; twenty-four-karat gold etched in the ceiling; lush gardens throughout the resort; many challenging golf courses to keep the enthusiast entertained; and an elegant restaurant named for his wife, Mary Elaine.

In 1989, the *Los Angeles Times* featured an article about the Phoenician, its extravagance, and the fact that it was financed by Lincoln Savings & Loan, one of Keating's subsidiaries. The newspaper described the marble-floored main lobby and the $25 million art collection and disclosed the cost to complete the resort at $300 million. The average room rate for the Phoenix market at the time was so low that experts estimated it would take at least forty years for the resort to turn a profit.

Keating could not financially sustain the Phoenician, even though he had managed to sell a 45 percent interest in the resort to the Kuwait Investment Office. Although the resort began paying its ordinary expenses, it was not bringing in enough cash to pay the debt it owed to Lincoln.

When American Continental filed its bankruptcy petition in April 1989, many of the American Continental bankruptcy lawyers soon took up residence at the resort. It was argued that the lawyers were staying there at well below the market cost for the rooms, so the lawyers were saving the creditors money. Many questioned that analysis. Couldn't the lawyers take up residence at one of the hotels that catered to professionals who were in the Phoenix area on a long-term basis? No one foresaw how the residency issue would be resolved.

Keating also owned an interest in the Hotel Pontchartrain in Detroit, Michigan. The hotel was dedicated on July 24, 1965, and had a modern architectural style, with bay windows providing views of the city's riverfront. In 1985, the Crescent Hotel Group, a subsidiary of Lincoln Savings & Loan, which was then under Keating's control, purchased the hotel for $19.5 million.

Keating then purchased the hotel outright from the hotel group for $38 million and placed it in the Hotel Pontchartrain Limited Partnership, which he controlled along with family members and other executives. The vehicle of the limited partnership shielded him and others from liability.

Moreover, the dramatic increase in the paper value of the hotel from $19.5 million to $38 million, the purchase price, was artificial, giving the appearance of a dramatic increase in real estate values. Keating used Lincoln and its subsidiaries to finance the sale, passing the risk of owning the hotel from himself and others to Lincoln.

Keating also had dreams of developing desert land west of Phoenix, near the interstate highway to Los Angeles and the Estrella Mountains, into a master-planned community. In 1988, he began constructing the community infrastructure and opening model homes when little was around other than a glider airport in rugged terrain.

The 20,000-acre community, located in Goodyear, Arizona, became known as Estrella, named for the Estrella Mountains in the Sonoran Desert. As with his other real estate transactions, the many intercompany transfers to create the community's infrastructure gave the appearance that the development was rapidly increasing in value.

As his companies' holdings became more substantial, they began to affect the market value of other residential and commercial properties in the Phoenix metropolitan area. He was creating financial statements that reflected a huge increase in net worth over a short period of time. It was an empire that would later cause a catastrophic collapse in the Phoenix real estate market.

Lincoln continued to generate paper loans for intercompany transfers, increasing the book value of its assets from $1 billion in 1984 to $5 billion by 1989. Keating had invested two-thirds of Lincoln's federally insured funds in high-risk real estate ventures and junk bonds. When it appeared that the regulators were going to shut down Lincoln, Keating filed a bankruptcy petition for his holding company, American Continental, in April 1989.

After I was assigned to the case, American Continental lawyers requested an emergency hearing. The lawyers accused the government regulators of violating the bankruptcy law. Without notice and when everyone was asleep, the regulators had seized Lincoln Savings & Loan, Keating's crown jewel. The regulators had effectively shut down the business operations of American Continental since Lincoln was the source of ready funding for all of Keating's entities.

American Continental requested a hearing the next day. Emotions were high. The American Continental lawyers were incensed. The regulators' lawyers, not so much. Since Lincoln, as a federal savings and loan, could not file a bankruptcy case and was most likely insolvent, the regulators argued that federal law pertaining to all savings and loans required the immediate seizure of Lincoln to protect the depositors' funds and wind up Lincoln's operations, minimizing the losses that would have to be paid ultimately by taxpayers. The regulators had put a receiver, or fiduciary, in place who was charged with protecting depositors' funds and winding up Lincoln's operations while maximizing payments to creditors and defrauded investors.

The seizure by the regulators should have been foreseen by American Continental. The regulators in San Francisco had been questioning Lincoln's operations for years, but the transfer of the regulators' review to the office in Washington, DC only delayed the inevitable. American Continental's bankruptcy filing meant the company would be under the control of the court and the creditors. Keating's loss of absolute control of American Continental and all its subsidiaries gave the regulators the chance to get the upper hand and seize Lincoln.

In a bold move, the receiver then seized control of all of

Lincoln's subsidiaries, including the Phoenician Hotel, fired the law firm representing the Lincoln group, and retained new legal counsel. New counsel for Lincoln and its subsidiaries had just found out about the hearing but were in attendance.

It was a novel legal issue. Was American Continental still in control of Lincoln and its subsidiaries, or had other federal law as to savings and loans permitted the seizure of Lincoln? To me, it seemed the receiver had acquired all the powers of a shareholder at the time he seized Lincoln. As a shareholder, he could appoint new officers or directors, decide what to do with Lincoln's assets, and employ any lawyers he desired. No one seemed to disagree with my analysis, and we began the hard task of trying to decide if American Continental could survive without a ready source of financing.[1]

Unfortunately, one of the more valuable assets was lost. Keating did not want just his real estate properties to be lavish. He needed to have an appropriate arsenal of airplanes and jets to fly, at a moment's notice, to his properties in Arizona, Michigan, or other locations. His planes needed a suitable hangar to be protected from the elements. The City of Phoenix accommodated Keating, renting to the company a hangar located at Sky Harbor Airport.

However, its concrete walls and floor did not seem appropriate. Keating had the hangar redone with luxurious offices, carpeting, and a valuable art collection. And, yes, the airplanes and jets were also nestled inside.

The issue was whether American Continental would be able to sell its interest in the hangar lease to some other company. The ability to transfer a long-term lease interest was possible under the bankruptcy law. The new tenant would acquire American Continental's interest and most likely be

1. Using a federal statute enacted later in 1989, an appellate court agreed with my overall analysis. In re Landmark Land Company, et als v. Resolution Trust Corporation, et als, 973 F.2d 283 (4th Cir. 1992).

able to pay a below-market rental for the hangar to the City of Phoenix. American Continental would receive much-needed cash from the transfer and possibly be able to sell the airplanes, art collection, office furniture, or other hangar assets as well.

There was one catch. American Continental had a limited period, as outlined in the bankruptcy law, to sell the lease. Unfortunately, its law firm missed the deadline. At a hearing after the deadline had passed, the lawyers tried to convince me not to worry. Wasn't getting as much money as possible for the lease what counted? Didn't everyone miss deadlines? The bankruptcy statute and case law were clear that some deadlines could not be missed, no matter what the problem. I ruled that the City of Phoenix lease had been automatically rejected or effectively terminated. American Continental had to vacate the hangar immediately.

Because there were so many moving pieces in the case, I usually set hearings in the case several times a week. One morning, as I took the bench, I noticed that the American Continental lawyers had a lot of cardboard boxes stacked around the counsel table at the front of the courtroom. Since no evidentiary hearings were scheduled that morning, I was unsure what was in the cardboard boxes. The courtroom was packed. All the American Continental lawyers looked a bit sleep-deprived. Something had happened.

One of American Continental's lawyers went to the podium and advised me that it was a sad day in the case. He had never suffered such indignities. He had had a sleepless night. He then went to the counsel table, grabbed one of the cardboard boxes, and brought it over to the podium. I could now see what was in the partially opened box. At the top was a random assortment of toothpaste, wrinkled shirts, and other personal items.

"Judge, in the middle of the night, I was awakened by a pounding at my hotel room door. I went to the door, calling out, 'Who's there?' A voice from the other side of the door said they were with Lincoln's receiver. They said I had to get out of the room . . . immediately. It was two o'clock in the morning!

"I told them, in colorful language, that was unreasonable. What authority did they have to do that? I was going to call the court and let you and everyone else know what was going on. But I realized I'd probably not get a hearing at 2 a.m., so I threw everything into a few boxes and suitcases and left. That's just not fair what they did! I can't say it was illegal. We had been told that the receiver wanted us out so as to get market rates for the hotel rooms, but in the middle of the night?" He paused, grabbed the box from the podium, and went back to the counsel table. I then asked what relief he was requesting. He said nothing.

I asked the receiver's lawyers if they had forced the American Continental lawyers out of the Phoenician at 2 a.m. They responded affirmatively. I then asked the American Continental lawyers if they had incurred any expenses in moving, and they said no. I admonished the receiver's lawyers for their actions in the middle of the night and told the lawyers we were breaking for the day to allow the American Continental lawyers to get settled in their new hotel rooms at another location and get some sleep.

The case continued day by day, with twenty or so easy-to-complex matters heard by me a day, several days a week. The volume of pleadings filed was unprecedented. I needed additional staff just to place the pleadings on the court docket, schedule hearings, contact counsel of the date and time of emergency hearings, and make sure documents were filed in the right place. There was no electronic court filing system in place in those days, so every paper pleading had to be reviewed and placed in the appropriate place for future access by the court, lawyers, and the public.

The hearings developed a certain pattern. Judy Wischer, who made $800,000 a year in 1989, was the president of American Continental, so she certainly could have been the appropriate executive who would usually testify as to the overall assets and liabilities of a company, its debt structure, its major creditors, and an overview of the financial operations. The problem was she didn't seem to have a grasp of the operations. We would have to stop the hearing because she didn't have the requisite information and have another officer testify.

At times, I had so little evidence from American Continental on matters which they had brought that I had to rule against them. Keating, who was chairman of the American Continental Board of Directors and had bragged to the newspapers as to his business acumen and thorough knowledge of all business operations, was present at every hearing, sitting in the back, but never testified under oath. Meanwhile all the investors at Keating's Lincoln Savings & Loan felt that they had been defrauded and filed a class action lawsuit in the Arizona federal district court.

As the case dragged on, it was clear that American Continental could not reorganize. No one wanted to lend it any money, given the recent press about fraudulent activities. Any assets it had were liquidated, but creditors would receive little on their claims.

The retirees who had purchased now worthless American Continental debt eventually obtained a civil judgment against Keating. Criminal proceedings had also been commenced against Keating, and a jury had convicted him of fraud. Later the Ninth Circuit Court of Appeals reversed the criminal conviction.

In 1990, federal legislation was enacted creating the Resolution Trust Corporation (RTC), a federal management company which took control of and liquidated assets of failed savings and loans. In 1990, the RTC placed the Hotel

Pontchartrain in receivership. The Detroit, Michigan, hotel was then managed by Radisson Hotels and was one of Lincoln's subsidiaries. In 1994, the hotel was sold to third parties at a substantial loss to United States taxpayers.

The Federal Savings & Loan Insurance Corporation (FSLIC) paid out $3 billion to the depositors and others who had sustained a loss because of Lincoln's fraudulent activity. Keating only owned Lincoln for five years, which meant that he had losses of roughly $1 million a day.

The depositors would continue to pursue insurance companies, law and accounting firms, and others they believed responsible for their losses. There were more than one thousand savings and loans that eventually failed, costing the taxpayers an estimated $124 billion. The losses would eventually deplete all assets of FSLIC.

Kuwait Investment Office sold their stake in the Phoenician for $140 million.

In 2021, the Estrella parcels were sold to builders for $212.5 million. In 1988, Keating had paid $100 million for desert land. Over thirty-five years, the Estrella parcels had turned out to be a poor investment. The compound annual growth rate was only 2.18 percent. With inflation at the average rate of 2.74 percent over the same period, the investment would had to have grown to a value of $258 million in 2023 to break even. In 2023, only 21,000 people resided in Estrella, with 7,600 homes having been completed. About 40 to 45 percent of the community has been developed, with another eight thousand to ten thousand future homes possible.

If Keating had invested $100,000 in 1989, with a projected 5 percent return, 3 percent inflation rate, and no taxes being paid, the funds would eventually have grown to $432,000,000 in thirty years. His investments in real estate had only led to massive losses to investors and the United States taxpayers.

Keating never recovered from the loss of his empire. He spent his final days living with his daughter.

In so many ways, the American Continental case reminded me of the Adela Holzer case when I was a student law clerk in New York. Many of the wealthy were indifferent to rules and constraints—even to the point that a few found it acceptable to defraud people.

CHAPTER EIGHT
I SHALL NOT ATONE!

From 1800 to 1978, the old bankruptcy law offered a fresh start to those who placed their assets before the court and agreed that most of those assets would be used to pay creditors to receive forgiveness of their obligations to creditors. Historically, a party that did not go through the process would not be released from the payment of creditors.

From time to time, other parties also wanted debt relief without going through bankruptcy proceedings. However, the Bankruptcy Code was clear: Forgiving the debtor as to repayment of a debt did not affect the liability of any other party for the same debt.[1] That third party had to pay the debt as agreed.

Mass tort litigation changed the game. An airplane manufacturer created an aircraft, a few of which might crash in the future;[2] a company manufactured intrauterine devices that

1. Section 524(e).

2. In the case of Piper Aircraft, 162 B.R. 619 (Bankr. S.D. FL 1994), the judge stated the company had been manufacturing aviation aircraft since 1937. Fifty thousand to sixty thousand of those aircraft were still operational in 1994. Unfortunately, because of design or construction defects, the judge anticipated that some of those planes would crash, even after the company

would cause injuries to women many years after the devices were implanted;[3] a car manufacturer that had known about a defective ignition switch for many years still manufactured and sold the defective automobiles to the public.[4] The bankruptcy courts found it difficult to find a solution to the massive claims that were being created and to the future claims that would surely arise but would not be known for years to come.

What started a rethinking of who should be forgiven for misconduct affecting thousands of people began with an asbestos bankruptcy case. In the 1940s and '50s, Johns-Manville Corp., later known by the same name but without the hyphen, manufactured asbestos, which was used in shipyards and construction on a widespread basis in the United States. Although, over the years, many were exposed to asbestos, there was no definitive link between asbestos and respiratory illnesses, including cancer, until the 1970s. Thousands died before ever receiving any payment for their medical expenses or suffering.

Allegations arose that Johns-Manville knew of the dangers of exposure to asbestos but hid the information from the public. Over time, thousands of lawsuits were filed connecting the exposure of individuals to asbestos to mesothelioma, a type of lung cancer, and other fatal illnesses.

In 1982, Johns-Manville, as the defendant in sixteen thousand asbestos-related lawsuits, filed bankruptcy reorganization

---

left bankruptcy, killing some persons, injuring others, or causing property damage. Of course, the problem was that these were all future claims of unknown persons, or their next of kin, who had a right to be compensated because the company's product was in the marketplace and there was no intention to recall it to ensure the safety of the public.

3. In re A.H. Robins Co., 63 B.R. 986 (Bankr.E.D.Va. 1986) aff'd sub nom. Grady v. A.H. Robins Co., 839 F.2d 198 (4th Cir.), cert dismissed, 487 U.S. 1260, 109 S.Ct 201 (1988).

4. Elliott v. General Motors LLC (In re Motors Liquidation Co.), 829 F.3d 1351 (2d Cir. 2016).

proceedings. The company wanted to limit its current and future liability for the effects of its toxic substance.

It proposed a complex plan that placed the victims' claims in a trust, paying any present and future claims over time. The trust would pay those who had been injured or might be injured in the future. All present and future litigation against the company would be dismissed. In 1988, the plan and trust fund were approved by the bankruptcy court.

Why had the bankruptcy court approved the plan? It reasoned that the insurance carriers were also liable, but if the individuals pursued the insurance companies and recovered, it would decrease the amount of money remaining under the policies to pay the victims in the company's bankruptcy case. As a result, the insurance policies became assets of the bankruptcy case, with the insurance funds pooled for creditors. The insurance companies were released, along with the company, as to any liability they might have.[5] Within a relatively short period of time, hundreds of thousands of claimants sought recovery from the trust.

Although the trust was initially funded with $3 billion in cash and the company's securities, by 1990, it was clear that given past, present, and future claims, the trust would soon run out of money. A judge divided claimants into those with serious illnesses such as cancer, who would receive priority, and those with less severe illnesses, who would have to wait. The company agreed to pay an additional $520 million over seven years.

In 1994, given the complexity of paying present and future claims of asbestos victims, Congress amended the bankruptcy law and codified a version of the "Manville trust" to provide more certainty as to how asbestos claims were paid. Congress did not provide a *method* to pay claims of victims who were injured by individuals or companies that were inten-

5. In re Johns-Manville Corp., 33 B.R. 254, 268 (Bankr. S.D.N.Y. 1983).

tionally, willfully, or maliciously engaged in other conduct or activities that were harmful.

The National Bankruptcy Review Commission stated that the 1994 amendments to the Bankruptcy Code, which focused only on how to treat asbestos claims, created uncertainty as to how to treat other mass tort claims and massive future liabilities. In the *Johns-Manville* case, one approach as to future claimants was to allow them to recover their medical expenses, lost wages, etc., if the conduct giving rise to the liability could be determined as of a certain time and then connected with the injuries that would subsequently occur.[6]

In many cases, such as with the airplane manufacturer, it was impossible to pinpoint which aircraft or parts were defective or, more importantly to the judge, who would be injured by the defective airplane or part in the future.

Moreover, the creation of a trust to pay future claimants has not been entirely successful as to the asbestos claimants. Litigation continues to this day,[7] reflecting how difficult it has been to provide a long-term solution.

As of the end of 2023, the trust was still paying on claims and had assets of $600,132,570. Johns-Manville is still in operation today as a subsidiary of Berkshire Hathaway Inc. and manufactures asbestos-free construction materials. The trust has had to revise the percentage paid on victims' claims to make sure payments continue to be made. At the end of 2023, victims were being paid only 5.1 percent on their claims' full amounts.

Soon, other companies involved in mass tort litigation wanted the same protections as the asbestos companies for any third parties that were also directly liable with the debtor

---

6. One judge stated that "the focus should be on the time when the acts giving rise to the alleged liability were performed." In re Johns-Manville Corp., 57 B.R. 680, 690 (Bankr.S.D.N.Y. 1986).
7. In re Johns-Manville Corp., 581 B.R. 38 (Bankr. S.D.N.Y. 2018).

company. The companies soon inserted in their plans releases of parent corporations, or third parties, for direct obligations that the third parties were supposed to pay if the debtor were unable to do so.

In December 2021, the release of parties that had not filed a bankruptcy petition arose in the Purdue Pharma LP bankruptcy case. Tragically, 614,000 parties filed claims for damages resulting from the opioid crisis, the amount of their claims aggregating more than the world's domestic product.

The name Purdue Pharma LP may not be a familiar name to most Americans. However, if one mentions the opioid epidemic that killed 247,000 people in the United States between 1999 and 2019, many remember and understand the gravity of the problem that caused needless suffering of friends, family members, and fellow workers.

How did Purdue Pharma become the center of the opioid tragedy? In the mid-1990s, the Sackler family, which included several doctors, had invented a drug named OxyContin, which they marketed to doctors as a better alternative to pain killers that were used at the time. The Sackler family owned and controlled the company, Purdue Pharma, and its affiliates that manufactured and marketed the new drug. Because the drug was later found to be highly addictive, patient demand skyrocketed and led to billions of dollars of sales by the company over the next decade.

However, by 2007, one of Purdue Pharma's affiliates had pleaded guilty to felony charges of mislabeling OxyContin. The many lawsuits filed by family members over loss of loved ones or by individuals who were addicted to the drug led to the Sackler family distributing billions of dollars of Purdue Pharma's and affiliates' assets to themselves over the next decade. By 2017, the family had dissipated 75 percent of company and affiliate assets.

In 2019, Purdue Pharma filed a petition to reorganize its business affairs. Of note is that none of the responsible

Sackler family members sought bankruptcy relief. However, the Sackler family wanted to ensure that once their company left bankruptcy, the opiate claimants and their families would not be able to pursue them legally for payment.

Any future claims that any claimant or claimant's family had against the company and the Sackler family would also be wrapped into the plan. What do we mean by future claims? An individual may have taken OxyContin but may not have been hospitalized or suffered any immediate medical issues or problems. However, perhaps in five years from now, the individual may begin exhibiting symptoms and medical complications resulting from exposure to the drug. Any expenses incurred by the individual from such future medical complications could only be recovered from the company or the Sackler family as permitted by the plan.

In 2021, the bankruptcy court approved the plan, and the district court reversed, stating that letting off Sackler family members was not legally permitted. The Second Circuit Court of Appeals reversed the district court and came up with a modified version of the plan. The parties then appealed to the US Supreme Court.

Forgiving family members, owners, or principals of a company for their bad behavior has become popular. Why? Because if the individuals who are engaged in such conduct file their own bankruptcy cases, they could potentially be found liable for their fraudulent, intentionally malicious or wrongful conduct and receive no debt forgiveness for the damages that they owe to their victims. Individuals engaged in such conduct place their companies in bankruptcy, attempting to use the bankruptcy law to shield them as well.

Over the years, experts have disagreed as to whether insulating family members or company principals from their wrongful conduct through the bankruptcies of only their companies was permissible. Bankruptcy courts, district courts, and courts of appeals also had different views of the law.

I believe the United States Supreme Court majority got it right in the *Purdue Pharma* decision. The majority and dissent agreed that the section which described what might be placed or contained in plans was the starting point of their analysis. For instance, the individual or company might decide to sell all assets or obtain financing to continue with any business operations. However, there was a catchall provision in the bankruptcy law that stated, "A plan may . . . include any other appropriate provision not inconsistent with the applicable provisions of [the bankruptcy law]."[8] What were the limits of that catchall section?

In the majority opinion, the justices concluded that there were several bankruptcy provisions that prohibited those who had not filed a bankruptcy petition ("non-filers") from receiving forgiveness of their obligations owed to their victims and creditors. So any plan that released or discharged non-filers was inconsistent with the text of the bankruptcy law and could not be approved. Settlements of victims' claims were always possible, but such settlements could not be contrary to one or more other sections of the law. The catchall section could not be used to release non-filers.

Bankruptcy law should also be construed or interpreted as a whole document. It has many parts that are interrelated and have to be read together. There are provisions of the bankruptcy law that allow forgiveness, or discharge, of debt only under certain circumstances. Individuals who defrauded others, or intentionally or maliciously harmed others, had to pay such victims in full for any damages they might have incurred.

Allowing individuals in the Sackler family to be released or forgiven from their obligations owed to opiate claimants would likely not be permitted if they filed their own bankruptcy petitions. Therefore, there was no basis to allow the Sackler family

---

8. See 11 U.S.C. §1123(b)(6).

to receive forgiveness of their obligations in their company's case when they would never directly receive such relief in any case that they filed unless the claimants consented.

Finally, from a historical perspective, the Sackler family would not have had their obligations forgiven. The dissent was unpersuasive in its analysis, relying primarily on prior cases concerning mass tort litigation as the basis for the release of the Sackler family. However, there was no reason to have a blanket rule of forgiveness of those individuals who controlled the corporations.

Ultimately, the *Purdue Pharma* decision is beneficial to any claimant who may have been victimized, allowing them to be heard as to (1) whether they should be paid in full or would accept a lesser percentage return, (2) whether they should be paid immediately or over time, and (3) whether they are treated fairly when compared to other creditors. If individuals or family members are to be forgiven of *their* separate debts or obligations even though they have not filed a bankruptcy petition, the claimants must consent to such relief. Given the trauma that certain claimants have suffered, that seems only fair.

A multistate coalition separately pursued Purdue Pharma and the Sackler Family to pay for substance abuse treatment and recovery resources that the states required as a result of the opioid crises.[9] In 2024, the US Supreme Court overturned a proposed $6 billion multistate settlement as being woefully insufficient. The parties went back to the drawing board, allowing the states to receive a proportionate amount from the settlement. For instance, Pennsylvania would receive $212 million in payments over fifteen years.

9. The attorney generals of California, Colorado, Connecticut, Delaware, Florida, Illinois, Massachusetts, New York, Oregon, Pennsylvania, Tennessee, Texas, Vermont, Virginia, and West Virginia secured the nationwide settlement.

In January 2025, a national multistate settlement was announced that required the Sackler family to pay $6.5 billion over fifteen years and Purdue Pharma to pay around $900 million. The states would use the funding to pay communities for opioid addiction treatment, prevention, and recovery programs. The settlement also required that the Sackler family relinquish control of Purdue Pharma and that the family no longer be able to sell opioids in the United States.

The Sackler family would *not* have immunity from future lawsuits, but a fund of $800 million would be available to them from settlement funds to pay the costs of any future litigation against them. There was also a provision that thirty million documents related to the Purdue Pharma and the Sackler family's opioid business would become public. Each state was to receive a proportionate share of the settlement, subject to court approval.

In March 2025, Purdue Pharma filed another plan of reorganization to address the issues raised in the June 2024 decision of the US Supreme Court denying approval of the Purdue Pharma plan.

The 2025 plan no longer contains nonconsensual third-party releases. The opiate claimants have two choices. They may either vote affirmatively for the plan treatment, in which case the Sackler family third-party release will be effective, or they may reject the plan, allowing them to pursue the Sackler family separately. The proposed plan will contribute the Purdue Pharma assets for distribution to creditors, with an expected $900 million cash distribution to creditors on the day the company emerges from bankruptcy.

The proposed plan also includes the multistate settlement as well as the payment of $850 million to individual victims. Upon confirmation, Purdue Pharma will be dissolved, with a newly created foundation to implement the plan and be controlled by the states, with the states to select the initial board of directors.

The 2025 Purdue Pharma plan will work its way through the trial and appellate courts. The opiate claimants must now affirmatively advise the court, creditors, and other parties whether they wish the proposed payments under the plan.

Of concern is the fact that a reserve of $800 million has been set aside in the plan for the Sackler family if opiate claimants pursue them in lawsuits. Why should the Sackler family be entitled to any reserve? We will have to see how the courts ultimately determine the fairness of such a reserve.

Some experts have complained that mass tort litigation continues to be advantageous for the company, with claimants having little say as to any payments they will receive. Apparently, most companies that file mass tort cases like to list an alleged victim's claim as having a value of $1 on any documents that they file with the court. If the alleged victim takes no action, the company may argue that any distribution to the alleged victim should be $1, the amount that has been listed by the company.

An alleged victim would be able to counter the company's value by filing their own claim, using judgments, orders, or other documents filed in state or federal litigation as the true value.[10] If the alleged victim was unable to finalize a judgment or order before the case filing, the alleged victim could request that the court estimate the value of the claim.[11] Granted the alleged victim would need to retain counsel to take these various steps, but at least, the alleged victim would have their day in court.

10. See 11 U.S.C. §502.
11. See 11 U.S.C. §502(c).

CHAPTER NINE

WHO SHOULD CONTROL A BANKRUPTCY CASE?

There is growing concern that certain agreements are being negotiated by attorneys among various parties, with the court not being advised of the terms of the agreements. These agreements have become known as "secret settlements." Have the attorneys usurped the powers of the court?

Lawyers are guided by ethical rules in state and federal courts. The rules may vary depending on whether the particular court follows the Model Rules of Professional Conduct first published by the American Bar Association in 1983, subsequently updated and revised, or the ethical rules enacted where the court is located.

Model Rules of Professional Conduct, Rule 3.4(f) has been adopted by many jurisdictions. The general rule is that a lawyer should not prevent a person from providing information to another party. If the person is not a client but has factual information that may be relevant or critical in resolving the issues in a particular lawsuit, the person should be able to advise another party and that party's attorney of that factual information.

Arizona Ethical Rule 3.4(f) follows the Model Rule and

states that a lawyer shall insist that a client refrain from giving information to the other side. And if the person is a relative, employee, or agent of the client, and if the lawyer reasonably believes that the person's interest will not be adversely affected from refraining to provide such information, the lawyer may request that they not provide information to the other party.[1]

The debate over whether settlements should be withheld from court review has gone on for decades. A.H. Robbins, which eventually filed a bankruptcy petition, allegedly hid the health and safety risks of the Dalkon Shield with nonpublic settlements while continuing to market the product.

Some states have enacted legislation trying to limit nonpublic settlements, and courts have independently required the disclosure of settlements that focus on health and safety issues. But other lawyers have negotiated around the ethical rule or legislation by creating noncooperation agreements in out-of-court private contracts that are not subject to court approval.

Moreover, there are other ethical rules which support secret settlements under certain circumstances. For instance, a lawyer should abide by a client's decision, including whether to settle a matter, unless the lawyer is assisting the client in conduct that is criminal or fraudulent.[2]

The lawyer's duty of confidentiality in representing the client would also require that the lawyer not reveal any information concerning the representation unless authorized by the client.[3] The American Bar Association, state ethics opinions,

---

1. AZ ER 3.4(f) "A lawyer shall not: (f) request a person other than a client to refrain from voluntarily giving relevant information to another party unless: (1) the person is a relative or an employee or other agent of a client; and (2) the lawyer reasonably believes that the person's interest will not be adversely affected by refraining from giving such information." Many other courts have an ethical rule that is similar to that of Arizona. The Arizona ethical rules may be found at A.R.S. Sup. Ct. Rules, Rule 42, Rules of Prof. Conduct.
2. See Model Rules 1.2 and 1.16.
3. See Model Rule 1.6.

and a number of experts concur that lawyers may generally keep the underlying facts in the case confidential as a part of a settlement.

There is also strong opposition to such nonpublic settlements which have come to be known as secret settlements. The Association of Trial Lawyers of America has denounced secret settlements as "detrimental to public health and safety, the proper functioning of the civil justice system, and the interests of individual victims." Civil rights and public interest lawyers are also concerned about secret settlements that affect the right of the public to be informed and that deter enforcement efforts in environmental and similar matters.

In 2002, the Model Rules were updated to allow a lawyer to reveal confidential information related to a representation of a client when a law or final order of a court directs the lawyer to disclose the information or if disclosure is reasonably certain to prevent "death or substantial bodily harm."[4]

Not all states have adopted the Ethical Rule 1.6 changes. Moreover, the ethical rule only affects the *lawyer's* duty of disclosure. The client may be bound by the secret settlement because the client may be in desperate need of medical treatment that requires the client not breach the secret settlement and lose all payments under the agreement.

Returning to the mass tort litigation that leads to the filing of a bankruptcy petition by a company selling cancer-causing consumer products or medical devices that may kill or injure women who use the product, the issue becomes how much should be disclosed during the confirmation process so that victims may make an informed decision as to whether to accept the plan treatment and be bound by the terms of the settlement or refuse to accept what is being offered by the debtor in a plan and continue to litigate the victims' claims in

4. A.R.S. Sup. Ct. Rules, Rule 42, Rules of Prof. Conduct, ER 1.6 (d)(5) and (6).

future litigation. Should corporate lawyers, through secret settlements, withhold critical information to victims?

Judges may also disagree that lawyers should control a case. In the Ninth Circuit, the bankruptcy court must review a proposed settlement and determine whether it is "fair and equitable." In other words, is the settlement in the best interest of creditors and other parties involved in the bankruptcy case?[5]

The party proposing the settlement has the burden of persuading the court that the settlement should be approved. It is the responsibility of the bankruptcy court to serve an independent role of oversight. Secret settlements should generally not be authorized and are subject to being set aside by the bankruptcy court once discovered.

Some judges also focus on determining what all relevant facts are in a matter before making a final decision. For instance, assume that one side, Party A, has retained an expert to study how much will be paid to the victims in a mass tort bankruptcy case. The expert opines that the victims will only be paid 10 to 15 percent of their claims over a fifteen-year period.

As a part of its plan, the debtor has filed disclosures with the court, which state that all victims will be paid in full during the same fifteen-year period. In a settlement between Party A and the debtor, they agree that the court and all other creditors will not be advised of Party A's expert opinion. Such manipulation of the facts to be presented in court is arguably similar to a secret settlement. Why should the other victims not at least be informed of the one expert's opinion in order to determine whether the settlement is fair to them?

5. See Federal Rule of Bankruptcy Procedure 9019, and Woodson v. Fireman's Fund Ins. Co. (In re Woodson), 839 F.2d 610 (9th Cir. 1988).

CHAPTER TEN

THE ROAD TO NOWHERE

Arizona is a land of forgiveness and endless skies. It's a place where developers may flourish, sometimes at the expense of many others. In the 1980s, there was desert land far from the Phoenix metropolitan area that was attractive to javelinas, bobcats, and coyotes. The White Tank Mountains were a rugged wilderness nearby and provided a boundary prohibiting easy access to Phoenix. The White Tank Mountains also blocked the Phoenix nighttime lights for those who wanted to get away from it all.

A thirty-mile stretch of a paved four-lane highway was proposed among the saguaros and arroyos. The paved highway would encourage housing and commercial development, yet it would seem like a desert oasis far from city traffic. It was projected that future development along the highway would include three hundred thousand residents.

The highway was called the Sun Valley Parkway. A developer worked with the county to arrange the financing for the highway. The county would use its authority to issue tax-exempt bonds to investors, who would provide the funding to build the parkway. In turn, the county would enter into a separate agreement with lead developers who would ultimately be liable on the construction financing. Finally, a trustee was appointed to ensure the receipt and transfer of payments to the bondholders.

The financing was expensive, complex, and risky, relying on those whose land bordered the parkway to repay the principal and interest on the debt through assessments against their land. Landowners would also have to pay the real estate taxes to the county treasurer.

In 1988 and 1989, seventy-five private landowners formed the Sun Valley Owners Association, which became the core group who would own the land and repay the financing. The landowners purchased forty-eight thousand acres along the parkway and constructed the parkway at a cost of $82 million. The marketing pitch to lure future landowners to the area? *A forty-five-minute drive is a breeze if you come from any other place in the world . . . People who come here from all over the country find the drive very, very palatable.*

At the time the parkway was being constructed, real estate values in the Phoenix metropolitan area were rising rapidly, which caused other vacant land in the West Valley to increase dramatically and unrealistically in value. Everyone wanted to purchase vacant land along the parkway. The dream was that the land would continue to increase in value, and the landowners would simply sell all, or a part, of their land to pay any assessments levied on their land for the financing as well as the real estate taxes.

However, just as the parkway was completed in 1989, a housing crisis swept the Phoenix metropolitan area. Residential properties dropped 75 percent in value within a relatively short period of time. No one ventured to the vacant land by the White Tank Mountains, with only five hundred motorists a day using the parkway.

However, the assessments against the individual landowners to repay the financing continued. Individual landowners and developers filed bankruptcy petitions.

The glorious parkway became known as the Road to Nowhere. Bottom line: It was unrealistic to rely on landowners and developers to pay the enormous debt that was created to build a paved highway in the middle of nowhere.

I presided over the many bankruptcy cases that were filed. Unfortunately, most of the landowners were hardworking Phoenicians who got caught up in the excitement of a "sure thing." They collectively felt they would soon have the equivalent of a royal flush in poker. Instead, they ended up on my calendar, describing their desperate situations.

They were not only going to lose their land along the parkway but also their homes. They had stretched themselves financially, taking out second, third, and fourth mortgages on their homes to invest in the West Valley and pay the costs of the financing. They had paid the real estate taxes and the other assessments against the parkway land to the point that they no longer had any savings or money in their bank accounts to pay the mortgages on their homes.

Many individuals engaged in moral shaming of those who had invested so unwisely. It's hard to describe how optimistic everyone was at the time. Newspaper articles described the highly touted real estate market in the Phoenix metropolitan area as only increasing in value. I can remember taking a shared ride to the airport during the daily increases in real estate prices; even the driver of the shuttle had become a real estate agent and was investigating the latest shifts in the mortgage interest rates for home loans for his clients while driving.

There were certain developers who gamed the system. They insisted on court hearings for the numerous parcels they held along the parkway. They knew that their land was worth substantially less than the debt they had to repay, but they persisted to the point of causing a backlog of cases in the court. A typical hearing was a fight over a desert parcel.

"Judge, the developer would like to call John Smith to the witness stand as an expert in the valuation of vacant desert land. He has not been certified as an expert in the valuation of such land. He is self-taught, has read a few books, and drove by one of the parcels but could not locate the other."

"The parcels that are the subject of the dispute today," the developer's attorney continued, "are adjoining parcels along the Sun Valley Parkway. One parcel has an arroyo or 'steep-sided gully.' The other parcel is flat desert land. My client has unpaid assessments on the parcels in the amount of $100,000. The debt payable by all the landowners along the Sun Valley Parkway is $92 million and climbing. If we are just given a chance to market all of the properties, my client will be able to pay his assessments, and all creditors will be paid in full."

Counsel for the creditor with a lien on the parcels suddenly rose to her feet. "Judge, I object to Mr. Smith testifying. He is not an expert in real estate appraising. And counsel has admitted that Mr. Smith could not locate one of the parcels. As for the parcel he did locate? It appears he never got out of his car but literally drove by it. Given the lack of traffic on the Sun Valley Parkway, one wonders how fast he was going as he took a fleeting look at the parcel. Perhaps he was going the speed limit of seventy-five, perhaps not."

Although the evidence presented was usually more detailed than I have outlined, the intent of the developer and others was to delay and keep the costs down by bringing in individuals who would never be able to give a fair valuation of the desert land while providing no facts that would show the developer or others would ever be able to pay the debt owed to the bondholders. Over time, I disposed of the issues in the Sun Valley Parkway cases. None of the landowners who filed bankruptcy petitions kept their land.

There has been a mixed history of development along the parkway after the stabilization of the Phoenix metropolitan real estate market. In 2000, Stardust Development Co. began to plan a twenty-one-square-mile residential community along the parkway. In 2004, the developer began construction of

Tartesso, which continues to this day. However, in 2023, there were concerns about the community's development with requests to change some of the residential uses to commercial.

In 2005, another developer began construction near the parkway of Sun City Festival, a community of 3,100 acres, with the grand opening in 2006. As of 2024, Sun City Festival is scheduled to be completed in 2028 with 7,200 homes. In July 2023, the population of Buckeye, the city in which the Sun Valley Parkway and Sun City Festival are located, was only 108,909, not the 300,000 originally projected.

In 2003, allegations of fraud surfaced. It was alleged that one of the developers had sold some of the parkway land to a third party without the consent of the landowners, pocketing profits from the sale. The lawsuit dragged on in the state courts until a 2015 judgment in the amount of $86.4 million was entered against the developer who had had acted improperly as to the landowners.

What happened to the Road to Nowhere? The Maricopa County Department of Transportation assumed maintenance responsibilities of the parkway, which has continued to this day. The county did not take on sole responsibility for the parkway's construction in 1989 because there was no established need for the parkway. Many argued that the developers had placed undue pressure on the county, which should never have provided the $90 million in tax-exempt bond financing.

Some of the landowners continued to hold their land along the Road to Nowhere. They never filed bankruptcy petitions, and twenty years later, they were able to sell their land and roughly receive what they had originally paid for the land in 1989. Upon reflection, they would have been better off investing in the stock market.

CHAPTER ELEVEN

WHY IS MY LOCAL MARKET FILING A BANKRUPTCY PETITION IN DELAWARE?

It's happening on Main Street but with little notice from those who are dramatically impacted. Bankruptcy cases are no longer heard locally. To the average American, that doesn't seem to be a problem; if a bankruptcy case is heard in Delaware, New York, or Houston, it has no impact on them. They should reconsider.

In mid-October 2023, I attended a nationwide conference on bankruptcy that had several panel presentations on the current state of the law and what bankruptcy judges thought the trends would be in coming years. At the end, there was a question-and-answer session where the audience was able to pose questions to the judges.

One panel included several judges from the District of Delaware and one judge from the Southern District of New York. Both Delaware and, to some extent, the Southern District of New York are two of the preferred districts where lawyers file the mega cases that affect individuals and companies throughout the United States.

What I found interesting was the unabashed promotion by the Delaware judges of their superior ability to handle mega cases. They discussed the complex and well-developed

Delaware state and federal law, how they readily handled emergency hearings on short notice, how they quickly entered orders that impacted the rights of various groups of creditors, and how they quickly resolved disputes leading to confirmation of plans.

At the end of the presentation, there were probably many lawyers who had sweet dreams of filing their next case in Delaware. There were also a few bankruptcy judges who were wondering why Delaware judges seemed a bit egotistical.

But there was a time when the Delaware bankruptcy judges depended on their colleagues. In the 1980s, Delaware was a sleepy district with few bankruptcy cases. In 1996, to get to its desired goal that 87 percent of all bankruptcy cases be filed in Delaware, the bankruptcy court aggressively marketed itself as the place to file a mega case. Procedures were streamlined to the point that many felt the ability of someone to be heard on an issue was being denied.

The Delaware bankruptcy court created the "omnibus hearing," where any number of matters in one mega case were placed on the hearing calendar, with the judge rapidly going from item to item and quickly providing a decision on the issues. Another reason to try Delaware was that some lawyers thought judges in other parts of the country were "rude, arrogant, and inconsiderate of business realities."[1]

Delaware bankruptcy judges also required that Delaware lawyers be retained in any case, which meant that major corporations had to retain Delaware counsel and their preferred bankruptcy counsel in any case they filed in Delaware. This increased the costs in a Delaware case.

Many lawyers and a few bankruptcy judges in other parts of the country began to grumble. Delaware was soon over-

1. "Courting Failure: How Competition for Big Cases Is Corrupting the Courts" by Professor Lynn M. LoPucki

whelmed with complex bankruptcy cases that the few appointed bankruptcy judges were struggling to handle.

The Federal Judicial Center, the research and educational arm for the judiciary, had prepared a report at the request of the Judicial Conference Committee on the Administration of the Bankruptcy System, which is the judicial committee that studies issues and proposes changes to the nationwide bankruptcy system. Although the report was intended to focus on potential amendments to the bankruptcy law, it also discussed the procedures being followed in the Delaware bankruptcy court. Bankruptcy judges feared that the report was casting the Delaware bankruptcy court in a bad light that would have an adverse effect on all bankruptcy courts.

In January 1997, the Federal District Court in Delaware, in a move that shocked the bankruptcy community, took back all chapter 11 reorganization cases being handled by Delaware bankruptcy judges. Known as "revoking the reference," the federal district court judges decided they could handle all bankruptcy reorganization cases. They had lost confidence in the bankruptcy judges' ability to administer cases before them.

The federal judges soon hit a brick wall. Under federal law, certain matters, such as criminal cases, are required to be handled on an expedited basis. Bankruptcy also is driven by hearings that must be set on an emergency basis. For instance, electricity may be turned off at a facility, workers may be rioting at the gates, and employees may be desperate for the payment of backpay. Judges quickly hear and decide such matters.

The district court judges soon determined that their hearing calendars could not accommodate the criminal and other expedited federal cases and the bankruptcy hearings that had to be heard daily. The bankruptcy cases were returned to the bankruptcy judges.

But the Delaware bankruptcy court was understaffed.

The administrative arm of the judiciary asked for bankruptcy judges across the country to volunteer for six months, or for as long as a year, to hear Delaware cases. Bankruptcy courts across the country volunteered to let their judges go to Delaware to help.

Some judges kept their regular number of cases in their home court and took on the extra burden of handling Delaware cases. Other judges took on fewer cases, with the other judges in their home court taking on the extra burden of hearing their cases. The bankruptcy judges responded to help their Delaware colleagues.

In 2025, it seems the Delaware colleagues and judges in the Southern District of New York and Houston have returned to promoting their courts as the most experienced in handling mega cases, much to the detriment of their colleagues in other parts of the country.

Recent bankruptcy case filings also reflect orchestrated inventiveness. Because the companies and their officers and directors want to insulate themselves from massive personal injury claims, they have resorted to a multistep process when filing bankruptcy petitions. One of the more recent examples of the trend is the bankruptcy filing of LTL Management, LLC, a Johnson & Johnson subsidiary.

Johnson & Johnson has been known for decades for its seemingly wholesome consumer products, such as Tylenol, Neutrogena, Listerine, and Johnson's Baby Powder. Unfortunately, talc, as one of the components of baby powder, picks up particles of asbestos as it is being mined. Beginning in 2010, certain individuals alleged that Johnson's Baby Powder caused ovarian cancer and mesothelioma, a certain type of lung cancer.

By 2020, thirty-eight thousand ovarian cancer and four hundred mesothelioma lawsuits were pending against Johnson & Johnson and its consumer subsidiary Johnson & Johnson Consumer Inc., incorporated in 1979 to manufacture and sell consumer products. By 2018, the average damage award was around $39.7 million. But pressure was being put on the consumer subsidiary, which was expending $10 to $20 million per month in defense costs. Although the consumer subsidiary had a $2.1 billion profit in 2019 and a $1.1 billion loss in 2020, it was still worth $61.5 billion if its future talc liabilities were not included.

Most of the ovarian cancer lawsuits have been consolidated into federal multidistrict court litigation in New Jersey. In multidistrict court litigation, a federal district court judge starts with a handful of cases (perhaps fifteen or sixteen) where the issues of fact and law are identified and then determined by juries. The jury verdicts in those cases will then serve as a paradigm for settling the other pending litigation.

Although Johnson & Johnson and its consumer subsidiary were solvent, the companies determined that filing bankruptcy would force all claimants suffering from cancer and their families to accept settlements within a shorter time. So what inventive procedure did they develop to speed the financial recovery of Johnson & Johnson and its subsidiaries?

First, Johnson & Johnson Consumer Inc. ("old consumer entity") merged into a newly formed Texas limited liability company with no assets or liabilities. Like a virus, the new Texas limited liability company divided into two new Texas entities, with Entity A receiving all the talc-related liabilities and some assets, and Entity B, the profitable operations of the old consumer entity. Then, at the end of the restructuring, the old consumer entity ceased to exist, with just Entities A and B remaining. The name of Entity A, the debt-ridden company, was changed to LTL Management, LLC and, in a heartbeat, became a North Carolina company.

It then filed a bankruptcy petition in North Carolina. Why? Because LTL was hoping to take advantage of "favorable legal precedent." This is lawyer talk for forum shopping, which means pick a place where a company has few connections (such as a deposit account, a local law firm that it has retained, or where it has been incorporated), file a bankruptcy petition in that location, and hope to get some favorable rulings that will allow some pesky legal problems to go away.

North Carolina was also the place where LTL was "domiciled," which meant it was where the company had been incorporated or created. The bankruptcy judge apparently had some concerns about what was going on and decided to transfer the LTL bankruptcy case to New Jersey, where the federal multidistrict court litigation was pending.

Creditors cried foul as to LTL's multistep procedure, which courts and experts soon described as the "Texas Two-Step," and the Third Circuit Court of Appeals weighed in on whether its bankruptcy case should be dismissed. It was. Was that a victory? No. First, the Third Circuit *assumed* the LTL bankruptcy case was filed in good faith. The circuit court dismissed the case because LTL was "not in financial distress." Although LTL had all the talc-related liability, it still had some assets and a backup agreement from Johnson & Johnson, the parent, to pay the liability claims.

However, the dismissal did not resolve whether the many steps used to file a bankruptcy petition in a favorable location far from creditors was appropriate. LTL immediately refiled its bankruptcy case. The creditors and other interested parties sounded the alarm, asserting that LTL was acting in bad faith. The bankruptcy court conducted a four-day trial on whether the LTL case should be dismissed again. Using the Third Circuit's prior decision as a guide, the judge focused on whether LTL was in financial distress. LTL faced billions of dollars in liability as a result of judgments already entered against it as well as countless lawsuits that were still pending, but it still had the assistance of its parent, Johnson & Johnson, as a funding backstop. The value of the backstop was approximately $30 billion, which was sufficient to cover LTL's near-term talc liability. The court's conclusion was that LTL was solvent. LTL's second bankruptcy case was filed in bad faith.

Whether the Texas Two-Step was a procedure that should be held by the courts as manipulative and, hence, sufficient to cause the dismissal of the bankruptcy case was not addressed. No federal circuit of appeal has yet to address the issue.

It used to be that bankruptcy cases were filed where the company had some connection to the community. I presided over the Pro's Ranch Markets case, which had seven stores in Arizona and four stores in Texas and New Mexico. It had been a family-owned business for over thirty years. In its filings, the company stated that a struggling economy—including a loss of construction jobs and the chilling effect of Arizona's passage of SB 1070, which made being "illegally in the country" an Arizona crime—caused it to file a bankruptcy petition in 2013.

Although portions of SB 1070 were found to be unconstitutional, the company still believed the law had an impact on its business. But Arizona consumers loved the company. Its fresh-made food allowed the company to be named 2012 Arizona Retailer of the Year by Arizona Food Marketing Alliance. The company wanted to save the jobs of over 2,200 team members. I determined at evidentiary hearings that the company should continue its operations and obtain financing. The company was eventually sold to a California company, which had similar operations and promised to keep the Pro's Ranch stores open.

What is critical is that local consumers had a vested interest in the stores. Since the company filed locally, they could continue to follow the case and be avid consumers of fresh market produce.

Today local companies are disconnecting from their communities, filing in places far from home and hoping to reorganize quickly with few hurdles from creditors. They have forgotten that Main Street cares, nourishes, and provides invaluable support to them.

CHAPTER TWELVE
BEWARE—THE DEBT YOU OWE MAY BE SETTLED IN ASIA!

About a year ago, I watched an international symposium on the latest developments in reorganizing multinational corporations. This area of the law, also known as cross-border insolvencies, has always been complex.

Certain countries, with the help of the United Nations, worked tirelessly together to provide a uniform law that was objective and might easily be adapted and enacted by many countries. Although there were not that many cross-border cases in the 1990s, many countries had encountered inconsistent approaches, time-consuming delays, and inadequate solutions that impacted whether businesses could be rescued.

In 1997, the United Nations Commission on International Trade Law (UNCITRAL) finally created a Model Law, which was to modernize, harmonize, and create a "fair insolvency framework" for companies or individuals that were experiencing "severe financial distress or insolvency" and had assets, operations, or other connections with several countries. In the legal area, it was preferred to have as much certainty as possible as to how to handle cross-border insolvencies, and the uniform Model Law seemed to be the answer.

In 2005, with some modifications, the United States enacted the Model Law as chapter 15 of the Bankruptcy Code, the US law on bankruptcy. In Arizona, I was the first judge to preside over a chapter 15 case and, somewhat ironically, the last for quite a while. Over the last decade, no chapter 15 cases were filed in Arizona until recently. Of course, part of the problem was that fewer bankruptcy cases were being filed in Arizona. Many companies were incorporated in Delaware, so even though they might have had a substantial presence in Arizona, they chose Delaware as the preferred place to file.[1]

In November 2024, Hong Kong began developing proposed legislation to attract the global business and financial community. The idea was to allow foreign-based companies to migrate their places of incorporation to Hong Kong "while conserving their legal identity." A paper published on the process in July 2024 further explained how "re-domiciliation" would work.

The foreign company would maintain its current identity. In other words, a new company or subsidiary would not be created. The company's assets and liabilities, property rights, contractual obligations, and legal processes would not be affected. But the company would also have the same rights and obligations as a company incorporated in Hong Kong. The domicile or place of incorporation of the company would be transferred to Hong Kong.

The problems that may arise with the transfer of an incorporation of a US company to another country may be considerable and not easily resolved. In essence, the incorporation of a US company is its birth. Documents are filed with one or more governmental authorities describing the individuals who will be in charge, the locations of those individuals and the

1. See Chapter 11 of this book for more information on attorneys filing bankruptcy cases only in a few locations.

new company, the individual or entity that will accept service on behalf of the company in case anyone wants to sue it, and other basic information, such as the type of business, whether service, retail, or manufacturing.

The company may have assets or liabilities in many locations. For instance, it may have manufacturing facilities or warehouses in several states or countries. However, although the company may do business in several locations or even in several countries, it has one place of incorporation.

A company may change its place of incorporation through a process called "domestication." The company may be seeking lower taxes or a state that may be more business friendly. However, states may vary in their requirements for domestication, so any such process should be carefully planned. But what if a company desires to domesticate itself in a foreign country? Since the laws in Hong Kong have not yet been finalized, it is unclear whether a transfer of incorporation to Hong Kong is the same or similar to domestication in the United States.

Even if a US corporation were able to transfer its incorporation to Hong Kong, would that be advantageous? In many cases, US companies incorporate in Delaware because they prefer to litigate matters there. They believe the Delaware judges are more sophisticated in commercial issues or the judges are more likely to rule in favor of the company. But how does a Delaware judge handle a US company that has migrated its incorporation to Hong Kong? Arguably the judge could dismiss the case, stating that the company is no longer incorporated and has no assets in Delaware. The company would no longer be able to take advantage of favorable rulings solely for Delaware companies. No company likes that type of uncertainty.

Indeed, understanding that there will be issues with migration, the proposed legislation in Hong Kong states that the country where the company was incorporated initially must permit the incorporation migration. Moreover, a certain majority of those in control of the company must also consent to the migration.

There is also the problem that the law in Hong Kong may not be favorable to US companies and creditors. Hong Kong previously did not provide for a reorganization process that included comprehensive restructuring of a company located in another country, such as the United States, Singapore, the United Kingdom, and, since 2006, even the People's Republic of China. Hong Kong was willing to recognize foreign insolvency proceedings commenced in another country, but only to the extent that the other country's law was consistent with Hong Kong's insolvency law and its public policy.

Will there be a change in Hong Kong's approach to accepting orders, judgments, and rulings in another country's insolvency proceedings? Unclear. In the 2021 decision of *In re Lamtex Holdings Ltd.* ([2021] HKCFI 622), the Hong Kong Court did look for the first time at a company's "center of main interests" in determining which country would control the reorganization process.

A company's center of main interests is an objective standard found in the Model Law adopted by the United States and many other countries and has been described as the place where "the company or individual is found or operates on a regular basis so that the company or individual is ascertainable by third parties." In a layman's analysis, it would be the place where the company has its executive offices or its principal place of business.

One court decision in Hong Kong does not provide clarity as to which country will control how quickly a cross-border company may reorganize, how expensive the proceedings will be for the company and creditors, and what types of plans a Hong Kong court will accept to restructure the company's debt. Ultimately, it is unclear whether the 2024 changes to Hong Kong law will prompt US companies to file there.

As for an individual, the center of main interests would be the individual's permanent home or domicile. Other factors may need to be considered if the individual's affairs are complex. Cross-border cases are particularly common in the European Union where individuals may be employed in one country but have their residences or domiciles in another country. In other cases, individuals may own real property in a number of European countries but have their residences or domiciles in yet another country. For individuals, the test to determine which country will control the reorganization or bankruptcy proceeding is based on different factors than that of an entity, such as where the individual is domiciled or resides and whether the individual intends to remain in the country on a permanent basis.

In contrast, it is unclear how receptive Hong Kong will be to such cases by individuals. Hong Kong follows legal developments in the People's Republic of China, but as of early March 2024, China was only beginning to accept requests for reorganizations by individuals. China had previously only focused on liquidation of individuals' assets.

Other Asian countries have vied to have US and other foreign corporations file bankruptcy cases in their jurisdictions. Singapore is the clear leader. In 2015, Singapore adopted the Model Law and established the Singapore International Commercial Court to handle foreign corporations' sophisticated, commercial cases. In 2022, Singapore expanded its insolvency law to allow courts to determine "any proceedings" concerning corporate insolvency, restructuring, or dissolution that were international and commercial in character.

Court rules concerning the legal profession were also expanded to allow attorneys from other countries to be involved with Singapore counsel in corporate insolvency proceedings. Foreign lawyers would supply the expertise as to their countries' laws; Singapore lawyers would handle how to shepherd the cases through the Singapore court system.

Could anything go wrong? In 2023, the Singapore court held that Lim How Teck ("Lim"), an unsecured creditor could bring an insolvency proceeding in Singapore to wind up the affairs of a Laguna, California golf course.[2] A few people in the US who also helped fund and build the country club were probably surprised.

In 1991, Laguna Golf issued 1,800 unsecured noninterest-bearing notes to finance the construction of a country club. Lim was one of those individuals who purchased a note. As is typical in cases where there are many creditors with similar rights, a trustee was appointed to act on behalf of all the noteholders. A document ("the Trust Deed") was drawn up specifying who would be the trustee and what actions the trustee would take. There was also a clause that stated individual noteholders were limited in actions that they could pursue, the idea being that the trustee would act in the best interests of all the noteholders.

In 2021, Lim and other unsecured noteholders were not repaid. Litigation ensued. Although Lim was not the majority noteholder and should have asked the noteholders' trustee to act, he decided, on his own, to wind up Laguna Golf's business affairs in Singapore. He filed a request (or petition) that the country club be placed in insolvency proceedings in Singapore, along with a challenge to the clause in the Trust Deed that stated he could take no action on his own until the trustee had first analyzed the situation and decided what steps, if any, should be taken on behalf of all noteholders. Keep in mind that the Trust Deed provided that the trustee was not bound to act unless a "significant portion" of the noteholders directed the trustee to act, and that action was probably deter-

---

2. See Lim How Tuck v. Laguna National Golf and Country Club Ltd. (2023)(SGHC 23).

mined by those noteholders with the largest claims even though they might be a minority in number.

By now you are probably thinking there's something unfair about one creditor who lives or has some connection to Singapore (maybe his favorite lawyer lives in Singapore?) putting a California country club in an insolvency proceeding in *Singapore*.

What happened in Singapore? Lim stated in court pleadings that he was not paid when his note came due. Laguna Golf countered Lim did not have the ability to start any action in any court. The trustee should have been the one to decide whether action should be taken, not a single unsecured creditor. Lim then argued that he had the necessary support from the other noteholders to file the Singapore insolvency proceeding, but he conceded he had not given *any direction* to the trustee.

At this point, one would think the court should have dismissed Lim's insolvency case, advised him and other noteholders to meet with the trustee, and figure out what the trustee's next steps should be. Instead, the Singapore court examined several cases from the United States relevant to the dispute. The court inquired whether there was the *possibility* that the trustee was not acting in a manner consistent with his obligations under the Trust Deed. Maybe the trustee should have taken some action but was refusing to do so? No, the court found that the trustee was never directed by a significant number of noteholders to act. Lim had acted improperly.

Lim also presented the argument that the trustee had a conflict of interest, which allowed Lim to act on his own. The court stated that a potential claim of a trustee's conflict of interest or that the trustee had not acted properly were insufficient allegations for Lim to act. One would need to wait until some action was taken by the trustee that was improper. Lim had lost again.

Then the court took a curious position. It said that if the

trustee were to file the request or petition to wind up Laguna Golf, he would need to provide the liquidators who would be appointed with relevant information to help the liquidators investigate the activities of Laguna Golf. The court concluded that just such a series of events meant that the trustee would protect his interest against the noteholders and any claims that they might have, rather than act according to his fiduciary duty to protect the noteholders' interests.

Let's pause and think about the court's conclusion. The court had no evidence that the trustee had violated his fiduciary duty. There was only the *possibility* that he might act improperly. The court should have ruled against Lim and advised that he would need to show facts that would support a breach of the trustee's fiduciary duty.

However, the court stated that although it was not making a factual finding that the trustee had acted improperly or that he had, in fact, breached his fiduciary duty under the Trust Deed, there was the *potential* for the trustee's improper action. The court then concluded that such *potential* for a conflict of interest was sufficient for Lim to act on his own and file the request or petition to wind up Laguna Golf.

If one were to defend the court's decision, one would argue that it would be human nature for the trustee to defend what he had done in the case and not provide all the information necessary for the liquidators to determine next steps in liquidating the company's assets.

Rather than put the trustee in such a moral and legal quandary, it was better to allow Lim to proceed with the bankruptcy case, remove the trustee from taking further action, and have the court appoint the liquidators to wind up the affairs of the company.

Most courts would allow only the trustee to act, wait until someone alleged the trustee had acted in some improper manner, and then hold a hearing to determine whether the trustee should remain in place. Until the trustee was removed, the trustee would decide whether to file a bankruptcy case.

In March 2025, the committee formed by Singapore's Ministry of Law issued a report analyzing Singapore's current cross-border system, along with proposed additional reforms. The report focused on four different categories for proposed changes.

Although debtors or creditors could apply to the court to take possession of a company's operations, 45 percent of the cases were unsuccessful in allowing the company to survive, putting together some type of arrangement to pay creditors, or obtaining the best outcome in winding up the assets of the company. Thirty-three percent of the cases were dismissed or withdrawn. That meant that only 22 percent of the cases were managed successfully by the court. Better management of the cases was required going forward.

The second category of concern was how to handle conflicts between classes of creditors, known as the "cross-class cramdown." Under the law, the court had the power to force a dissenting creditor class to accept its treatment under a plan. The difficulty had been that a majority of 75 percent in value of the creditor class had to consent.

Assume that there were one hundred claims in a particular class, and the aggregate value of all those claims was $1,000,000. Claims in the amount of $750,000 had to agree to the proposed treatment of their claims. Reviewing the cases indicated that it was almost impossible to reach the 75 percent threshold.

The report also stated that shareholders should be included in the mix as a separate class. Shareholders would be given the opportunity to provide funding or new value to the distressed company in order to receive a shareholder interest in the new company.

The third category focused on providing a framework and more tools for efficient debt restructurings. The law required the company, at a general meeting of shareholders, to approve the disposal of all or almost all of the company's assets. However, it was important to recognize that, as a company was determining whether to file a bankruptcy petition, it was more important to consider the rights of creditors who had a higher priority in payment of their claims over shareholders as to whether the company should be sold or liquidated. Giving the vote to shareholders gave the shareholders' veto power over what action should be taken. The report recommended that a neutral third party, known as a restructuring officer, be appointed by the court to oversee the restructuring process.

The fourth category recommended an expansion of the Model Law in Singapore. One area allowed enterprise groups or affiliated companies to file a single insolvency proceeding. A group representative would oversee the group filing. The other area to be added would allow recovery of insolvency-related judgments, which would allow for the easier recovery of assets found in multiple countries.

Whether one views the Singapore court's ruling as to a US golf course or the proposed 2025 changes to Singapore's cross-border insolvency law, there are potential problems for US companies. A foreign court may interpret a clause in one of the company's documents in an unanticipated manner. Or current provisions under the Singapore Model Law may not be consistent with established reorganization procedures in other countries. The uncertainty should cause US companies to think carefully about whether insolvency proceedings should be maintained against them in other countries.

Are there any problems for you as a US investor? Indeed. A US investor may end up in a Singapore insolvency proceeding because a single noteholder with some ties to Singapore could act on its own.

PART THREE
INDIVIDUAL BANKRUPTCY

CHAPTER THIRTEEN

IF YOU FAIL, MAY YOU TRY AGAIN?

In 1996, during a full day of hearings in Prescott, Arizona, a young man I'll call Will apologized for being in my court. He told me he had always worked hard and never contemplated bankruptcy. But his pay had been cut as part of budget-saving measures; the federal government then furloughed him, with no pay, during the federal government shutdowns from November 14 through November 19, 1995, and December 16, 1995, to January 6, 1996.[1]

Will was a park ranger who spent most of his time in remote areas protecting animals or assisting individuals in need of rescue. He had no savings. He lived paycheck to paycheck, and he couldn't pay his bills. He just needed a little time. I gave it to him.

While I was a judge, people I met often asked me, "Why do you allow individuals to get a free ride? They don't budget. It's a moral failure." There are many reasons why individuals seek bankruptcy protection. One reason is they live at poverty level. Another is the burden of high medical debt—even for

1. The Interior Department, which houses the National Park Service, was shut down both times.

Americans who have health coverage. And student loan debt —which was once eligible for forgiveness under the old bankruptcy law—can now lead college-educated Americans into bankruptcy.

In 2005, Congress passed the Bankruptcy Abuse Prevention and Consumer Protection Act of 2005 (BAPCPA), which was an oxymoron. Consumers were abused, and creditors were protected. BAPCPA burdens consumers with many new requirements before they can even commence a bankruptcy case.

Let's assume that you are a small business owner, and recent flooding, hurricanes, or other weather events have caused you temporarily to close your business. Your retail inventory of cutting-edge T-shirts currently sits in five feet of water. You also silk-screen the T-shirts at the back of your store, and all that equipment is underwater. The new truck that you recently purchased and financed through Big Bob's Car Emporium is stalled by the back door as you tried unsuccessfully to move inventory before floodwaters engulfed your vehicle. The water has permanently destroyed the truck's engine.

Given your situation, you've maxed out the credit line on the credit card you usually use for business operations. So you've taken to using your personal credit card that you normally use for vacations in Cancun to purchase critical inventory and equipment for your business. Still not having enough money, you've also taken cash advances on the personal credit card in the amount of $5,000.

Although state law requires you to insure your truck that you purchased from Big Bob, you believe that any insurance funds that you receive for a total loss of your truck are insufficient to pay your auto loan.

As for your business operations, you decided to self-insure, so any money that you put away in a savings account must now be utilized to pay for the cleanup of the property, purchase new furniture, and pay your ten loyal employees a nominal wage to keep them on board until you can open your doors. Since you decided not to operate your business through any type of entity, you are personally on the hook if creditors show up at your door trying to collect their debts. It may take you up to a year to get back to your normal business operations.

Fearing that creditors will try to collect while you are vulnerable and that you may lose your home, you decide to start a bankruptcy case.[2] Normally, an individual who needs bankruptcy relief must receive credit counseling 180 days prior to commencing a bankruptcy case. The counseling is provided over the phone or internet, and one may request that the requirement be waived if there is some type of emergency.[3]

Nevertheless, you, who are reeling from the disaster, couldn't get access to credit counseling before you filed. Your case has been flagged for dismissal, and you request an immediate hearing before the judge to explain your desperate situation. The judge grants your request for a waiver of credit counseling, and you manage to survive another day.

You learn that the credit counseling requirement was added in 2005 at the urging of creditors, who convinced Congress that individuals were constantly gaming the system and they should be repeatedly required to convince the court and the creditors that they were acting in good faith.

Showing that the individual had reviewed their financial situation through credit counseling before filing a bankruptcy case was just one of the many roadblocks created by credi-

2. See Section 101(51) of the Bankruptcy Code on the definition of what is a small business debtor.
3. See Section 109(h) of the Bankruptcy Code.

tors.[4] You let out a sigh. *Why don't creditors understand that emergencies happen?*

Big Bob, who sold and financed your truck, is livid that you have sought bankruptcy. He believes that your business is profitable since you were able to take money out of the business to purchase a new truck from him. He tracks you down as you are taking a break from mopping up the retail area, having a sandwich for lunch. He argues that you must pay him, over time, the full purchase price of the truck.

You gag on the processed tuna sandwich that you've purchased from a nearby laundromat vending machine. "Impossible!" you yell. "The vehicle is out back by the loading dock, full of water. It's crap, and I'm not paying you a dime for it. I'll give you any insurance proceeds that I receive, but I don't think the insurance will cover the total debt that I owe you."

You're worried by Bob's sneer. "My friend, you're destined for the wage-earner part of the bankruptcy law, which states that if you've acquired anything of value within the year before you started your bankruptcy case that I've financed and got a lien on, you're going to have to pay me the full purchase price." He chuckles. "Right now, you owe me $50,000, even if the truck is worthless."[5]

You think Bob is dead wrong. You seem to recall that you filed under the part of the bankruptcy law that deals with small businesses that want to pay their business and personal debts over time.[6] You make a mental note to wade through the floodwaters to dry land where the bankruptcy court is now

4. Public Law 109-8 added Section 109(h), with an effective date of 180 days after April 20, 2005.

5. See the aptly named "hanging paragraph," underneath Bankruptcy Code Section 1325 (a)(9).

6. Public Law 116-54, Subchapter V-Small Business Debtor Reorganization (August 23, 2019) as amended.

located and see if you can find a lawyer there to help you out. You push Bob out the door, slamming it behind him.

There's another knock on your door. You sigh. *Now what?* You crack open the door, and a lean man in a polyester suit forces the door open with his waterproof boot. He's been wading door to door collecting debts. He reminds you of the $5,000 advance that you recently took on your personal credit card for silk-screening equipment, insinuating that your silk-screening is only some hobby that you are pursuing. As you shove his foot out of the way, slamming the door shut, you yell a single word from your days as a frustrated artist and part-time dockworker, shouting at Big Bob through the closed door, "It's not my hobby. It's my business." Another item to jot down to discuss with a lawyer.

As you've been fighting off creditors at your door, your bankruptcy case has been dismissed. You forgot to file some schedules that disclosed the assets and liabilities that you had. But you're not worried. Don't people just repeatedly file cases?

You file another bankruptcy case, hoping to do everything by the required date the second time around. However, the law now assumes that you, as an individual, may be acting fraudulently, so your right to be protected from creditors in the new case is more limited.

For instance, if you have a mortgage on your home or you've purchased business equipment where the seller has retained a lien on, or interest in, the equipment in case you don't make payments, the bank or creditor may simply bide their time until thirty days passes after the filing of your new case. The bank or creditor will then advise you that if you miss a payment going forward, they will begin foreclosure proceedings to take your home or take steps to seize your equipment.

But you've filed a new case, you argue to yourself. Shouldn't you be entitled to have a chance to get it right the second time? Unfortunately, the 2005 amendments to the

Bankruptcy Code require an individual to understand that *they must act within the thirty days* of the second case filing to request that the court enter an order protecting the individual from creditor's actions to recover or seize the individual's property.[7] Moreover, the creditor has the power to request that the court put certain controls in place even if you get a court order. For instance, if you miss a loan payment or fail to insure your property, the creditor may soon be at your door to get the property back.

You still haven't figured out how to protect your assets and pay your creditors over time. You have no business income, and you are not sure when the local, state, or federal government will provide you with some type of interim payments to keep your head literally and figuratively above water.

You don't talk to a lawyer since you think they are all too expensive, and you decide to dismiss your case a second time. This was probably one of your worst decisions ever. You have now gone from the frying pan into the fire!

Belatedly, you go to the bankruptcy court self-help center, read articles, watch videos, and ask the attorney volunteering that day at the center a few questions. You learn you should not have dismissed your second case. "Now that I understand what's going on, filing a third case is OK, right?"

The volunteer attorney pulls you aside and says, "It's not OK. Since you've filed so many cases within a short period of time, the law assumes that you're filing the case in bad faith."

You shudder. "But I'm an honest person! I've lived through a hellish weather episode, my business is still underwater in every sense of the word, my equipment is rotting in the humid air and polluted water, and my ten employees need me to open my doors ASAP!"

Now it's the turn of the volunteer attorney to sigh. "I believe you, but changes in the law force individuals like you

---

7. Public Law 109-8, Section 362(c)(3)(A).

to *prove* that you've been through very difficult times and that you need bankruptcy relief. By proof, I mean evidence like photos of your destroyed business and facts to support that you were unable to obtain insurance on your business. You need to show that the insurance on your truck, even if it is a total loss, will not pay Big Bob in full and that you want to pay Big Bob over time.

"You must provide your most recent bank statements showing you have no savings and little money in your checking account. You need to show that you have no cash hidden away and you are uncertain when you will receive relief funds from any source. Hell, you may even want to provide a few weather reports to show how bad it was in your area.

"You have a heavy burden to persuade the court. It's not the usual burden in a civil case. You must prove to the court that what you say under oath and in your documents will persuasively show the court that you are acting in good faith. Only then will the court enter an order protecting you from creditors calling you about unpaid bills or seizing your home or your business equipment if you've missed payments on loans. Let's move to a side office that the court provides for attorneys and discuss next steps, including whether you wish me or some other attorney to represent you."[8]

You learn that you probably qualify as a small business debtor. Bob was wrong! He thought you filed chapter 13, the usual part of the bankruptcy law that individuals with regular income must use, but you saw a part of chapter 11 that allows individuals with small businesses to pay their creditors over time. The attorney advises you that you were correct in moving to the small business reorganization chapter. You feel confident that Bob can't force you to pay the purchase price for the truck in your new small business case.

You also believe that you have a good argument that the

---

8. Public Law 109-8, Section 362(c)(4).

$5,000 cash advance on your personal credit card was for your business, and as a result, you probably don't have to pay the credit card company in full. You have now gotten your credit counseling, so you may move forward with your third case.

As the sun slowly sets on the horizon, you are glad that there is someone there to help you. The attorney is knowledgeable and will most likely provide the evidence to the court that will allow you to remain in bankruptcy, file a small business plan, and use government assistance and income from your business once it reopens to pay certain creditors in full and pay others with smaller or lower priority debts a substantial percentage of their debts over time. It may take you five years to make all the payments under your plan, but in the end, you will get the debt forgiveness that you deserve, having survived a horrific storm.

CHAPTER FOURTEEN

THE TORTUOUS ROAD OF AN INDIVIDUAL SEEKING BANKRUPTCY RELIEF

Although counterintuitive, bankruptcy has always been expensive for an individual trying to get financial relief. Before the 2005 changes to the bankruptcy law, it cost an individual $712 just to begin a liquidation case. These were not complex cases. The individual surrendered certain assets to a bankruptcy trustee to be sold, with the proceeds used to pay the creditors.

In 2005, the filing fee was increased by 51 percent to $1,078. Was it a way to dissuade impoverished individuals from getting access to the bankruptcy courts? Absolutely. There was no policy reason to raise the filing fee so dramatically other than an erroneous belief that it was a moral failure of individuals to need bankruptcy relief at all.

Other changes in 2005 required an individual operating a small business to provide reports on profitability (how much the individual's business has recently earned and lost) and an estimate of and actual cash receipts and disbursements going forward and to promptly file tax returns and pay any taxes owing.[1] Other forms must be filed as well, and there is little

1. Public Law 109-8, Section 308.

room for error. An individual may find that within a short period of time, the bankruptcy case has been dismissed, and the creditors are free to collect their debts.

After 2005, individuals were also generally required to file their cases under the provisions of the Bankruptcy Code that forced them to pay their creditors over a five-year period even if it was difficult, if not impossible, for the individuals to have sufficient monthly cash on hand to make such periodic bankruptcy payments.

Most people were filing bankruptcy petitions because they were employed but living paycheck to paycheck. If they already had little money on hand, how would they be able to make the additional monthly payments required under a five-year plan?

And if they didn't make all the payments over time, unless they could show they had a terminal illness or were destitute, they would never receive forgiveness of their debts. By comparison, before the 2005 amendments to the bankruptcy law, individuals could choose whether to make payments to creditors over time or surrender certain assets to be sold and used to pay creditors. The benefit of choosing the latter path, the liquidation route, was that the individual received the benefit of immediate forgiveness of her debts rather than having to wait five years.

One bankruptcy judge described the 2005 changes to the Bankruptcy Code as "confusing, overlapping, and sometimes self-contradictory."[2] There are many provisions that unnecessarily take away a judge's discretion, are effectively punitive, and are decidedly pro-creditor. The litigation over what the 2005 changes really mean continues to this day.

---

2. In re Donald, 343 B.R. 524, 529 (Bankr. E.D.N.C. 2006).

WHAT CAUSED the dramatic 2005 changes to the Bankruptcy Code? The intense lobbying efforts of the credit card industry beginning in the 1990s were one of the primary causes. However, one might describe the credit card industry as having a checkered history, beginning well before the 1990s. Although humans first created debt in 3500 BCE, America certainly perfected the modern idea of how to obtain credit quickly and conveniently.[3]

Legend has it that Frank McNamara forgot his wallet while dining out in New York City in 1949. An urgent plea to his wife led her to furnish the necessary cash for him to leave the restaurant with his head held high. Frank pondered the problem: What if there was an easy way to pay a bill if he forgot his cash in the future?

Whether Frank's wife saved him is up for debate, but he did come up with the concept of paying a bill with a card. The card would be a credit card, which required card members to pay off their balances each month. The original cards were made from cardboard or flexible, transparent material like film. Frank's Diners Club card became wildly popular in the 1950s. In 1959, there was a competitor in the lucrative market—American Express—and the credit cards became plastic.

By 1958, banks got into the business, with Bank of America creating its first "general purpose credit card," which it sent to over sixty thousand residents in Fresno, California. The bank had a different idea as to how to sell credit to the World War II generation. Many had served their country, and they wanted a refrigerator. The card had a credit line that could increase or decrease as necessary, allowing cardmembers to purchase anything and pay off the purchase over time.

In the 1960s, Mastercard came up with a similar idea as

3. See David Graeber's bestseller *Debt: The First 5000 Years* as to our ongoing fascination with debt.

that of Bank of America. Why worry about a substantial purchase? Why not just allow card members to roll their debt to the next month and beyond? Of course, for such a privilege, a convenience fee would have to be paid. Mastercard invented and perfected a new way to make a lot of money.

In 1966, the Chicago Debacle occurred, which led to congressional hearings about whether credit cards should be banned. Certain Midwestern banks had sent out five million credit cards to everyone imaginable, including convicted felons and toddlers. Apparently, even a few dogs were advised of their need for credit. It was rumored that cats were too smart to open the alluring envelopes. However, Congress soon moved on to other issues, and technical advances in the 1970s made the credit card business profitable. It should also be noted that during this period, banks sent out one hundred million credit cards.

Times began to change. Many banks that had national charters were caught in a regulatory environment that prohibited them from raising their interest rates during inflationary times. In the late 1970s, Citibank was going broke. It was lending out money at 12 percent, but inflation was running at 20 percent. It had lost $1 billion in its credit card business.

However, in 1978, the United States Supreme Court changed the game in *Marquette Natl. Bank of Minneapolis v. First of Omaha Service Corp.*, 439 U.S. 299 (1978). Since First of Omaha was a national bank, the interest rate that it could charge customers was governed by federal law. Federal law permitted the bank to charge interest on any loan at a rate that was allowed by the state where the bank was located.

First of Omaha was located and made credit decisions in Nebraska, where it was chartered. The National Bank Act of 1864 encouraged and facilitated a national banking system, which allowed for loans to be made to citizens in other states. As a result, the Nebraska interest rate on loans could be exported to the residents of Minnesota, even though the

Nebraska interest rate was considered usurious under Minnesota law.

Citibank considered the *Marquette* decision as a basis to change its credit card operations and become profitable. New York had usury laws in place that its legislators had refused to lower. What if Citibank moved its credit card division somewhere else? Federal banking law allowed banks to set up operations outside their home state if the legislature of the new state invited the bank to set up operations there.

In 1980, most of the states had usury laws similar to New York's. The exception? South Dakota was in its own dire straits and decided to eliminate its usury laws to stimulate business. Citibank seized the opportunity. If South Dakota would invite Citibank to set up its credit card operations in the state, Citibank would move four hundred jobs there. South Dakota proposed a special emergency bill that was introduced and passed in the legislature in one day.

Eventually Citibank moved three thousand high-paying jobs to the state. Delaware was quick to change its laws as well, with Chase, Manufacturers Hanover, and Chemical moving there.

From 1980 to 1990, the credit card industry earned enormous profits. Meanwhile, the credit card debt of the average household increased from $518 to $2,700.

By 1990, interest rates on credit cards were running around 18 percent per annum. In November 1991, at a fundraising lunch, President George H. W. Bush wondered whether credit card interest rates had gotten too high. The very next day, the Senate passed legislation to cap credit card interest rates at 14 percent. Panic ensued in the banking industry, and the stock market took a nosedive. Then Vice President Dan Quayle stated in a television interview that if the House acted similarly and the legislation was presented to President Bush for signature, the president would likely veto it. Calamity averted.

Nevertheless, growth in the industry slowed. Analytics were created to find the cardmember who would have high balances but would never have a payment default. The cardmember would roll over the balances month-to-month but always pay the minimum balance due. Eventually credit lines, or the amount of credit that could be borrowed, increased dramatically. The minimum payment due each month was kept the same or reduced.

An example? The credit card company would increase the credit line from $2,000 to $5,000 but still only require a cardholder to pay the same minimum monthly payment of $100. The cardholder, intrigued, would purchase goods up to the new credit limit of $5,000 but still only pay $100 per month. In six months, the credit card company would increase the credit line to $10,000. The cardholder, unable to resist what appeared to be a good deal, would charge an expensive vacation on the credit card up to the limit of $10,000. The cardholder would continue to pay only $100 per month. In the space of nine months, the credit limit for the cardholder had increased from $2,000 to $10,000. A $10,000 credit card debt that accrued interest at a rate of 18 percent per annum, with payments of only $100 per month, would take the cardmember 137 months (over 11 years) to repay. The credit card company would rake in interest rate fees as profit over a prolonged period.

Was the pitch of credit card companies appealing to the average consumer? Absolutely. The average household debt increased from 1990 to 2015 from $2,500 to $7,500.

In 2024, President Biden and his administration, through the rule-making authority of the Consumer Financial Protection Bureau (CFPB), eliminated billions of dollars in fee revenue charged by banks. The CFPB estimated that banks had collected $280 billion in just overdraft fees over the last twenty years. Smaller banks and credit unions were not affected. Of particular concern were two-thirds of the overdraft fees being charged by only 175 banks, primarily when debit card transactions caused a customer's balance to go below zero.

The May 16, 2024, decision of the United States Supreme Court in *Consumer Financial Credit Bureau v. Financial Services Industry* parried the constitutional attacks by the industry, holding the director of the CFPB could receive funding from the Federal Reserve System for reasonable operating expenses of the bureau. It appeared that the rule change limiting fees might go into effect. But for how long?

In January 2025, a new leader took control of the CFPB and shuttered the agency. All employees were told to stay home and not do any work. Since its inception in 2009 after the financial crisis of 2008, the CFPB has helped consumers collect $21 billion in monetary compensation, loan principal reductions, canceled debt, and other funds.

In 2025, before it was closed, it had a budget of $823 million. The Federal Reserve provided the funding for the agency through quarterly transfers. Many Republicans are happy with the dismantling of the CFPB. Consumers, on the other hand, may sorely miss an advocate for them.

CHAPTER FIFTEEN

ON LIFE SUPPORT

We think that health insurance and the Affordable Care Act will protect us from financial catastrophe. The latest research shows that is not the case. In fact, in 2019, 530,000 families or two-thirds of the people who filed bankruptcy petitions did so because of medical issues that placed them in precarious financial conditions.

Many families are either unable to pay the high cost of medical care or must take time off from work, affecting the amount of their take-home pay. In many cases, individuals choose insurance policies with high deductibles to save money, only to find they're responsible for paying enormous out-of-pocket costs before their insurance company pays any of their medical costs. A recent study found that only 40 percent of Americans had even $1,000 available for emergency expenses.

Bankruptcy is not the solution for anyone with a chronic illness that generates ongoing medical expenses. In the late 1990s, I presided over a case filed by Walt (since I am speaking about his medical issues which were disclosed on the record at various hearings, I am using a pseudonym to protect his privacy). Walt was a Black man in his fifties who had kidney failure because of untreated high blood pressure over a prolonged period.

At a hearing before me one day, his attorney explained what happened to Walt.

"Judge, he just didn't take care of himself. He loved eggs and fried foods, and he worked hard. He didn't see a doctor on a regular basis. He didn't have the time. He had high blood pressure but ignored it. Then fatigue overwhelmed him, vomiting, swelling in his legs, and he ended up in the emergency room. He was chained to a dialysis machine when he came to his senses. And still is.

"The worst part is . . . there is no happy ending to the story. His chances of receiving a transplant of one or both kidneys are slim. He is on the waiting list, but it could take years before he gets to the top of the list, and he needs a near-perfect match with the donor. Right now, he must receive dialysis treatment every day. He can't be off the machine for any length of time, so he can't work anymore. And now he must face a creditor, someone on whom he depends for his very life, who demands an outrageous amount of money.

"I've never seen anything like it in all my years of practice. We need you to sort this out. And even when you listen to us and even when we show you he owes this creditor so much less, it won't be over.

"Each day Walt lives, he needs ongoing care. His medical expenses will grow day by day, year by year, until he dies. And I just don't know what to do about a debt he will never be able to pay. He will live in a state of penury, now and forever. This bankruptcy case will only take care of the debt that he owed on the date he commenced his case, not the new debt that he incurred the next day and every day thereafter. And I can't keep filing bankruptcy cases every time his medical expenses get too high."

Evidence was presented that the company had overcharged, double-billed, or had created phantom charges that could not be adequately explained. The medical bill was in the range of $200,000. I reduced the bill to around $50,000, which would be forgiven once he got his discharge, or forgiveness of debt, in his current bankruptcy case.

But Walt had filed chapter 7, a liquidation proceeding, and the debt he owed the creditor was determined as of the commencement of the bankruptcy case. I could only resolve that debt—not any future debt that arose for treatments to keep him alive.

For the foreseeable future, he would continue to incur almost limitless medical costs that would not be resolved. The bankruptcy law did not let him file a bankruptcy case at relatively short intervals to allow for the forgiveness of massive, ongoing debts. As his attorney had declared, his medical condition placed him in a perpetual state of penury.

Policymakers should consider expanding Medicare, or other medical coverage, to cover catastrophic medical expenses at little or no cost to those who cannot afford to pay. If one is living at the poverty level or is in the middle class, as so many are after the COVID- 19 pandemic, the individual is simply unable to increase the private insurance premium to obtain the requisite medical coverage.

Again, the solution seems to be that the government should provide an expansion of Medicare to those who don't otherwise qualify so that they may obtain more affordable insurance coverage for chronic illnesses.

CHAPTER SIXTEEN

UNTIL DEATH US DO PART

Student loan debt statistics have been described as "shocking." At the end of the first quarter of 2022, Americans owed $1.59 trillion in student loan debt, according to the Federal Reserve Bank of New York, an increase of $14 billion over the fourth quarter of 2021. The average graduate receiving a bachelor's degree owed $28,400 in federal and private debt.

Student loan debt has increased by $250 billion since 2019. The individuals in default only saw their financial woes increase with the lowering of their credit scores, which only made it harder to access credit at an affordable interest rate. The policies of the Department of Education have reduced the default rate on student loans. However, borrowers who drop out before they obtain their degrees or who are the first in their families to seek a college degree are the most likely to default. Research has shown that Black and Hispanic students are disproportionately affected by the student debt crisis; they are more likely to attend for-profit colleges that don't lead to high-paying careers, and they borrow more money to attend.[1]

1. Black and Hispanic students were encouraged to attend college, often

Black college graduates owe an average of $25,000 more in student loan debt than white graduates.

It is extremely difficult for student loan borrowers to get relief in bankruptcy. During my legal career, including the twenty-eight years I served as a bankruptcy judge in Arizona, I have watched a steady erosion of the pro-debtor provisions of the bankruptcy laws regarding student loans.

Under the current bankruptcy law, borrowers must meet the Brunner test, named after the case of *In re Brunner*, 46 B.R. 752 (S.DN.Y. 1985), which introduced three criteria of "undue hardship" borrowers must meet before their debt is forgiven: The borrower is living at the poverty level, will continue to do so for the foreseeable future, and has made good faith efforts to repay the student loan debt. If a debtor cannot meet one of the criteria, the debt cannot be discharged. The *Brunner* decision is followed, with some modification, in nearly all of the circuit courts of appeal.

The United States Supreme Court, in *Biden v. Nebraska*, vitiated the president's efforts to provide relief to millions of borrowers through his secretary of education. President Biden took other executive action, and the secretary of education forgave student loan debt of defunct for-profit schools and set up procedures to allow more flexibility on loan repayments. However, such efforts were short-term solutions.

Many of the actions that President Biden and the secretary of education took, such as putting a pause on the repayment of student loans or forgiving student loans that were provided by schools engaged in misconduct, were undone or suspended after President Trump was inaugurated.

On April 21, 2025, the US Department of Education announced that the Office of Federal Student Aid would

---

attended for-profit schools which did not advance their careers, and had families at lower income levels that took out too much debt to advance the students' studies.

begin collecting defaulted federal student loans on May 5, 2025. As of the end of April 2025, the Department of Education estimated that 42.7 million borrowers owed more than $1.6 trillion, and within a few months, around 10 million borrowers, or almost 25 percent of the federal student loan portfolio, would be in default. The department stated that only 38 percent of borrowers were current on their student loans.

The current administration's position on whether social security may be garnished to repay federal student loans is unclear. On June 1, 2025, a few news outlets reported that the administration would begin garnishing up to 15 percent of social security checks at some point in the summer. On June 3, 2025, other news outlets reported that the Trump administration had paused student debt collections for social security recipients. What happens next appears unclear.

Although social security recipients may have a brief respite, the Trump administration will garnish wages or offset student loan debt against any tax refunds borrowers may receive in payment of student loan debt. The federal government does have such authority.[2]

THE LATEST ATTACK on student loan recipients has been the passage of the Big Beautiful Bill Act on July 4, 2025.[3] High school and college students will see a dramatic change in loan repayment plans from many proposals to just two choices

2. The Debt Collection Improvement Act of 1996 allows the federal government to withhold social security benefits to collect delinquent taxes or other debts owed to federal agencies. The individual still receives the first $750 per month, but any benefits above that amount are offset up 15 percent of the benefits to repay student loans and other debts.
3. The bill has the official title of the One Big Beautiful Bill Act or the Big Beautiful Bill.

beginning July 1, 2026. They have little time to prepare. If they do not obtain the financing that they need within a short period of time, they may find that they will be unable to pursue their studies.

The new legislation corrects what the current administration describes as a policy that "forced people never setting foot on college campuses to pay the costs of elite Ivy League degrees." Of course, the administration has forgotten about students who obtained loans to attend community colleges or public universities[4] who will also now be forced to consider only two options.

The SAVE (Saving on a Valuable Education) plan, Income Contingent Repayment (ICR) plan, and Pay As You Earn (PAYE) plan will not be available to new borrowers after July 1, 2026. The SAVE plan was launched in August 2023, applicable to federal student loans, offering borrowers lower monthly payments based on income and loan forgiveness in less time. The ICR plan was also an income-driven plan based on many factors. Borrower's income, family size, and what funds were available from discretionary income (versus income that was necessary to keep the family fed, clothed, and sheltered) were considered in determining what the borrower could repay on a federal student loan over a twelve-year period.

The PAYE plan, another income-driven plan for federal student loans, capped monthly loan repayments at 10 percent of annual discretionary income divided by twelve. The aggregate amount of the loan to be paid was also capped at what one would pay under a standard repayment plan over a ten-year period. However, instead of making payments over a ten-

4. For instance, the land-grant colleges or universities were created pursuant to the Morrill Acts of 1862 and 1890 and the Equity in Educational Land-Grant Status Act of 1994, which allowed federal lands to be designated to the states to establish institutions to broaden higher educational access to students wishing to study agriculture, mechanical arts, and military science.

year period, the borrower was allowed to stretch the period to twenty years. The drawback was that the borrower had to make the loan repayments over the entire twenty-year period to receive loan forgiveness.

After July 1, 2026, the two options available for new borrowers will be the standard plan, which shortens the loan repayment period from between ten to twenty years but is not tied to earnings, or the Repayment Assistance Plan (RAP), which is tied to earnings but requires students to pay for thirty years before the student loan debt is forgiven.

Under the RAP plan, if the borrower earns $10,000 or less annually, she pays $120 annually or $10 per month. On earnings of $10,001 to $20,000 annually, she will pay 1 percent of her annual income. For each $10,000 incremental increase in income, the percentage payment will go up by 1 percentage point. For instance, on income between $20,001 and $30,000, the borrower will pay 2 percent of her annual income. On income of $30,000, the borrower will pay $600 annually or $50 per month. If the borrower earns more than $100,001 annually, the percentage payment will be capped at 10 percent of annual income.

Current borrowers under SAVE, ICR, and PAYE plans will have no choice but to watch their plans migrate to an amended version of an income-based repayment plan over a two-year period from July 1, 2026, to June 30, 2028. After July 1, 2028, all remaining borrowers under the SAVE, ICR, and PAYE plans will be enrolled in the RAP plan or another income-based plan if available.

There is one area where there is a potential silver lining. Because of a last-minute ambiguous change by the Senate to the Big Beautiful Bill, there is the possibility that borrowers enrolled currently in another income-based repayment plan other than SAVE, ICR, or PAYE may be able to retain that plan or enter into a more favorable plan than RAP after July 1, 2028.

Under the prior law, the alternative repayment plan was tied to discretionary income, which was defined as 150 percent of the federal poverty line. In 2025, for the forty-eight contiguous states, the yearly income was $23,475 for one person up to $64,725 for a family of six. The annual discretionary income was higher for Alaska and Hawaii because of the higher cost of living.

Each year the borrowers determined their discretionary income, took 15 percent of that amount as the required loan repayment, and repaid that amount in equal monthly payments over the next year. The borrowers paid their loans over a twenty-five-year period, with debt forgiveness at the end of the payment period.

Under the Big Beautiful Bill, the new income-based repayment plan (the IBR plan) will require borrowers to pay 10 percent of their annual discretionary income over a twenty-year period, with forgiveness of the debt at that time. This leaves open the possibility that borrowers may retain their plan under the prior law or switch to the IBR plan under the Big Beautiful Bill. Either option is better than the RAP income-based plan, which requires student loan repayments over a thirty-year period.

The Parent PLUS loan, which is a federal student loan provided to parents of dependent undergraduate students, has also been modified. On July 1, 2026, and after, the parents will be responsible for the repayment of the loan and must be the biological or adoptive parents of the student who is required to be enrolled at least half-time in an eligible school. The student must also meet the requirements for federal student aid. The new Parent PLUS loan will be capped at $20,000 per year and the aggregate amount of $65,000. The new loans will also be ineligible for any income-driven repayment plans or student loan forgiveness programs, including public service.[5] These loans will also be tied more closely to the costs of attendance at the school, such as tuition, and not all costs incurred by the student, such as rent for an apartment during the school year.

An exception to the lack of an income-based repayment plan for a Parent PLUS loan is if the parent currently has several such loans that have been consolidated. It appears that under the new law, the parent may continue with the repayment plan even after July 1, 2026. Unfortunately, if the parent has several Parent PLUS loans that have not yet been consolidated, the parent has only until July 1, 2026, to consolidate the loans, or the parent may be cut off from any income-based repayment plan as well as the possibility of eventual loan forgiveness.

The graduate loan program, known as Graduate PLUS, will be eliminated as to new borrowers after July 1, 2026. Currently a graduate student is allowed to borrow up to the full cost of attendance. That will end. Stafford loans for graduate students will continue but will be limited to an annual limit of $20,500, and a lifetime cap of $100,000. As for professional students, such as those attending medical or law schools, the annual loan amount will be capped at $50,000, with a lifetime cap of $200,000.

The Big Beautiful Bill has also modified the ability to have student loans forgiven through public service. Previously, a borrower could have a student loan forgiven if the individual worked for a nonprofit or was a government worker and made loan repayments, pursuant to an income-driven or a standard repayment plan, for a period of ten years.

The Department of Education, which has the mission of eliminating itself, is preparing regulations that prohibit student loan forgiveness for organizations that "engage in activities with a substantial illegal purpose." Will nonprofit organiza-

5. See below. The public service loan forgiveness program has been changed.

tions or state or local governments whose missions are different be disqualified, forcing borrowers to seek public service employment elsewhere? Moreover, there is concern that the Department of Education will simply issue its new regulations without getting congressional approval.

THE DIFFERENT POSITIONS recently taken by administrations as to how student loan debt should be repaid ignore the history of how we got to this place of unforgivable debt.

Under prior bankruptcy law, student loans could be forgiven, just like any other consumer debt. There were no conditions. But then student loans became profitable for the government and the private lender.

In 1976, an Amendment to the Higher Education Act, which also amended the bankruptcy law, was a game changer. It required that education loans not be forgiven unless a period of five years after the loan was entered into had passed or the borrower could show that they would experience an "undue hardship" if the loan were repaid. It was left to the courts to determine what undue hardship meant. The Bankruptcy Reform Act of 1978, the Bankruptcy Code or the new bankruptcy law, incorporated the changes.

In 1990, the Crime Control Bill changed the waiting period from five to seven years and added additional types of loans that were difficult to forgive under the Bankruptcy Code. Finally, on October 7, 1998, President Clinton signed the Higher Education Act Amendments, which eliminated the waiting period altogether. Then, only undue hardship could free a borrower from student loan debt in bankruptcy.

Over the course of two decades, lobbying efforts by financial institutions successfully eroded individual rights. Since the federal government was guaranteeing the loans issued by these for-profit financial institutions, it was in the interest of the government that the loans be difficult to be forgiven. But what about the human toll?

In 2012, I presided over a case that involved a woman, I call her Mary, who took out student loans in the 1970s and then decided to work in the public sector. Mary made sporadic payments on her loans over the years, owned a home, got divorced, then remarried. She never made a lot of money. If she had filed a bankruptcy petition in the early '80s, she probably would have been able to discharge her loans after seven years. She had her records back then. But Mary didn't think about bankruptcy.

Mary retired, sold her home, and moved to Arizona. Her husband did odd jobs, and they collected social security. Then the student loan collector came a-knocking. The collector demanded immediate payment. She filed a bankruptcy petition. Mary had no records of her payments over the years, and tellingly, the collector was having difficulty calculating the total amount owed. By the time she appeared in my courtroom, she was seventy-three years old, and she owed $584,854.99.

At a subsequent trial, the creditor presented no evidence, but Mary had little documentation to support her position as to repayments on her student loans or her salary over the years because she had taken out the student loans so long ago.

I saw incredible inequities in this case. I reasoned that if she had filed her bankruptcy petition prior to 1998, she most likely would have been entitled to a discharge of her student loans based on the passage of time. She also worked in the public sector for many years, so her service might have afforded her the ability to discharge her student loans after ten years. Mary was living at the poverty level, her life expectancy was a factor as to how long she could continue to make student loan payments, and she had made sporadic payments over the years.

Given the law at the time, I used ten years as the baseline

that she would have paid on her student loans given her public service. Next, I considered that had she filed her case prior to 1998, she would have been able to discharge all her student loan debt after seven years. Considering the increase in time from seven years to ten years, I determined that she would pay her student loan debt for three more years but only based on whatever her income level would permit.

If her social security income was only able to pay for her necessities of life, she need not pay any amount on her student loans. At the end of three years, even if she was only able to pay a small amount of the debt, her student loan debt would be forgiven. The parties stipulated to a form of judgment that followed the parameters of my ruling.

I presided over numerous bankruptcy cases like Mary's, where individuals were living at poverty level, had been unable to obtain gainful employment for a variety of reasons, and spent a substantial portion of their available income, after rent and food, on repayment of student loans.

The student loan crisis continues to be a nationwide problem. Although receiving initial media attention, judicial efforts have been unsuccessful. In the decision of *In re Tingling,* the Second Circuit Court of Appeals reaffirmed, in Spring 2022, that the Brunner test would stand. The US Congress must make some changes.

We allow the financial markets to take innumerable risks, yet we refuse to allow an individual to be forgiven for choosing to pursue an advanced degree.

CHAPTER SEVENTEEN

SOMETIMES THE IMPROBABLE IS TRUE

It seemed to be a typical day. I had the usual assortment of status conferences on various matters that had only recently been filed. Most attorneys were on the path to resolving their disputes.

Around 4 p.m., an attorney representing an individual I'll name Mr. Smith outlined the facts in the case. He stated that Mr. Smith had been seriously injured in an automobile accident by a drunk driver. He had the documentation to show Mr. Smith's injuries, the medical and legal costs his client had already incurred, the blood-alcohol level taken shortly after the accident of the drunk driver who hit his client's car head-on, the police record showing the driver had been arrested and incarcerated, and the driver's plea of guilty in a subsequent criminal proceeding.

The attorney stated that the individual who had filed the bankruptcy case, or debtor, was responsible for the injuries to Mr. Smith and had to pay all the expenses and costs incurred by his client. For purposes of the narrative, I'll call the individual, the debtor, Mr. Adams.

The bankruptcy laws on the consequences of driving and injuring people or damaging property while under the influence of alcohol are clear. An individual who has filed a bankruptcy case will be held responsible for any death or personal injury they caused from the operation of a motor vehicle, vessel, or aircraft while intoxicated after using alcohol, a drug, or another substance.[1] The individual is required to pay back the injured party or parties for all damages, in full, with interest, no matter how long it takes.

The attorney for Mr. Smith seemed to have sufficient evidence to resolve all the issues before me in a relatively short period of time. The effect would be that Mr. Adams, the individual who filed the bankruptcy case, would be responsible for payment in full of all damages he caused by his drunk driving, no matter how much the costs and expenses were and no matter how long it took him to repay the injured Mr. Smith.

The costs and expenses were around $100,000 at the time of our status conference. Given Mr. Adams's financial situation, it would probably take him twenty years to pay off the debt so long as he remained employed.

I looked over at the attorney for Mr. Adams. He remained seated at the table, lost in thought. His client, the debtor, was seated next to him. The attorney rose slowly, collecting his thoughts as he faced me. He hesitated.

"Judge, in all my years of practice, I have never seen a case like this. What I am about to say will seem improbable to you. It certainly was to me when I first heard the story. I will say that I have looked at the documents that my client, Mr. Adams, has shown me, and I believe him. As crazy as it seems, I believe him. I think you will find a way to sort this out.

"My client was not driving the car that injured Mr. Smith, the poor man who is here today. In fact, my client was nowhere near the scene of the accident. He has witnesses who will affirm where he was on the date and at the time of the accident.

1. See 11 U.S.C. §523(a)(9).

"What happened? A clear miscarriage of justice. The drunk driver who injured Mr. Smith stole my client's driver's license. The drunk driver had that license on him at the time of the accident. He used that license for identification when he was arrested, arraigned, and when he pled guilty to the criminal offense.

"How can I say this? No one cared. No one carefully looked at the license then at my client. My client is innocent. My client owes Mr. Smith, the injured man, nothing.

"Since my client was about to have his poverty-level wages garnished to pay the damages owed to Mr. Smith, I decided that I had to file a bankruptcy case for my client immediately before he lost his home, his family, everything, for an act he did not commit."

The attorney for Mr. Smith responded.

"Judge, the other side is telling you a fairy tale. How could so many people in the criminal justice system make so many mistakes?"

I knew both attorneys since they had practiced before me for years. But I had never heard such an argument before from any attorney. The debtor's attorney was right—what he said was improbable. But what if it were true?

I decided to do something unusual. Under the evidentiary rules governing proceedings in the bankruptcy court, a bankruptcy judge has the power to appoint an expert witness.[2] Judges usually don't appoint their own experts, allowing the parties to develop the evidentiary record. However, there are several reasons why a judge should step in and exercise her discretion. A party in a lawsuit may not have the financial wherewithal to hire an expert or may be unable to find someone who will testify on their behalf.

In certain cases, the experts who do testify may present extreme or unreliable positions to the judge. The judge may

2. Fed. R. of Evidence 706.

reject such expert opinions, preferring to appoint a qualified individual who will provide a realistic opinion upon which the judge may rely. Finally, in a few cases, the impartiality of the expert may be questioned.

Of course, some attorneys question why the judge should be involved in the legal process at all. To me, what is important is finding out what happened, then applying the law to the facts. Gamesmanship or, worse, presenting an inaccurate or false record to the court causes the public to lose confidence in the courts. The public may begin to believe that there is no justice and that insiders, the wealthy, or the powerful control all the outcomes.

I talked to the attorneys and their clients about the unusual situation we were in. Both sides seemed to believe that they had investigated the matter and were entitled to relief. I suggested to them that it made sense to bring in a disinterested third party who was aware of how the criminal justice system worked and have that party investigate what had happened. For instance, a third party could get a specimen of the debtor's fingerprints and compare it with the records on file at the state court criminal proceedings. The attorneys readily agreed to the idea. I also proposed that they split the cost of the expert fifty-fifty. Again, there was a ready agreement.

They asked me if I knew of anyone, and I said I did not. However, I set up a schedule for them to look for individuals to serve as experts and provide me with a list of proposed names. I would also look for a suitable person to serve as an expert witness. Ultimately, I would look at the list of names, select the most qualified individual, and advise them of my selection. I set a date for a future status conference to discuss with them the expert that I had selected and next steps in the case.

At the next status conference, the attorneys advised me that they had not found any suitable experts, but they did agree to allow my proposed expert to be appointed to resolve their issues. My expert witness was a former FBI agent who was an expert in fingerprint analysis. He had also testified as an expert at federal criminal court proceedings. He was highly recommended by many sources.

I worked with the parties to draft a form of order appointing the FBI expert and outlining the tasks that we wanted him to perform. We required him to file a report of his analysis and to testify before the court if either side requested it.

Several weeks later, the FBI expert filed his report. He had taken a specimen of the debtor's fingerprints and had accessed all records of the police and the court as to Mr. Adams's arrest, appearance at court hearings, pleadings filed with the court, including the plea of guilty, and incarceration. The improbable had become reality. Although the driver's license picture of Mr. Adams bore some resemblance to the mug shot of the criminal who took over his identity, it was clear that the various governmental agencies and the state court had failed the debtor.

The criminal had stolen Mr. Adams's driver's license and had used it, repeatedly, throughout the criminal justice system. Because Mr. Adams had no criminal record, the criminal was treated as a first-time offender and received a lenient sentence. When Mr. Smith then filed a civil complaint seeking damages for his medical and other costs arising from the accident, Mr. Adams was served, but he believed there had been some horrendous mistake. He did not respond or take any other action. At that point, Mr. Adams had a criminal record and a default judgment entered against him in a civil proceeding for substantial damages. He finally sought the help of a bankruptcy attorney.

After reading the expert's report, the attorneys accepted it as being thorough and persuasive. They did not ask the FBI expert to testify at a later hearing. Mr. Smith and his attorney agreed to dismiss the bankruptcy lawsuit against Mr. Adams and have the state court criminal and civil judgments set aside.

About a month after the final status conference in the case, I received a call from my expert witness. I thanked him for helping me resolve a most unusual case. He assured me he was glad to be of service. I asked him if he had been paid. He chuckled and said Mr. Smith's attorney had paid his client's half, but he had received nothing from Mr. Adams or his attorney.

I asked if I could be of assistance in setting up a further hearing to see if there were any issues as to his payment. The FBI agent said he was happy to "right a wrong" and did not need to be paid by Mr. Adams.

He did express one final concern. He said that Mr. Adams needed to petition the appropriate agencies and the state court to expunge his criminal conviction and record. He was worried that Mr. Adams might have some new interaction with the legal system, and his criminal record would show up and be a detriment to Mr. Adams getting relief or being heard.

The FBI agent offered to undertake the task of correcting the various records. I thanked him again for trying to help Mr. Adams but said that I would contact Mr. Adams and his attorney as to what action, if any, they desired the FBI agent to take. I did follow through with Mr. Adams's attorney. The attorney said they would determine what they wanted to do to expunge the criminal record. I never heard from anyone after that.

CHAPTER EIGHTEEN

THE BANKRUPTCY RECIDIVISTS

In Arizona, there are some individuals or certain properties that seem to be destined for the bankruptcy law hall of fame. They may disappear from the news for a time. The owners may then rise from the ashes of past financial mistakes, looking for mercy, ever hopeful that this time they have everything on their side. Is it the perpetual sun that blinds individuals from the reality of a situation? Whatever the cause, it occurs frequently.

I remember one individual who had desert land near a small city sixty-five miles southeast of Phoenix and fifty miles northwest of Tucson. The city was founded in the 1880s as a place for workers to rest while tracks were being laid for the Southern Pacific Railroad. The extent of the railroad workers' comfort was a couple of boxcars on a railroad spur. It was discovered that cotton could be grown in the desert area, although water was limited.

In 1987, aerobatic pilots loved the nearby airport with one runway because they could do stunt flying all day long, with no control tower or air traffic to impede them. The individual had dreams of developing one or more golf courses near the runway, then building golf course homes nearby.

Unfortunately, no one was interested . . . not even the aerobatic pilots. But the individual was ever hopeful. So he filed a bankruptcy petition, hoping to get a little time to sell his land or find an investor who would help develop a master-planned community far from the crowds. When he found no investor or financing, his case was dismissed. Dismissal did not deter him. He just filed another case. He became a repeat filer, or what was known as a bankruptcy recidivist.

Each of his parcels was placed in a limited liability company—no surprise since it allowed him to limit his personal liability. A bank financing his purchase of a few desert acres would be able to foreclose and sell the parcel if he didn't make payments on a loan, but at least the creditor could not pursue him if the desert land turned out to be worthless.

It is a testament to his ability as a salesman that he was able to convince many financial institutions or investors to give him money that allowed him to amass hundreds of acres of desert land in an area with just a one-runway airport and no control tower as the local amenity. Given the amount of desert land that he had, he was able to have at least ten bankruptcy cases pending at any time. He, of course, requested that the court grant administrative consolidation of his cases to allow his assets and liabilities to be managed efficiently. Once there was administrative consolidation, one judge would handle all cases. He became so well known that bankruptcy court staff would greet him by name when he strolled into the clerk's office.

I was the lucky judge who was assigned to all his cases. Over time, various creditors requested hearings to show me that there was absolutely no progress on any development near the small city in Pinal County. Evidence was presented that the recidivist was not independently wealthy, and he could not interest anyone in investing in his dream of golf courses in the middle of nowhere. Slowly but surely, I dismissed his cases. Over time, he found it more and more difficult to refile his cases because he ran out of money even to pay the filing fees to commence his future cases. And like the desert wind, he vanished.

When I drive on the interstate on my way to Tucson, I still see the aerobatic pilots and no one playing golf on a golf course with no shade. I see no homes near the interstate. A private for-profit prison company has built four prisons in the area from 1994 to 2008. In 2020, the company agreed to house detainees from Hawaii, Nevada, Idaho, and Kansas. Notable people in the community are five professional football and baseball players and a professional skydiver. The city's airport is still one runway with no control tower. The city has become the skydiving capital of the world, has one eighteen-hole golf course, and is ten miles from the only Civil War battle that took place in Arizona.

However, there is no master-planned community. The few hardy souls who skydive, occasionally play golf, or hunt for the Civil War battlefield must have recreational vehicles or camp out under the stars. Along Interstate 10, there are a few weathered signs that proclaim a real estate development will soon come to the area.

Some properties, even in tony areas of Phoenix, also seem destined to multiple bankruptcy filings. One such property is Copenhaver's Castle on Camelback Mountain where multi-million-dollar mansions ascend the steep slopes. Properties on the mountain have outstanding views of the Phoenix valley below and the other mountain ranges that surround the metropolitan area. However, the castle has seemed to struggle over the years. Even as late as 2016, neighbors were complaining about the debris around the castle and the chaotic construction site. In 2021, the castle still had an uncertain future.

Camelback Mountain—so named because of its distinctive shape with a huge rock hump in the middle and protruding boulders that seem to form the head and snout of a camel at one end—has a commanding view of the Phoenix metropolitan area. Dr. Copenhaver, an orthodontist, purchased a mountainside lot for $4,000 in 1967 at an altitude of 1,800 feet. The zoning did not permit any construction farther up the mountain, but he was promised spectacular views of the valley below from his lot. He spent twelve years blasting mountain rock, using the stone to build or serve as walls for his Moorish castle. He created arches, towers, fortress-like walls, parapets, secret passages, a steep driveway, and a dungeon.

The doctor described the castle as a "Moorish fortress of medieval Spain." Bob Villa of *This Old House* even took a tour of the property in 1987. The castle had twenty rooms on eight levels, having seven thousand square feet of living space. The YouTube video of the castle showed the indoor waterfall and reflecting pool, the beautifully carved wood of the walls and furniture, the landscape paintings found throughout the many bedrooms, and the art collections that adorned the living areas.

Villa even found the secret passage to enter the dungeon, which was an elaborate wine cellar with an entire wall of exquisite crystal. The dungeon in the video was so dark that it was difficult to tell what else was there. Villa described the darkness as "creepy." In the video, Dr. Copenhaver made a plea to viewers to donate to his nonprofit, which would provide orthodontics to needy children.

He also hoped to complete the renovation and open the castle to tours, with the proceeds also going to his nonprofit. The stone mansion became an iconic landmark that Phoenicians dubbed Copenhaver's Castle after the doctor who labored for years scratching and blasting rock out of an unforgiving land.

Unfortunately, Dr. Copenhaver was unable to obtain the necessary funding to complete the renovation, and the castle fell into hard times. In 1989, the doctor filed a bankruptcy petition, hoping to restructure or obtain financing. The property was later sold, but the new owner also struggled to maintain the property and find a use for the property in a residential area.

A second bankruptcy case was filed by the new owner, and it was randomly assigned to me. Lenders who had provided renovation financing were not being paid, and they soon requested that the bankruptcy case be dismissed or that they be able to proceed outside of the bankruptcy proceedings to sell the property at an auction and try to recover the money they were owed.

I set a hearing on whether the creditors should be able to get any of the relief they requested. Pictures of the castle were presented at the hearing. What I saw was fascinating but not the unique home in Villa's video. Gone were the indoor waterfall, the designer furniture, and the art and crystal collections. It looked as if the doctor or the new owner had sold most of the valuable possessions.

However, the dungeon was still there. It had become a dramatic medieval room with chains, metal tongs, and rough-hewn furniture. Clearly the new owner was creating a haunted mansion that might be a fun place to visit on Halloween. The creditors succeeded in presenting sufficient evidence that the castle should be turned over to them, and I granted their request to take back the castle.

The castle continued to change hands over the years, with no one having the ability to renovate and open the property to the public. In 2012, after remaining vacant for seven years, a new owner, who owned an armored vehicle company, purchased the castle for $1.45 million, hoping to restore it and provide others with an opportunity to see a historic landmark.

He apparently spent $5 million renovating the property. He created a new website and toyed with the idea of renting out the castle to various groups for events. However, new hillside ordinances in Phoenix with "heightened requirements to safeguard adjacent properties" that were downhill from the renovation site might have made any changes to the property cost prohibitive.

The owner never filed a bankruptcy petition. In 2021, the owner was still engaged in a renovation of the property. The castle may now have earned the title of the longest renovation project ever undertaken in Phoenix.

Most people would be appalled that there are bankruptcy recidivists. But the bankruptcy law has been revised over time to control repeat filers, so I really did not mind them. They usually were optimistic people and fairly easy to direct to get them back on track.

If the bankruptcy judge is allowed enough discretion, the judge may accommodate those repeat filers who have finally gotten their act together versus the individual or company that is engaged in fraudulent activity.

Many individuals who repeatedly file cases are surprised by the deadlines that require them to take credit counseling, file their bankruptcy schedules, pay their back taxes, and so on by a date certain or their cases are dismissed. If the court has a self-help center staffed by volunteer attorneys, the number of bankruptcy recidivists is greatly reduced.

In the Ninth Circuit and the US Court of Appeals for the Federal Circuit, any entity must be represented by an attorney.[1] Although not a universal rule, many federal district and circuit courts have the same requirement.

Since attorneys are officers of the court and bound by ethical rules, they do not file multiple bankruptcy cases unless the underlying facts change. For instance, an entity may have a plan accepted by its creditors and start making payments to creditors under the plan. Later the entity's management may determine that the entity is still having financial problems

1. In the Ninth Circuit, see the decision of C.E. Pope Equity Trust v. US, 818 F.2d 696 (9th Cir. 1987).

because of an economic downturn, the entity has unprofitable divisions that must be sold, embezzlement by an entity official has occurred, unfair competition from a competitor has occurred, etc. The attorney will need to file a new case, arguing that there has been a change in circumstance that requires additional relief.

CHAPTER NINETEEN
SOMETIMES SMALL IS BETTER

There used to be a restaurant on the west side of Phoenix that catered to families with small children. As a promotion to attract more families, the restaurant offered free pizza to the child who read the most books in a month, quarter, or year. One of my kids was a voracious reader, so he received many free coupons. We liked the restaurant, choosing it many times for a relaxing dinner.

The restaurant's atmosphere was Mexican, with fountains, wall murals, tiled arches, and Saltillo tile flooring. The restaurant was owned by a family who strolled among the diners, making sure everyone was comfortable. Of course, we enjoyed the experience so much that we often ate there even when we had no coupons. The family's promotional idea was a huge success.

Over time, the restaurant changed, and we stopped visiting. The family decided to expand its operations by owning restaurants in other locations and franchising its brand in the Southwest. The family created an entity, Famous Restaurants, to facilitate the franchising of the Garcia family name throughout the Southwest. Financing became necessary to fund the expansion, and Heller Financial became the secured creditor willing to assist the family. The expansion occurred rapidly, straining operations.

Moreover, in 1992, Arizona was experiencing the effect of the collapse of its savings and loan institutions, which began in 1989 with the bankruptcy filing of the American Continental Corporation. In May 1990, the Arizona unemployment rate was at 5.3 percent, but it peaked at nearly 9 percent in January 1992. The collapse of one area of the economy was dramatically impacting the restaurant industry. Famous Restaurants needed to file a bankruptcy petition to try to preserve some value in the restaurant chain.

One of the issues that soon arose was whether a law firm that had previously represented the restaurant chain could continue to do so once Famous Restaurants filed a bankruptcy case.

One of the advantages of bankruptcy is that an entity that files a bankruptcy case becomes a fiduciary for its creditors. As a result, the entity's operations are scrutinized. For instance, the entity must get court approval if it wishes to sell all of its assets. The entity may engage in its usual business operations, but retaining attorneys, accountants, or other professionals requires court approval. The creditors gain the right to scrutinize the entity's financial information and may request that the entity provide additional information if fraudulent activity is suspected. Ultimately, the entity must convince the creditors and the court that it has a viable plan to reorganize, or the court will dismiss the bankruptcy case. Any attorney representing the debtor entity must follow the ethical rules of the state where the bankruptcy court is located.

Moreover, the bankruptcy law imposes separate requirements on debtor's counsel to ensure that the law firm does not have an adverse interest, or conflict, with the debtor filing the case or its creditors.[1] For instance, what if, before the bank-

1. See 11 U.S.C. §327.

ruptcy filing, the law firm has represented the debtor in various lawsuits and transactions and has provided erroneous legal advice leading to questions of whether the law firm has committed malpractice?

The law firm's tendency will be to protect what it has done even at the expense of what is best for the debtor and its creditors. The law firm has an adverse interest and will not be allowed to represent the debtor once the bankruptcy case is filed.

Another example of an adverse interest may be that the law firm has previously represented the debtor and one of the creditors on conflicting claims. The law firm has obtained confidential information from the debtor and creditor, which should bar the law firm from proceeding to represent either side in the bankruptcy case. Moreover, since the claims are in conflict, the law firm is unable to provide the duty of loyalty, competent representation, and confidentiality of the information to each client.

The bankruptcy law also requires that debtor's counsel be disinterested, which is defined under the bankruptcy law as not being a creditor, equity security holder, or insider of the debtor; not being a director, officer, or employee of the debtor within two years before the filing date of bankruptcy; and not having a materially adverse interest because of a direct or indirect relationship, connection, or interest in the debtor or any of the various classes of creditors or shareholders in the case.[2] The focus is on whether the law firm has some type of direct or indirect relationship with the debtor that will cause the law firm to act in its own self-interest.

If the law firm is unable to meet the ethical requirements under applicable state law or the bankruptcy requirements, the law firm may not represent the debtor in the debtor's case. If the law firm hides information that would normally force it

2. See 11 U.S.C. §101(14).

to withdraw from representing the debtor, the court may punish the law firm by disqualifying the law firm from representing the debtor going forward in the case and may require that any compensation paid to the law firm be disgorged and potentially paid to the creditors

In the case before me, the law firm previously representing Famous Restaurants had requested permission to continue to represent the company on general corporate law issues after the bankruptcy case was filed. However, one of the firm's partners had also served on the board of directors for Famous Restaurants. They stated that the law firm would only be retained on a limited basis, not as the bankruptcy attorney for the debtor. The insider status of the law firm's partner would lead the law firm to defend the legal advice previously given to Famous Restaurants while the partner was a member of the board. I denied the law firm's request to represent the debtor even on a limited basis.

Unbeknownst to me, the law firm continued to represent the debtor. When the law firm later filed an application seeking approval of its legal fees and expenses and their payment, I denied the relief. The opinion came to stand for the proposition that any law firm, whether acting on a limited basis or as bankruptcy counsel, must have the bankruptcy court approve its employment with a court order before the law firm may be paid from assets of the company.[3]

Although Heller provided some interim financing to the family, it was clear that the family needed to rethink its restaurant operations for the long-term. An investor was found to acquire eight restaurants and operate them under the Garcia brand name. The family would keep one of the restaurants, the original one in west-central Phoenix. The family proposed a plan that was accepted by creditors, and later the bankruptcy case was closed after creditors were paid.

3. In re Famous Restaurants, Inc., 205 B.R. 922 (Bankr. D.AZ. 1996)

Today the family still operates the original restaurant. In January 2022, one of the other restaurants sold for nearly $3.4 million. The seller was a limited liability company that owned and operated at least eight other Garcia locations. The bankruptcy case allowed the family to recover financially and continue to operate its restaurant over the next thirty years. An investor was able to infuse capital into the other locations, operate those restaurants over the same period, and sell one of the locations for a substantial sum of money. Bankruptcy was an economic reality, but it allowed the restaurant to remain open. Bankruptcy had been a type of relief value during difficult times.

CHAPTER TWENTY

EVERYONE MAKES MISTAKES

One of my friends sends out texts and emails that all end with the statement "Don't expect perfection." Although I think many judges, including me, do strive for perfection, we settle for doing the best job we can under, at times, difficult circumstances. After all, no one wants to appear before a judge who says, "I know nothing about this area, so I'm hoping you can agree on the facts and let me know what the law is." If not perfection, most people do expect something magical to happen when they appear in court.

In bankruptcy, people hope their debts will go away, their businesses will succeed if they just read one more self-help book, or they will be able to keep their luxury vehicles. They come with boxes of documents at the first hearing the court sets, hoping they can have everything resolved by the end of the day.

The wood-paneled courtroom, the raised bench where the judge sits, the imposing wooden tables near the bench, and the wooden rail with the swinging gate that admits few to the inner area near the judge create a formal, perhaps intimidating, environment for the uninitiated. Nevertheless, movies and television series lead individuals to have unrealistic expectations, believing they will succeed. Some win their cases, but unfortunately, most of them lose.

Over the years of talking with non-lawyers, I have found that most think there is a clear winner in every case, one that's obvious from the day the bankruptcy case is filed. However, if they are in court, it is usually because there is a dispute as to what happened. Memories are imperfect, so two individuals may remember an event differently. Documents may help to clarify what happened, but not always.

I presided over one case where an individual accused another of engaging in fraud. They had been friends for many years, buying and selling Arizona real estate to each other or to third parties. Individual A, whom I'll call Bill, entered into a contract to sell desert land to his friend, whom I'll call Dave. Neither was a lawyer, but that didn't stop them from drafting their own contracts. Their standard contract did not state that time was of the essence, and their contract deposits were generally refundable. Their previous transactions over the years had also allowed for extensions of time, if requested, for one or the other to make final contract payments.

At the trial, Bill insisted they had agreed that Dave would pay the full purchase price, in cash, within ninety days of the date of the contract. If Dave did not pay on time, Bill could sell the land to a third party. Dave argued that Bill would not accept his late offer of cash nor grant an extension of time to pay, which Bill had done in other real estate transactions. Bill countered that not only had Dave not paid on time, but he had also not requested an extension of time to do so. Since he had a ready buyer, Bill sold the land to a third party.

When the dispute arose between Bill and Dave, the third party refused to return the land to Bill even though Bill agreed to return all the funds that the third party had paid for the land. Real estate is generally considered unique, so if a party purchases land, the party may refuse to return the land to the original seller. As a result, Bill and Dave could not force the third party to return the land to one of them.

Clearly the dispute that brought them to the bankruptcy court had destroyed their friendship. At times, emotions made it difficult to get through a trial day.

However, had Bill engaged in fraud? From my standpoint, no. Was Dave entitled to recover the land from the third party who had paid a fair price for the land? No. Did Dave have a claim for damages against Bill? As it turns out, no. Dave had not paid the full purchase price by the contract date and had not requested an extension of time from Bill to make the payment. Dave had lost the right to recover any damages.

Long after the case was closed, I learned from Dave's attorney that Dave was upset that he couldn't convince me that Bill had engaged in fraud. My response to the attorney was that I could only rule based on the evidence presented and if I had made an error, Dave could have appealed the matter and had another court look at the issues. The attorney said Dave did not have the funds to retain him on appeal, so nothing was done. Dave later committed suicide on the land that he was not able to purchase.

It's difficult for me to process what happened to Dave even so many years later. A long-standing friendship had come to a bitter end. So many deals had been based on their mutual trust. An innocent third party had also purchased the land, which left the parties and me with few remedies. Dave may have loved the land, but so did the innocent third party who had done everything correctly to acquire it. And since the parties had lost trust in each other and blamed each other for what had happened, emotions led to mutual accusations that were not true. I did have a detailed written record that an appellate court could have reviewed. Sadly, Dave did nothing further.

CHAPTER TWENTY-ONE

BANKRUPTCY AFFECTS EVERYONE

At this point, you have discovered the ancient routes of debt forgiveness and that bankruptcy has been in the US since colonial times. Mass tort litigation, its prevalence in society today, and the numerous bankruptcy petitions filed by major companies mean that any one of these cases has hundreds of thousands of claimants, with millions of family members and friends affected by the medical and financial issues of the victims.

Individual retirement or brokerage accounts may contain derivatives that are financial bets between parties that could unravel at some future point in time and cause the accounts to decrease dramatically in value. Experts now opine that a well-rounded brokerage account may need bitcoin, a volatile investment. How many retirees will find that their security net has failed them and resort to bankruptcy relief?

The recent hurricanes in the Southeast demonstrate that thriving communities may be destroyed in a matter of hours, and catastrophic wildfires in Hawaii or California may require long-term planning and assistance to recover. Many may have to resort to filing bankruptcy petitions to get a breathing spell before they are able to return to their homes, reopen their businesses, and repay creditors.

How the 2025 tariffs will affect small businesses is the latest unknown. Many small businesses have appealed to the US Chamber of Commerce for assistance. Small businesses may have run out of, or are running low on, preordered inventory from China and other foreign countries.

Small business owners still need to pay their operating expenses, such as rent, utilities, wages, loan repayments, even though they are receiving little or no income. Many envision that small businesses may need to file bankruptcy petitions to weather the coming financial storm.

Whether you will be involved, in some way, in a bankruptcy case is likely. You may be a debtor filing your own case because you are repaying a student loan and living at the poverty level; you may be a creditor who has rented out real property to a destructive tenant and find yourself receiving filings from the bankruptcy court as to whether you will get paid and when; or you may have been injured by a defective product and become trapped in the company's bankruptcy case, hoping to be paid something as an innocent victim.

Even I was involved in a bankruptcy case as a claimant. In 2005, I was going through a divorce proceeding. Our home needed to be sold, which seemed easy, because it was during the heady days when the Phoenix real estate market was on fire.

New homes were being built in the far reaches of the valley. Daily newspapers touted lots for new homes were increasing in value at the rate of $10,000 per day. Desperate people camped out overnight, hoping to purchase a new home lot as soon as a builder released them. It was frenetic, yet no one saw an end to the boom times.

I decided to build a new home in a community that had just had its infrastructure completed. The community was in the far west valley near planned freeways to be finished in a three- to five-year timeframe. I chose a builder that had a solid reputation in the Phoenix market. It was also a national homebuilder that had a presence in several other states.

At the time I signed the construction contract, I was notified that Engle Homes had been acquired by a publicly traded homebuilder. The name of the acquiring company was TOUSA. The salesperson said that Engle was solid financially, but its acquisition by TOUSA would only strengthen Engle's balance sheet. TOUSA and its subsidiaries were the thirteenth largest homebuilding business in the US with operations in Florida, Texas, mid-Atlantic states, Arizona, and other Western states.

In 2006, Engle completed my home, and I moved in. Engle provided me with a ten-year homebuilder's warranty to cover problems with materials and workmanship or structural issues.

In 2008, TOUSA filed a bankruptcy petition in the Southern District of Florida. Because the creditors had lost confidence in the management team, the creditors replaced management with independent experts in turning around troubled companies. Allegations of fraud soon surfaced. Creditors became focused on holding various parties responsible for destroying all the solvent companies that were subsidiaries of TOUSA. Engle was one of those solvent companies that was trapped in the complex fraudulent conveyances.

Shortly prior to filing bankruptcy, TOUSA had been engaged in a costly joint venture with another company that had failed. TOUSA had obtained a $500 million loan for the venture. The lenders concluded that other assets must be pledged in payment of the loan, known as "upstream guarantees," in case TOUSA was unable to make the debt payments. The lenders required the assets of the solvent subsidiaries to repay the TOUSA debt if TOUSA defaulted. The subsidiaries received nothing of value in return.

In 2012, the Eleventh Circuit of Appeals upheld the bankruptcy court's decision that the pledging of assets by the subsidiaries to TOUSA were fraudulent conveyances because TOUSA had provided nothing to the subsidiaries for pledging their assets to repay the massive debt that TOUSA had incurred.

Lenders involved in the asset transactions found themselves at the center of the controversy. As a result, the lenders' actions were scrutinized and set aside. Some estimates were that lenders would have to pay as much as $420 million to creditors. Many felt the decision would have a wide-ranging impact on lenders and their ability to save troubled borrowers.

What was forgotten was the impact on the subsidiaries. Engle went out of business, as did many of the other subsidiaries. After TOUSA filed bankruptcy in 2008, the Great Recession occurred. Some Arizona homebuilders did go out of business because of the collapse of the Phoenix metropolitan real estate market, but other homebuilders survived. TOUSA's bankruptcy affected Engle's ability to obtain financing during the recession and expedited its demise.

During TOUSA's case, I received notice that I was listed as a creditor with a possible claim. Because I had received a ten-year warranty for my home and had at least eight years remaining on the warranty, there was the possibility that I would have structural or other issues with my home that would require me to contact Engle to make the necessary repairs. The warranty was only backed by Engle, not by a third-party insurance company. I was at the bottom of the list of claimants in a case—an unsecured claim. The only lower claimants in the case were the shareholders of Engle.

Worse yet, I only had the *possibility* of a claim, which is known as a contingent claim. My home might go for ten years with no issues for the builder to repair. On the other hand, I might discover three years down the road that my home had a structural issue.

Such contingent claims are difficult to value in a bankruptcy case. The bankruptcy law does permit the estimation of such claims for the purpose of receiving some type of distribution in a debtor's plan.

However, in my case as an expert in the field, I believed that my claim had little value. Why? I was at the bottom of the list of creditors, and in reviewing the case, it was unlikely that I would ever receive any distribution. Moreover, I would be required to file my claim in the Southern District of Florida. As an out-of-district claimant, I would be an easy target for TOUSA's attorneys. They would contest my claim, requiring me to represent myself before the Florida court or retain a Florida attorney to represent me. Litigation in Florida would take time and be costly. If I represented myself, there would be the costs of travel and staying at a hotel. If I retained an attorney, there would be the hourly costs of the attorney and expenses that might be incurred. Based on my analysis, I decided to do nothing. My home made it ten years with no issues.

Someday, you may find yourself involved in a bankruptcy case as someone who needs a fresh start, is owed money, or is an investor. Initially, you may be surprised. Have you done something wrong? What will you do next? Although you may believe you don't need to consider what happens in bankruptcy until someone forces you to do so, that is short-sighted. Bankruptcy affects everyone—even you. You may just not realize how yet.

PART FOUR
AN UNCERTAIN FUTURE FOR BANKRUPTCY COURTS AND JUDGES

CHAPTER TWENTY-TWO

WHERE ARE ALL OF THE EMPLOYEES?

Imagine we are now five years in the future. We have used our newly invented time machine to drop in on Barb's apartment to see how she's handling her financial problems. She is trying to file a bankruptcy case, but she seems to be having trouble. We will be able to see and hear Barb, but given the new cloaking technique of our time machine, she will be unable to see or hear us.

As we arrive, we see that it's midnight, and Barb has just electronically filed her bankruptcy petition. Her small business, employing her and a few artists, has fallen into hard times. No one wants to purchase her abstract art. We know this because her apartment is stacked, wall to wall, with abstract art. She's been ignoring warnings from her utility, with past-due notices scattered on the floor. One of the notices advises her that her power will be shut off in twenty-four hours. Over the next twenty-four hours, the temperature in Phoenix is projected to be a high of 125 degrees F. Her computer screen blinks. It's a message from the bankruptcy court.

> *Hi, Barb! It's Bonnie, the Model 5000 Bankruptcy Bot. I'm sorry . . . your bankruptcy petition has been rejected. You forgot to attach a statement as to your earnings and liabilities that makes sense.*

In disbelief, Barb throws a book at the screen, yelling, "Manager! I need to speak to a manager."

Bonnie replies in dulcet tones, "I'm sorry, Barb. We have no employees, only judges. Your estimated wait time to speak to a judge is two days. Have a nice day!" The screen goes dark. You sigh at Barb's predicament. We jump into our time machine and arrive back to the present day.

Perhaps I have exaggerated a bit as to what will happen soon. But it seems every day I listen to or read news about the Department of Government Efficiency (DOGE).

Under the direction of Elon Musk, DOGE was charged with "reducing government spending, workforce size, and the number of federal programs." No one opposed reducing waste in the federal government, but the cuts should have been strategic. Instead, DOGE became embedded in many federal government agencies, reducing employees who had just been promoted or hired without analyzing what those individuals did. The result was that many federal agencies lost critical employees within a short period of time and had to act quickly to rehire them.

An analysis of DOGE's first one hundred days reflected that savings had not materialized in a meaningful way, federal agencies were not more efficient, and DOGE had not been transparent as to what it had done at the federal agencies.

In June 2025, the detrimental impact of DOGE became apparent. Although only 15 percent of the federal workforce was in Washington, DC, the layoff of federal workers accelerated. Forty-three percent of the area real estate agents saw more real estate sales, and over half of the agents stated that the job cuts were affecting the market in some fashion.

One federal worker laid off in February 2025 had hoped to purchase a home in the area where her son would be attending kindergarten. However, since she was still unemployed in June 2025, she was seeking other alternatives. Two-income families found themselves in financial difficulty as well, being forced to consider leaving the DC area even though only one of them was a federal worker who was laid off.

Even the federal courts, a separate branch of government, have been affected by DOGE. For instance, the General Services Administration (GSA), an agency within the executive branch, handles many of the real estate and other contracts for the judiciary.

The Phoenix office of GSA was closed, with most services to be handled by the Tucson office, a two-hour drive from Phoenix. So if the air conditioning went out or there was a plumbing issue at one of the Phoenix courthouses, the court needed to contact Tucson. This caused a few judges to muse whether they should bring in their own plumbers if their toilets didn't work.

Another issue arose when DOGE thought the Federal Public Defender was part of the executive branch's justice department. DOGE decided to terminate the real estate lease for the Phoenix office used by the Public Defender's appellate group. Although the real estate lease was negotiated by GSA, the Public Defender has always been a part of the judiciary. Hopefully DOGE recognized that the appellate office needed to have a workspace somewhere and corrected its mistake.

DOGE is not going away any time soon. One may expect that the federal courts, a de minimis part of the federal government, will be affected in the future.

Of course, having some affinity for figures, I checked online for the Treasury Department's analysis of actual US government spending for Fiscal Year 2022. It was $6.27 trillion. Although somewhat counterintuitive, Fiscal Year 2022 was from October 1, 2021, to September 30, 2022.

In the federal budget, the term "mandatory spending" is what is required by law, such as social security, Medicare, and Medicaid. Mandatory spending is about two-thirds of the federal budget. Discretionary spending is what must be appropriated each year by Congress. Although national defense was 12 percent of the Fiscal Year 2022 budget, it was about 45 percent of discretionary spending. Finally, supplemental spending is appropriated by Congress when a need arises that is not originally in the budget—think of the spending necessary in the Fiscal Year 2020 for COVID.

At the very end of the Treasury Department's analysis, one learns that most of the federal government, such as the Treasury Department (which includes the Internal Revenue Service), the Department of Agriculture (which includes the US Forest Service that fights wildfires), the Department of Energy (which keeps watch over our nuclear weapons and waste), the Department of the Interior (which includes the Environmental Protection Agency), *and all courts*, is between 2 to 3 percent of the entire budget. It's considered discretionary spending. Some are trying to eliminate or reduce discretionary spending, but how is that possible? Do we fire the employees who are with an agency in the Department of Energy who have the expertise to safeguard our nuclear weapons?[1] Do we fire US Forestry Service firefighters who are a part of the Department of Agriculture? There is nothing "discretionary" about many federal agencies and "nonessential" about the employees who are a part of them. There is nothing wrong with reducing federal government spending, but one needs to

1. It seems that hundreds of workers (the agency says only fifty) were fired at facilities where nuclear weapons were being constructed. Unfortunately, someone also locked the employees out of their federal government email accounts, so it has been difficult for the agency to reverse course and hire the employees back. The agency's response? "We are trying to reach the probationary employees to hire them back, but we don't have a great way to contact them."

use a scalpel and analytical thinking to make the appropriate spending cuts.

The federal courts, as indicated, are a de minimis part of the entire federal budget. In the Fiscal Year 2021 Annual Report, the US Courts spent $7.7 billion, or roughly .122807 percent of the total federal budget (yes, there is a decimal point in front of the percentage figure). $6.2 billion was devoted to court salaries. Court physical security, internet security and equipment upgrades, providing counsel in criminal cases to those who cannot afford attorneys, juror compensation, etc., made up the rest of the budget. Bottom line: The courts are a coequal branch of the federal government that is funded on a shoestring. The courts have embraced technology in an era of decreased funding. But how far can one go with efficiency?

The budget for the bankruptcy courts is also determined by how many bankruptcy cases are filed each year. But bankruptcy filings are cyclical. And the number of cases filed is not a true measure of how much work a judge or staff member will need to devote to a particular case. For instance, while I was still serving as a judge, the Administrative Office of the US Courts devoted about six months to a study of how much time a bankruptcy judge was in court hearing matters, what types of matters took the most time or the least, how much time a judge spent reading memoranda of law or pleadings prior to a trial or hearing, how much time a judge spent trying to settle cases of colleagues, etc.

Although complex reorganization cases of corporations of over $100 million in assets or liabilities (the so-called "mega cases") took a great deal of time, the study found that one could not solely rely on case filings to determine the workload of bankruptcy judges. And the bankruptcy courts do provide some funding to the federal government through charging bankruptcy filing and other fees.

The bottom line is that the federal courts still struggle to get the requisite funding. There is a fear that at some point the court budgets will be cut to such an extent that the courts will no longer be able to function effectively. No one really cares whether the federal courts are adequately funded or not until that person desperately needs court help. That someone could be in Barb's situation, a person who is unable to file a bankruptcy case or get any help until it is too late.

We must work together to make sure the bankruptcy courts are adequately staffed. No one wants to have the electricity shut off or have a creditor seize desperately needed funds from a bank account without having emergency recourse to a bankruptcy court to stop everything that's going on, sort through the issues, and provide some relief to those who need it.

CHAPTER TWENTY-THREE

HOW SHOULD ONE HANDLE THE ISSUE OF JUDICIAL DISABILITY?

We want to remain relevant and help society for as long as possible. There is also the dignity of work that allows us to define who we are. It's hard to let go. No one wants to feel as if they are being warehoused.

Federal district court and appellate judges are appointed by the president with the advice and consent of the Senate. Their appointments have been described as for a "lifetime," but the Constitution says they may serve during their "good behavior."[1] Most federal judges like being independent, but power and prestige are also inherent in the position, making the individual reluctant to retire. Bankruptcy judges, appointed under Article I of the US Constitution, only serve fourteen-year terms and are appointed by the federal circuit courts. Bankruptcy judges usually stay for one full term. They may also ask for reappointment to a second fourteen-year term. Although many younger individuals have recently been appointed to the federal courts, there are many judges who have continued to serve in their golden years.

1. See Article III of the US Constitution which states that federal judges "hold [their] offices during good behavior."

The American Bar Association (ABA), an organization of lawyers, judges, and professors, recently considered the plight of Federal Circuit Court Judge Pauline Newman in an article. The article focused on the ninety-five-year-old judge's potential competency issues, stating she apparently flunked security training, was overly concerned about being hacked, and engaged in behavior toward court staff that was described as paranoid. Aliza Shatzman, who is an attorney, served as a former law clerk for another judge and speaks and writes on judicial accountability, stated in an ABA article:

> [I]n all three branches of government, questions around whether leaders are serving well beyond their capacity to serve the people have only grown more dramatic in recent years . . . Modern medicine may enable us to live longer, healthier lives. Yet it is clear that some judges—who are among the most powerful people in our constitutional system—insist on remaining on the bench until long after they are fit to handle the rigors of federal judicial service. Judge Newman's story is a very dramatic recent example of a dangerous ongoing trend.

As Shatzman points out, the problem is endemic to all three branches of the federal government. For instance, the *median* age of the voting US House lawmakers is 57.9 years, and the Senate's *median* age is 65.3 years in the 118th Congress (2023–2024).[2] As of September 2022, the median age of federal judges was sixty-eight years. As to the aging of the federal judiciary, Shira Scheindlin, a Federal District Court judge in the Southern District of New York, remarked, "I

---

2. The median age is a more reliable number since it provides us with the midpoint in a dataset with 50 percent above the midpoint and 50 percent below, whereas the average age of a certain group may skew the numbers.

[have] seen too many judges stay too long . . . It's a problem. It's just a problem. Some judges get too old to do it well."

Many federal judges with lifetime appointments retire and become arbitrators or neutral evaluators to assist the courts and allow the parties to settle difficult issues at reasonable costs. Other federal judges transfer from active to senior status, presiding over fewer cases. A federal judge's transfer to senior status also allows the US president, with the advice and consent of the Senate, to appoint a new active judge to the appropriate court.

As for Judge Newman, she received her BA from Vassar College in 1947, an MA from Columbia University in 1948, a PhD from Yale University in 1952, and an LLB from New York University Law School in 1958. In her legal career, she specialized in intellectual property, rising to the level of director of the Patent, Trademark, and Licensing Department at FMC Corporation from 1969 to 1984. In 1984, President Ronald W. Reagan appointed her to the United States Court of Appeals for the Federal Circuit (Federal Circuit Court). As of June 20, 2025, she was ninety-eight years old.

The federal judiciary has the authority to handle its disability issues.[3] The Newman proceedings began when a complaint was filed with the Federal Circuit Court by a person with sufficient facts to cause a special committee to be appointed by that court. I have been able to review the May 16, 2023, public order entered by the Committee of the Federal Circuit Court (the committee), which is still considering the issue of Judge Newman's mental or physical disability.

After an investigation by the committee, a series of orders were entered requiring Judge Newman to provide the committee with additional information. Judge Newman's

3. The applicable statute is 28 U.S.C. §§351-364, the Judicial Conduct and Disability Act.

attorney submitted a "letter brief" in response. It appears that although the committee allowed Judge Newman until May 23, 2023, to advise the committee as to whether she would submit to a neurological evaluation and neurological testing by a doctor chosen by the committee and provide additional medical information, she chose to file a separate lawsuit attempting to block the committee's order as her response. Her counsel advocated for a neutral tribunal, not the judges of her court, to determine whether she had a mental or physical disability. The Federal Court of Appeals determined its only recourse was to suspend her from her duties until she complied with turning over her medical records and sitting for a neurological examination. Newman's suspension was renewed by the court in September 2024.

Some of the facts described in the committee's May 16, 2023, order are disturbing yet heartbreaking. From day-to-day, Judge Newman could not remember how to log in to or where she had saved her files on her court computer. Her disagreement with one of her staff members escalated to the point that multiple court employees heard her say that the staff member should be removed from the building and arrested. Court employees who have worked with her for many years said it was painful to watch her struggle to pass, on multiple occasions, mandatory security training or see her unable to perform routine tasks that she easily navigated in her eighties.

At one point, she advised court employees that she did not need to comply with one of the Federal Circuit Court's internal rules, even though she and her colleagues had approved the rule in 2018. Her reason: Chief Judge Howard T. Markey had told her she could take up to thirty days, not the five days mandated for other judges, to comply with the rule. The problem? Chief Judge Markey had not been a member of the Court for thirty-two years and died seventeen years ago.

There is no mention of any family member or friend to

assist her. Has she outlived everyone who loved or cherished her? I suspect her lawsuit to block the committee's actions and reinstate her will ultimately be dismissed since the applicable statute states judicial disability is to be handled by the judicial council of the federal circuit court where the judge serves, which is already being done.

The federal judiciary continues to age. In the future, we will need to determine what is the best, perhaps more compassionate, way to handle judicial disability issues.

CHAPTER TWENTY-FOUR

WILL JUDICIAL MISCONDUCT CONTINUE TO BE AN ISSUE?

Judges deal with disputes, so you would expect that in any given lawsuit, there will be winners and losers. One side will praise the sagacity of the judge; the other side will declare that the judge is clearly incompetent. It's hard to make everyone happy. Moreover, there are certain constraints on what a judge can do or say. For instance, judges cannot discuss litigation that is pending before them or provide an opinion on an issue that they may hear and decide in the future. So the public rarely, if ever, hears from the judge when there is some outcry as to their decision in a particular case.

Over the years, the various courts, commissions, or bodies overseeing the conduct of judges have developed rules, guidelines, or advisory opinions to provide some guidance to judges and the public as to what is proper or improper judicial conduct. The gray area, of course, is that a judge must avoid "even the appearance of impropriety."

What do those words mean? If the judge is hearing a complex matter that will last for several months or longer and you are one of the parties in the lawsuit, how would you feel if you saw the judge at a private lunch with the lawyer on the opposing side of your case? Or what if you saw the judge playing golf with the lawyer on the other side? Is the judge acting improperly? Does it appear to be improper? Although the judge will argue that they only discussed their families or their subpar golf games, how will the judge ever convince you of that? Obviously, it is preferred that a judge analyze personal or social events carefully. For the judge, it may be best to eat at one's desk or avoid social gatherings if there's a major trial underway.

The ABA and others involved in the legal field have drafted a proposed model code of conduct for judges. One of the proposed ABA rules, or canons, states that a judge or candidate for judicial office shall not engage in "political or campaign activity that is inconsistent with the independence, integrity, or impartiality of the judiciary."[1]

If a judge is running for reelection or an individual is a candidate for a judicial office and a wealthy lawyer or law firm channels a substantial contribution to the judge's or candidate's campaign, has the judge or candidate engaged in improper conduct? The ABA's Model Code, although a gold standard, has not necessarily been adopted by all courts or bodies overseeing the conduct of judges. However, if the judge or lawyer candidate wins, even if the candidate's conduct is deemed appropriate under applicable law, that new judge probably feels obligated, on some level, to that donor.

As to why some courts or state legislatures overseeing the licensing of attorneys don't adopt the ABA's gold standard, there are many factors. The wealthy and powerful want to maintain control over the selection of judges, some judges believe they can put blinders on as to the donor's influence and rule fairly, and other judges may lack courage to buck the system that has always been in place.

Let's say a few months after the hotly contested election, the newly elected judge is presiding over a contentious matter,

1. Canon 4, ABA Model Code of Judicial Conduct.

and the donor happens to be representing one of the litigants in the case. At the end of the trial, the judge must carefully consider the evidence presented. What if it's a close call as to who should win? One might argue that it is only human nature to rule in favor of the lawyer or law firm that helped elect the judge. So long as there are elections of judges, there will be questions as to whether a particular judge has been influenced by moneyed interests that have helped the individual get elected.

However, even bankruptcy judges who are appointed by the federal circuit courts through a merit selection process may have their conduct called into question. In October 2023, David R. Jones, a bankruptcy judge from Houston, Texas, suddenly resigned after the Fifth Circuit Court of Appeals filed a misconduct complaint against him.

Jones was removed from working on or hearing any bankruptcy cases or consulting with any judges on a case. Two aspects of his conduct were called into question: Did such a well-respected judge violate federal judicial ethical rules, and had he acted improperly in championing amendments of local court procedures to attract major corporations to his federal district? The jury is still out as to whether his local court procedures were improper.

Judge Jones obtained his law degree from the University of Houston and was a partner at the Porter Hodges law firm. At one point, Jones and Marvin Isgur practiced at the same law firm, and Isgur considered Jones "his stubborn adopted son." Both Jones and Isgur were later appointed bankruptcy judges in Houston.

Although Jones was appointed in 2011, by 2015, he had become chief judge of the Bankruptcy Court for the Southern District of Texas and began promoting his court as the place for mega corporations, or corporations with over a $100 million in liabilities, to file their bankruptcy petitions. Judge

Isgur, the seasoned professional, was proud of Judge Jones's innovations.

The Fifth Circuit Complaint 05-24-90002 stated that there was "probable cause," or a reasonable belief or sufficient evidence, to believe that Judge Jones had engaged in misconduct. In 2017, Judge Jones and Elizabeth Freeman, a partner at Jackson Walker LLP, purchased a home in which they resided. Jackson Walker, a nationally known Texas bankruptcy law firm, frequently appeared in complex reorganization cases before Judge Jones. For several years, Judge Jones approved $1 million in fees for legal services rendered by Freeman. Jackson Walker stated that it did not learn of the Jones–Freeman romantic relationship until a 2021 court hearing. At that time, the firm told Freeman to stop working on and billing clients for any cases assigned to Judge Jones. Jackson Walker believed that it had appropriately handled the matter. Freeman left Jackson Walker in late 2022 to form her own law firm.

When practitioners began to question the ethical conduct of Freeman and whether Judge Jones was complying with the guidelines governing judicial conduct, Freeman and Jones stated that since they were not married, they could keep their romantic relationship a secret and it was appropriate for Judge Jones to determine whether Freeman's legal fees were reasonable in amount and actually necessary in the bankruptcy case.

Federal judges are bound by the Code of Conduct of United States Judges. Canon 2 states that a judge should avoid even the appearance of impropriety. It is an objective standard by "reasonable minds," with knowledge of all the facts and circumstances after a reasonable inquiry. Would a reasonable person conclude that the judge's honesty, integrity, and impartiality had been impaired? Canon 3 also states that a judge should, among other things, avoid favoritism.

It appears that Judge Jones did not believe he was violating any of the ethical rules for judges because he was not married to Freeman. In contrast, the Fifth Circuit Court of Appeals filed a misconduct complaint against Judge Jones because it believed that his approval of the substantial compensation paid to Freeman, with whom he had a romantic relationship, was improper.

Judge Jones has since resigned. The Fifth Circuit will probably dismiss its complaint against him. The maximum penalty that would have been meted out to Judge Jones would have been removal, and that's already been accomplished through Jones's resignation.

Dismissal of the misconduct complaint does not end all the investigations or actions that may ensue. There is the possibility that other lawyers may face misconduct allegations for having known of the romantic relationship between Jones and Freeman but failing to report it. There is also concern that Judge Jones's approval of Freeman's fee applications, which may have aggregated as much as $1 million while Freeman was a partner at Jackson Walker, may cause bankruptcy cases to be reopened and reexamined as to whether her attorneys' fees were appropriate or should be disgorged by her.[2]

Realizing the seriousness of the disgorgement issue, Randy Crane, the chief United States district court judge of the Southern District of Texas, stated that he was prepared to consider any requests to reopen cases. Bankruptcy judges are considered officers of the federal district court where they are located. So, as the chief district court judge for the district where Jones was located, he was a potentially logical party to review the actions of Jones.

The office of the United States Trustee, which handles various issues in bankruptcy cases including the reasonable-

2. The *Wall Street Journal's* independent review of court records determined the $1 million amount of fees awarded to Freeman. Also see 11 U.S.C. §330 as to the standard that a judge must apply in approving legal fees for an attorney in a bankruptcy case.

ness of attorneys' fees, had requested that Judge Crane investigate at least thirty-three cases where Jones had awarded fees to Jackson Walker, Freeman's former law firm.

At a hearing before Judge Crane, the United States Trustee argued that Jackson Walker had failed to disclose the romantic relationship between Freeman and Jones and should be required to disgorge $18 million, or all the fees that the firm received in the thirty-three cases.

All cases against Jones have been transferred to the Western District of Texas, a federal district independent from Jones' district. A judge in that district is now sorting through the issues in the various cases.

There is another issue of concern. After the 2001 *Enron* reorganization case was filed in Delaware, even though its headquarters were in Houston, Jones, as a bankruptcy lawyer, had expressed concern about the loss of attorneys' fees to Texas counsel. In 2015, when Judge Jones became chief judge of the Southern District of Texas Bankruptcy Court, new procedures were adopted for complex reorganization cases, with those cases either being assigned to Judge Jones or his mentor and colleague, Judge Isgur.

Statistics show that Jones soon became the most active judge in the United States. From 2016 onward, eighty-one cases or 11 percent of the major reorganization cases with over $100 million in liabilities were assigned to him, 8 percent to Judge Isgur. To reflect how much has changed in the bankruptcy field, one need only look at the location of the other bankruptcy judges who presided over complex reorganization cases with over $100 million in liabilities. Seven judges in Delaware were listed as being in the next tier (from about fifty to a low of thirty cases per judge), and a judge from the Southern District of New York presided over only twenty complex reorganization cases.

Bankruptcy cases may be filed in many locations. It may be where the corporation has its assets, its corporate headquarters, or its place of incorporation. However, from a policy standpoint, should the most complex reorganization cases with liabilities over $100 million be heard by ten bankruptcy judges in Houston, Texas; Delaware; and New York City? The answer is no. Given the merit screening process concerning the appointment of bankruptcy judges, judges in Boston, Chicago, or Phoenix are equally capable of administering complex cases. Unfortunately, moneyed interests, such as financial institutions or large investors, seek a path of least resistance in having cases determined in a manner that they find most beneficial.

CHAPTER TWENTY-FIVE

WILL TRIALS BECOME EXTINCT?

What will be the role of courts in the future? Some say courts are not to deliver justice but to resolve disputes. In providing a fair result through a settlement, justice is achieved, but disputes are resolved expeditiously, in a nonconfrontational manner, and on a cost-effective basis.

Alternative Dispute Resolution, or a means to resolve a dispute without a trial, is utilized in the court system. A "third-party neutral" is used, which the ABA has defined as a "mediator, arbitrator, conciliator or evaluator, who assists the parties, represented or unrepresented, in the resolution of a dispute."[1] Many courts prefer to utilize a lawyer as a third-party neutral.

The lawyer is bound by the rules of the court and a code of professional, or ethical, conduct. It allows the court to have better oversight of the process, removing the individual if necessary. Courts also have confidence that the lawyer, as an officer of the court, will provide a more honest assessment of the possibility of the parties settling a dispute.

1. American Bar Association, Rule 2.4, Model Rules of Professional Conduct (8/16/2018).

Once the plaintiff files a lawsuit, the defendant, or opposing party, will respond to what the plaintiff has alleged in her complaint. The court will then schedule a conference to determine whether the parties can stipulate as to any facts and whether they have exchanged documents in support of their respective positions. At the same scheduling conference, the court will set a date for the trial and encourage the parties to explore a settlement.

In some cases, the court will mandate that the parties meet and discuss settlement. Many suggest that a mandatory settlement conference, versus one where the parties voluntarily agree, has the effect of creating an adversarial atmosphere where a settlement is less likely to happen.

When neither party is represented by a lawyer, courts will still encourage the use of a third-party neutral. However, a lawyer, as a third-party neutral, is placed in a difficult position. Unrepresented individuals tend to think of the person as their lawyer or advocate, rather than someone who is neutral.

The lawyer is placed in the unenviable position of providing additional disclosure to both individuals, reminding them that she cannot provide legal advice but only serves to review their respective positions and to try to find a common ground on which everyone may agree. Whether a lawyer or not, for those neutrals who try to settle cases that involve highly emotional issues, such as employment or family disputes, special training is required.

Some courts certify certain individuals to serve as neutrals, sometimes called mediators, in their local rules or procedures. The benefit of the certification process is that the individual must take a certain number of hours of training by an approved organization, with further training required at specific intervals. If the court is a specialized court, such as the bankruptcy court, the individual may also be required to be an expert in that area of the law.

A list of trained neutrals or mediators is usually available on the court's website or may be obtained from the clerk's office of the court. The parties may then review the list and, in many cases, agree on a neutral for the court to appoint. A court appointment usually sets up the parameters of the neutral's duties: the issue or issues to be resolved, how the neutral's costs will be paid, how the parties will present their positions to the neutral (orally, in writing, both?), any facts upon which the parties agree, legal cases that may limit or narrow the issues that need to be resolved, and when and how often the parties will meet in an effort to settle the dispute.

If the parties are unrepresented, wish to keep the costs of litigation as low as possible, and/or the factual or legal issues are easy to resolve, the use of neutrals makes sense. Since most of the disputes before the courts now fall into one of the categories that I have listed, the courts will have many fewer trials.

Trials will continue but on a less frequent basis. Courts will still need to resolve those disputes that are not factually driven but pose legal issues that are complex. If the legal issue is not resolved with clarity, the court will be faced with repeatedly considering the same or similar legal issue, sometimes daily, which is certainly a waste of valuable limited resources. The resolution of a complex but frequently occurring legal issue is essential to the smooth functioning of a court.

CHAPTER TWENTY-SIX

SHOULD CAMERAS BE PERMITTED IN FEDERAL COURT?

I have never watched an entire state court trial on television. Usually, one or more commitments force me to move on. However, I found the Rittenhouse trial in November 2021 in Kenosha, Wisconsin, fascinating. There was a great deal of footage in the public domain. As a result, how would he succeed on a claim of self-defense as to those individuals he shot? Was some other drama about to unfold?

On August 25, 2020, a riot broke out in Kenosha, Wisconsin, after a white police officer shot Jacob Blake, a Black man. During the trial, there was grainy footage of Rittenhouse running through the streets with his assault rifle on that night. Rittenhouse, seventeen at the time, had come to Kenosha to protect property. Rittenhouse was later charged with shooting three men, two fatally.

Rittenhouse took the stand in his own defense. He did not live in Kenosha, not even in Wisconsin. He lived in Antioch, Illinois, and did not have a driver's license. As I recall, he lived with his mother, and she drove him to work. However, one of his friends, Dominick Black, had a car. Black had dated Rittenhouse's sister, and Black soon considered Rittenhouse to be like a brother. Black also had an assault rifle, which he showed to Rittenhouse. Not surprisingly, Rittenhouse decided he wanted one as well. Black purchased the assault rifle for him since Rittenhouse, at seventeen, could not legally purchase or possess one. Black and Rittenhouse, with their assault rifles, set off for Wisconsin to somehow help in a situation for which they had no training. On the witness stand, Rittenhouse was awkward, unclear at times in his testimony, yet compelling as a young man trapped and frantic in a chaotic situation that he chose. The jury believed him. He was found not guilty of all charges.

The Rittenhouse trial was streamed live. The news media, focusing on the public's right to be informed and the First Amendment (freedom of the press, speech, assembly), stated that cameras should be always allowed in the courtrooms. However, after the trial, the judge expressed concern about allowing cameras in his courtroom in the future. Cameras might sensationalize the proceedings, distract the lawyers or judges more frequently, and expose identified witnesses to harassment or worse. Despite concerns, most state courts allow cameras in the courtroom while federal district courts ban them.

I can certainly see the appeal of watching an interesting trial. But then that was part of my job. The main argument for cameras in the federal courts would be transparency—allow the public to see what is going on and be assured that it is fair. It would also allow the public to learn about and have confidence in the justice system. The lawyers carefully prepare their cases and present to the judge or jury the best evidence and arguments in support of their respective positions. However, rarely is it the full story.

As a result, the lawyers are engaging in a type of performance, which can get out of hand at times. Some argue that allowing cameras in federal court would focus more on sensationalism, rather than resolving the disputes. The judge may also engage in actions that are not fully understood by the public. For instance, at the end of the trial, the judge in the Rittenhouse trial allowed the defendant to reduce the number of jurors who had heard the evidence and who would ultimately decide his guilt or innocence in jury deliberations, randomly picking those jurors who would be excused from further service and allowed to go home.

Empaneling extra jurors for a trial is usually necessary, particularly in a long trial, since one or more jurors may need to be excused because of medical or other emergencies, and the law requires that a reduced number of jurors remain available when jury deliberations begin. The judge stated that allowing the defendant to pick the jurors to be excused was always his procedure in criminal cases to assure the defendant of fairness. Outsiders objected, stating that such treatment appeared to be preferential to the defendant.

In allowing cameras in the courtroom, is the public really learning about the justice system or simply engaging in a type of voyeurism? We want to be shocked or amazed. Perhaps the trial has become a type of entertainment, although, at times, it may become more of a horror movie; that is reality.

Some lawyers state that cameras should never be permitted in the courtroom, arguing that live broadcasts allow witnesses to see and listen to trial testimony and then alter their own testimony. Of course, although such witnesses should never engage in such conduct, lawyers argue that it happens. Moreover, some witnesses are just not camera ready and appear angry or untruthful when, in most encounters, they are personable and honest.

Many trials may get out of hand. Lawyers or witnesses may perform to the cameras, an oral ruling by the judge may be misunderstood by the public, there may be intimidation of the witnesses, or witnesses may improperly view trial testimony shown on television before appearing in court. Unfortunately, there is legitimate concern that cameras in the courtroom may be prejudicial to a party and may result in the public losing confidence in the justice system.

CHAPTER TWENTY-SEVEN

THE ALLURE OF ONLINE DOCUMENTS

While I was watching a show on cable from the comfort of my couch, an unwelcome commercial suddenly appeared. Although it is not necessarily a better choice, I decided to switch to the shopping channel. A woman was earnestly pitching new software that allowed anyone to do their wills and other necessary estate documents online. For just $130 per person, or $199 per couple, the online company would send a code that the individual or couple could use to create an account. The software would then ask a series of questions to determine what type of will or other document might be needed, then walk the individual or couple through all the necessary steps to draft a will or anything else that might be required. The final documents needed to be notarized, but they would be valid in any state. It all seemed so easy.

I am a strong proponent of everyone having access to the courts. I was an advocate for and one of the creators of the Self-Help Center in the Arizona Bankruptcy Court. The center provides information through videos and forms and is staffed with a volunteer attorney, usually several days a week. The volunteer attorneys are there to answer routine questions.

If the volunteer attorney is presented with a complicated matter, the attorney may agree to represent the individual at a lower cost or for free if the individual is without a job or in a lower income bracket. The attorney may also refer the individual to other Arizona attorneys if the volunteer attorney is unable to help.

So isn't the online document company just another type of self-help center? The document company might be a wonderful solution for a married couple with a cat. What if they tragically die in an accident? Who will take care of Beauty, the beloved cat? Certainly, a will would ensure that Beauty would become the pet of a devoted human that the couple both agree on. An individual's or couple's affairs may quickly become complicated if they have children, have real estate in several states, or don't want their assets to go to certain family members.

How does the online form handle the complexities of our lives, even though we believe that our lives are in order and all solutions are straightforward? How does the software handle the nuances or unanswered questions of the law, or how does it exercise critical thinking to solve a problem when the statutes and case law are unclear?

We know that even the best generative AI today still misses the mark in analytical writing and may have an answer to a particular question that is nonsensical, which is described as the system "hallucinating."

Although AI is constantly improving as more data is absorbed, there is concern that individuals filling out online forms will be unable to discern whether AI has provided the correct answer. AI is not signing the online forms under penalty of perjury; rather, it is the individual accessing the software. The individual will be sanctioned by the court, having her bankruptcy case dismissed, or she'll be threatened with a criminal proceeding for perjury. And the online document company will suffer no consequences.

As for the document company that is offering online forms, perhaps it has a staff of attorneys on call in every state who review the documents when the computer system alerts them to a potential problem. But then what? If the attorney interacts with the individual or couple, are they then charged more money?

Perhaps the forms are set up so that if an individual types in "I own real and personal property in Illinois and Arizona," the computer suddenly goes to a screen that says "ALERT—THIS IS COMPLICATED. WE ARE TERMINATING THIS SESSION. CONSULT AN ATTORNEY." Of course, the individual would probably want their $130 back. Or what if the program does not ask all the necessary questions, so the documents do not provide the legal relief that the individual or couple seeks?

A friend advised me that she had filled out documents online and loved the process. I suggested that she ask one of our mutual lawyer friends to look at her documents. It would cost my friend perhaps $200 to $300 for a review, but I told her it was worth the price to make sure everything was in order. She would not want to pass on to a better world only to learn that her loved ones had to pay $2,000, $3,000, or more for a mistake that had been made by an online service.

Whether one focuses on online document companies or the use of AI, there is no doubt that the legal field will change dramatically. Recent graduates of law schools will no longer be needed to handle time-consuming document review. Some law firms may become controlled by partners with no desire to hire those newly admitted to the bar. Other law firms may be more creative, training young associates to handle more complex matters while partners become focused on acquiring new business. Perhaps the lawyer of the future may need a degree that includes topics normally found in a master of business administration as well as a juris doctor degree.

AI may be utilized effectively by financially sound law

firms, but small firms or newly admitted attorneys may find the cost of AI beyond their means and be unable to compete with the established firms. Individuals who can afford AI and who are appearing pro se, or without the assistance of counsel, in court may use technology for fraudulent purposes, manufacturing pleadings or cases that are entirely fictional to win a case.

Courts will have to use AI on a frequent basis to check what is being filed with them and mete out the necessary penalties to those who use it improperly. Of course, there is no doubt that courts will also use AI to make their tasks easier, such as reviewing documents that have extensive financial information that may be sorted, reviewed, and analyzed better by AI than any individual.

CHAPTER TWENTY-EIGHT

BANKRUPTCY IN A HOT, DRY, FIERY WORLD

In early November 2018, twenty-six thousand people lived in a small community nestled in the foothills of the Sierra Nevada. There were 12,000 homes and 1,500 businesses. On November 8, a community was engulfed by fire and swept away. Eighty-five people died in the fire; 90 percent of the homes were destroyed. Paradise had been lost. Many later focused on the causes of the fire, such as climate change or global warming, the effect of a lack of proper forestry management, and faulty power lines that sparked fires and should have been buried underground.

A reporter visited Paradise five years later and still found it struggling to survive. Under California law, utilities may be held liable for damages resulting from a fire if the company sparked the blaze, even if the company was not negligent. PG&E, a California utility whose downed power lines caused the Paradise fire, pleaded guilty to eighty-four counts of involuntary manslaughter and agreed to provide $220 million as a settlement to help rebuild the community it had destroyed. Paradise also received $1 billion in federal and state assistance.

In rebuilding Paradise, an effort has been made to make it climate resilient. Electrical and broadband cables have been buried underground, excavation routes have been widened, thousands of trees have been removed, and the community has created a siren system to warn residents of impending emergencies. Paradise residents have also teamed with Habitat for Humanity to build structures that can withstand wildfires, such as using fire-resistant construction materials, covering vents, and upgrading windows, to reduce the risk of embers causing homes to explode in flames and to allow homes to endure wildfires' radiant heat.

However, few residents have returned. There are only 9,000 residents, 4,000 homes, and 450 businesses. The community is no longer self-sufficient, relying on PG&E money to provide essential services. It is estimated that the PG&E money will be exhausted in twenty years. By that time, the community must double its number of residents and businesses to survive.

Another drawback to returning Paradise to the vibrant community that it once was is the cost of fire insurance premiums, which have increased to five figures for some residents.

But there were economic consequences beyond rebuilding communities that arose from climate change or global warming. On January 29, 2019, PG&E, one of the nation's largest utilities, filed a bankruptcy case, seeking to continue its operations and hold creditors at bay while proposing a plan to pay creditors over time. The stock of the utility was reduced to "junk" status since the liabilities resulting from the Paradise fire seemed astronomical in amount and impossible to pay.

Ultimately, the company was able to reorganize, paying $25.5 billion to its creditors over time, establishing a trust fund in the amount of $13.5 billion, and settling with insurance companies for $11 billion. As part of its plan, PG&E was also granted access to a $21 billion wildfire fund created and funded by California. To have PG&E act more responsibly, the California Public Utilities Commission also set up a process to revoke the utility's license to operate if the utility did not live up to its legal responsibilities. After confirmation of its plan, PG&E remained a shareholder-owned utility, although many requested that it become a public-private or public utility.

Many wildfire victims remained angry that the utility was able to reduce its liabilities in bankruptcy and continue to operate when it had a "history of negligence and ineptitude."

The victims had reason to be concerned. The 2019 case was not the first time that PG&E had availed itself of bankruptcy protection. In 1996, California Governor Pete Wilson signed legislation partially deregulating the state's energy industry. In 2001, Enron Corporation, a now-defunct entity as a result of what occurred in its bankruptcy case learned of California's deregulation and stepped in to take advantage of the energy market.

California initially had adequate generating capacity for the demand of consumers and industry. However, Enron created artificial shortages of power. For instance, it took power plants offline at a time when there was peak demand. Enron traders then sold power at premium prices, sometimes as much as twenty times the normal value. Unfortunately, PG&E's retail market prices were capped by the state, so when the cost of electricity skyrocketed because of Enron's manipulation, PG&E could not raise rates. It began sustaining massive losses that forced it into bankruptcy. Enron had created an energy crisis.

Enron's corruption and fraudulent activity were uncovered, not only in the energy market, but also in its accounting records, which hid the immense losses it had sustained. It, too, filed a bankruptcy case in 2001.

Whether Paradise will succeed given the changes in the environment is unclear.

Another community that has arguably been destroyed by climate change or global warming is Lahaina, Maui, Hawaii. As of January 2025, Lahaina is still recovering from one of the deadliest fires in US history. In August 2023, 102 people were killed, and thousands were displaced. A firestorm swept from the mountains down through the town, leaving only ashes. Those who have relocated to other areas of Maui fear that what is being done to rebuild the town is not enough and that if they return, they will be subjected to another wildfire.

Others have returned to the area where they used to live, residing in RVs and makeshift shelters. Median rents have increased by 44 percent between 2023 and 2024. FEMA has leased homes to 1,200 families and provided subsidies to another 500 families. In March 2025, those living in FEMA temporary housing may need to start paying rent if financially able. In February 2026, all housing assistance is scheduled to expire.

In the meantime, the state has begun to take measures to try to prevent another catastrophe. Fire sensors are being placed in the area with the hope of detecting a fire in the early stages. The utility, Hawaiian Electric, is upgrading its equipment and intends to shut off electricity if extreme weather is imminent. The rebuilding process is overwhelming. Long-term affordable housing must be constructed, the infrastructure must be replaced, health and social services must be provided, and businesses must be rebuilt.

Litigation has been ongoing. Over six hundred cases were brought. The Hawaii governor was instrumental in negotiating a settlement to award $4 billion to the victims and end the litigation. However, the insurance companies objected to the settlement filed with the court, arguing that they had already paid out over $2 billion in claims and wanted to be reimbursed for those payments. In 2025, the Hawaii Supreme Court will rule on whether the settlement may go forward.

Although some victims will also use bankruptcy as a vehicle to pay back their creditors over time since they have perhaps lost their homes, their jobs, or access to regular income, it may be impossible for them to propose a viable plan to repay creditors. Rebuilding in a fire-ravaged area, only to be subjected to mudslides or enduring repetitive wildfires, could mean that individuals are never able to recover over the long term.

Insurers, in turn, will leave the markets where environmentally caused events occur, leaving individuals to self-insure. Insurers may also raise rates so high that few can afford insurance. Finally, insurers that make unwise financial decisions may be subject to being wound up or dissolved under the insurance laws of individual states.

It is unclear what the long-term solution is to environmental catastrophes.

CHAPTER TWENTY-NINE

BEING CHIEF

Most federal chief court judges handle administrative duties as well as a caseload. The administrative duties focus on the business of running the court. The federal government utilizes a decentralized budget to fund each court, sending disbursements that are tailored to the needs of that court. The decentralized budgeting process also allows for more transparency as to how the courts are using federal funds.

In June 2001, I became chief judge of the Arizona bankruptcy court. My court was provided with allocations that allowed us to focus on technological advances. For instance, our court was willing to be a "beta court," testing new technologies before they were disseminated to other courts nationwide. As a result, we shifted our staffing needs, hiring individuals who had advanced programming skills and were ready to implement cutting-edge technology. We were able to roll out new programs, along with other beta courts, that became the foundation of a nationwide conversion into fully electronic courts with no paper files.

Based on local needs, we also devoted courthouse space to

a self-help center, with the ability to assign a court employee to oversee the center's operational details.

Along with colleagues, the chief judge also determines the future needs of the court. At our meetings, we discussed how many cases were being filed, what resources we needed to administer those cases, and the approval process for any resource acquisition. We generally arrived at a consensus as to how we should proceed.

When I was chief judge, we had a critical need to expand and renovate two courthouses, one in Phoenix and the other in Tucson, and acquire lease space for a new hearing site to meet the needs of the communities in Northern Arizona.

In October 2000, the Sandra Day O'Connor Courthouse in Phoenix was completed, but it could not accommodate the space requirements of the bankruptcy court. We had to move to an older courthouse that had been closed because of asbestos contamination at the location.

It was a complex renovation, and I was glad that I was able to work with the General Services Administration (GSA), which owned the courthouse, and the architects that it had retained. The first step was asbestos abatement or encapsulation, then removing all tenant improvements until only the concrete slabs remained.

We developed the space requirements for the bankruptcy court, including the number of courtrooms, the type of technology that would be installed in each courtroom, the layout of other public areas of the building that would be used by the court, and the judicial rooms or chambers, which would be in secure areas. The bankruptcy court would be the primary tenant in the building, with the remainder of the space being rented by other federal government agencies.

The second renovation was the James A. Walsh Courthouse, Tucson, Arizona. In 2000, it was closed because of asbestos found on the property.

Completed in 1929–1930, the Walsh Courthouse was also

a US post office, a gathering place where residents could exchange the latest news and pick up their packages and mail at the mailboxes and windows staffed by postal clerks.

The courthouse was constructed in the neoclassical style, a simplified version of classical features that was utilized in most federal buildings of that time. The south or main facade had terra-cotta sheathing as well as some brickwork. Rather than classically round columns, the facade had vertically embedded columns made from flat, smooth, or polished stone. As an acknowledgment of its surroundings and a softening of the neoclassical style, it also had a mission-style roof. In 1974, the post office portion of the facility was closed, but the mailboxes and other finishings remained. In 1983, the courthouse was listed on the National Register of Historic Places.

My Tucson colleagues James M. Marlar and Eileen W. Hollowell wanted to restore the courthouse consistent with the style and materials reminiscent of when the Walsh Courthouse was first opened. For instance, they wanted to preserve the old mailboxes and some of the other finishes used when the post office was open.

We also had to keep in mind that the National Park Service allowed property to be remodeled as the owner wanted, so long as the owner followed any state or local regulations. Listing in the National Register also protected the property from demolition or other "negative effects."[1] It seemed the best way to proceed with the renovation was to preserve the importance of the courthouse to the community, including its history as a post office.

I also assisted on the project along with GSA employees and the architects. Monthly meetings were initially set up to

1. The listing triggered a review process, which included potential comment to the Advisory Council on Historic Preservation for federally funded projects. Since the US Congress allocated funding for the renovation, the courthouse was a federally funded project.

plan the project in two stages. The first phase was to renovate that portion of the courthouse that would allow the bankruptcy court to function. It was completed in 2002. The second phase of the project was to finish the upper courthouse floors. That phase was completed in 2008.

We started with asbestos abatement or encapsulation. New technology was placed in the building, and several courtrooms, chambers, and staff areas were finished to allow the court to function. Later, the old mailboxes and other post office finishes were burnished, fresh paint was applied to the original murals on the main entrance ceiling and walls. The wood paneling, light fixtures, and artistic detail in the ceremonial courtroom were restored to their past beauty. Finally, the other courtrooms, staff offices, and chambers on the upper floors were renovated.

I owe a debt of gratitude to Judges Marlar and Hollowell for their care, insight, and hard work on the renovation.

My final project was obtaining a hearing site in Northern Arizona. The bankruptcy court had been utilizing the federal district court building in Prescott, Arizona, as an additional hearing site for the convenience of residents of Northern Arizona. Unfortunately, many federal court trials were placed on the hearing calendar, and the bankruptcy court lost access to the site.

Since I was handling the Prescott calendar at the time, I was charged, as chief judge and as the judge who was most familiar with what the requisite space requirements were, with working with the GSA and court personnel to negotiate a lease near Prescott, Arizona.

I ultimately found new construction in nearby Prescott Valley, which allowed me to build out the tenant improvements that the court needed: a small courtroom, an adjoining room that I would use prior to or in between hearings, and a small hallway where the court security officers could screen individuals.

Because I anticipated that many attorneys would appear telephonically or by video, I had to make sure the technology would accommodate them. Working with GSA and court personnel, I was able to enter into a lease agreement in only three months.

Chief bankruptcy judges no longer have the ability to be involved in the space planning projects that I have outlined. Many services may now be shared between the federal district and bankruptcy courts. Certainly, cost savings may occur if courts pool their resources.

However, the needs of the courts may differ. They have different stakeholders, such as the Office of the United States Trustee, which is a part of the Department of Justice and may be heard at bankruptcy hearings. In the bankruptcy court, there are many administrative-type hearings that must be heard on an accelerated basis. Courtrooms are used more frequently to allow the many bankruptcy cases to be administered more efficiently.

The federal district court stakeholders are the US Attorneys' Office, which is a part of the Department of Justice, and the Federal Public Defender's Office, which is part of the court system.

The federal district court hearings may be set on a motion or similar calendar that allows for brief argument from the parties, but most court hearings will be criminal matters or complex civil cases, which may require a trial to resolve. Courtrooms are used less frequently, but if a complex trial has begun, a courtroom may be used daily for a prolonged period.

As a result, sharing courtrooms or court personnel between the courts is not currently feasible in many areas.

There is the fear that in touting the economic benefit of combining the services of many courts, many bankruptcy courts will be unable to function.

CHAPTER THIRTY

LET'S CELEBRATE BANKRUPTCY FLEXIBILITY AND CREATIVITY, NOT MANIPULATION

In the future, bankruptcy laws should be creative and flexible without preferring one group over another if they have the same rights. Creativity and flexibility lead to better results for creditors.

In New York City, many commercial leases are for ten or fifteen years, sometimes longer. If a company executes a long-term lease and still has eight years left on the lease, there is a reasonable chance that the lease will be below market. In other words, a long-term tenant will be paying less rent for the same type of commercial space as another tenant that has just signed a lease contract.

The Bankruptcy Code allows the tenant to sell or transfer its rights in a lease to maximize funds that will be distributed to creditors in a plan. So a long-term tenant who files a bankruptcy case may want to market the lease to the public for a quick sale or transfer of rights, with the ability to receive enough money in return to fund a plan to pay creditors.

What if a debtor wants to transfer its rights in a lease but the new tenant wants to use the real property in a different manner and the landlord refuses to consent to the new use? In the 1982 decision of *Matter of U.L. Radio Corp*, Judge Galgay came up with a solution that benefited all parties.[1]

The tenant Radio Corporation executed a lease agreement in 1979 with Jemrock Realty Company, landlord, to operate a business that sold and serviced televisions and appliances. The business was in a residential apartment building that also had a grocery store, a Chinese restaurant, a liquor store, and 170 apartments.

Radio Corporation had the right to assign the lease to a third party but needed the landlord's consent, which could not be "unreasonably withheld." In 1981, Radio Corporation was not in default under the lease.

Radio Corporation decided that it wanted to liquidate its assets and pay creditors in full. It filed a bankruptcy case on May 20, 1981, moving forward with its plans to liquidate. The proposed tenant was Just Heaven Restaurant Ltd., which wanted to operate a small bistro. The president of Just Heaven also provided his personal guarantee, ensuring the financial ability of Just Heaven to make rental payments until the end of the lease. Just Heaven also agreed to provide soundproofing at the restaurant since the lease provided that any noise at the location would be a breach of the lease, which could lead to lease termination.

Radio Corporation filed a pleading to assume the lease and then assign it to Just Heaven. Radio Corporation would receive from Just Heaven the sum of $2,000 per month until 1988, at which point the debtor would have paid its creditors in full. Jemrock objected, refusing to permit the change in use from a television/appliance store to a restaurant. From Jemrock's standpoint, the change in use was a default under the lease.

Judge Galgay had a difficult issue to resolve. Radio Corporation had complied with all provisions of the bankruptcy law

1. 19 B.R. 537 (Bankr. S.D.N.Y 1982).

except as to how the change in use should be handled. The law provided that Jemrock receive adequate assurance that Just Heaven, the proposed new tenant, could perform for the remaining term of the lease.

If the debtor were successful in assigning the lease to Just Heaven, it would not only receive payments to fund its plan, but it would also no longer be liable for any future payments or compliance with other terms of the lease.

The judge concluded that assignments were preferred; therefore, a change in the premises' use would not necessarily be a bar to an assignment. A change in use would only be prohibited if the landlord could show a "substantial detriment" would occur if a change in use were permitted. A restaurant, laundry, and liquor store were already tenants in Jemrock's building. Just Heaven had also agreed to put in soundproofing. Being practical yet flexible, the judge approved the change in use and allowed Radio Corporation to assume and assign its lease to Just Heaven.

Businesses have been given many more opportunities to be successful under the Bankruptcy Code. The principals should propose plans that are suitable for the businesses they operate. Gaming the system, as outlined in previous chapters, should not be permitted.

CHAPTER THIRTY-ONE

IS A MINIMALIST APPROACH TO BANKRUPTCY THE SOLUTION?

A few experts have proposed a minimalist approach that reduces the footprint of the bankruptcy system. In September 2022, Senator Elizabeth Warren introduced legislation that would establish a new chapter for individual debtors that would be similar to the current reorganization subchapter concerning small businesses. The debt limit for individual debtors would be increased to $7.5 million and allow individuals to take advantage of simplified procedures to receive forgiveness of debt. However, the legislation also would repeal chapter 7, allowing individuals to liquidate their assets and promptly receive forgiveness of their debts, and chapter 13, the reorganization chapter for individuals, which was substantially modified in 2005 to have an adverse impact on consumer debtors.[1] The legislation did not get any traction but is indicative of the new approach.

Another approach limits the relief that bankruptcy may provide. Bankruptcy would only focus on debts. Bankruptcy would modify or discharge those debts arising from "traditional contractual relationships, rather than any obligation

1. Consumer Bankruptcy Reform Act of 2022 (S 4980).

that would be expressed in non-monetary terms." This approach would limit the relief that could be accorded to debtors. For instance, revisiting the bankruptcy judge in the Radio Corporation case who allowed a change in the use of a leased premises arising from the transfer of the lease from a tenant who was not in default in the payment of rent or any other monetary obligation to a new tenant would arguably not be permitted under a debt analysis.

The second change would be for bankruptcy not to be used in mass tort litigation. Bankruptcy has been used in unintended ways to "harness its intense powers to work around principles of fairness and justice." This would force individuals to resort to multistate litigation or class actions to obtain a judgment against tortfeasors and then bring those judgments to the bankruptcy court to be resolved. But what about those who are injured in the future by a defective product or the malicious actions of a corporation and its principals? How would they get relief? Would they have to file a separate lawsuit many years later, and if so, would the entity that caused the injuries and its principals still be in existence or alive?

Most businesses are more complex in debt structure and how they operate than individuals. There are already subchapters providing for the bankruptcy of railroads and the liquidation of stockbrokers and commodity brokers under the Securities Investor Protection Act and chapter 7 of the Bankruptcy Code. The reorganization or liquidation provisions must also accommodate public companies.

A better solution is to revamp chapter 11 for certain businesses that have many stakeholders, such as victims who have suffered catastrophic injuries or investors who have set up complex repayment priorities of their debts which require substantial new infusions of capital or financing to propose plans of reorganization.

As for individuals, they should have their own chapter. It

should be less complex and streamlined, with fewer forms to be completed. Individuals should be able to elect whether to liquidate their assets, pay their creditors immediately, and receive forgiveness of their debts or pay their creditors over time if they are able to do so, only receiving a fresh start when they have made all payments under a multi-year plan.

Individuals are also entitled to retain certain property, known as exempt property, which entities are unable to claim. The retention of exempt property has been a critical bankruptcy law component for a long time to ensure that individuals have a chance for a fresh start and will not be a public burden. For those individuals who are sole proprietors or operate small businesses, they may continue to file under the subchapter that has been created for them.

Since the 1930s, chapter 9 has allowed municipalities to reorganize. Because of the Tenth Amendment to the US Constitution, the sovereignty of the states and individual liberties are preserved over powers that are not explicitly given to the federal government.[2]

Although Article I of the US Constitution states that bankruptcy laws are enacted by Congress, each state retains its right to determine whether any municipality may seek bankruptcy relief and to control the day-to-day operations of the municipality. Bankruptcy judges describe the process as the municipality continues with its daily operations, negotiates any proposed plan, decides whether to increase or impose taxes if it has the authority to do so, and obtains financing to fund a plan. A judge's only duty will be a thumbs-up or down as to whether the plan should be confirmed.

If the plan is not confirmed, the municipality may propose one or more new plans. However, if the municipality ulti-

2. The Tenth Amendment states "any powers not specifically delegated to the federal government by the Constitution, nor prohibited to the states, are reserved to the states or the people."

mately fails to confirm a viable plan, the state may disincorporate or dissolve its status as a legal entity. Because of constitutional constraints, municipalities need to have their own chapter.

Since the United Nations has drafted the Model Law on cross-border insolvencies, which has been adopted by many nations, the Model Law should continue as a separate chapter under our bankruptcy law.

PART FIVE
PROPOSED SOLUTIONS TO THE BANKRUPTCY SYSTEM

CHAPTER THIRTY-TWO

BECOME AN ADVOCATE

The bankruptcy system has become more complex since the 1780s, but it is still critical to a functioning economy and providing relief to individuals and companies. I would be remiss not to point out some proposed solutions that will make our system fairer and more responsive to all.

1. **Provide Easy Access to the Courts**

While I was chief judge of the Arizona Bankruptcy Court, I focused on making the court more accessible to all. Arizona has always had a lot of independent souls—some would say ornery—who want to do things on their own. In the early 2000s, about 30 percent of our court's total filings were made by individuals who were not represented by counsel. In 2000, Arizona had a population of 5,130,632, and the Central District of California, which encompasses numerous counties around Los Angeles, had a population of 17,079,662.[1] Yet in

1. The statistics are from the 2000 census. The Central District of California includes the counties of Los Angeles, Orange, Riverside, San Bernardino, San

the early 2000s, Arizona was number two in the Ninth Circuit, behind the Central District of California, as to the number of case filings, and we had a higher percentage of individuals who were filing without counsel. We had to be innovative to handle the caseload.

The first step was to bring everyone to the table. We couldn't bring in everyone that was filing a bankruptcy petition, but we could ask the document preparers to meet with us.

In many federal districts, document preparers are shunned. Many judges are concerned that document preparers take away business from small firms or firms that specialize in consumer bankruptcy law. Other courts do not certify document preparers to make sure that they understand how to complete documents and electronically file them. As a result, the judges do not want to take the time to review documents that are improperly prepared.

However, in Arizona, it is not realistic to ignore them. Document preparers have long been a critical component of the legal system. Many individuals prefer to represent themselves in federal and state courts, but they need an inexpensive way to file the necessary court forms.

The Arizona Supreme Court, acknowledging the preference of a large part of the population that used the court system to handle legal affairs with minimum assistance, began enacting rules that allowed document preparers to fill out the forms and file the documents with the court. The court also made sure that the document preparers were competent to handle such tasks, were not charging excessive fees, and were not providing legal advice.

As a result, a list of certified document preparers was soon created and filed with the Arizona Supreme Court. The

---

Luis Obispo, Santa Barbara, and Ventura. In 2000, these counties had a population of 17,079,662.

Arizona Bankruptcy Court soon allowed certified document preparers to file documents with it.

To ensure that individuals had access to the courts, I worked with others to go from paper filing to an electronic filing system. I had to bring document preparers to the table as well as attorneys, bankruptcy trustees, and court staff to create local rules that would allow the greatest number of individuals to file electronically. As a result, we were one of the first courts in the nation to go fully electronic.

For those who did not want the assistance of a document preparer, we opened self-help centers at our courthouses in Phoenix and Tucson, stocked with helpful videos, forms, and instruction booklets for individuals to review before they filed a bankruptcy petition. If the individual indicated to court personnel at the self-help center that they had a legal question, court personnel would direct the person to the volunteer lawyer who was there to answer any basic legal questions. If the individual needed help with a legal issue, that volunteer attorney could agree to represent the person or refer them to another attorney.

We found that the self-help center increased the number of individuals who sought assistance of counsel. Fears that consumer lawyers would suffer economically because of the self-help center were unfounded. Our self-help center still exists today and has been recognized on a nationwide basis for its excellence.

2. **Give Relief on Student Loans**

In 1978, when the Bankruptcy Code was first enacted, it was more pro-debtor than any prior bankruptcy law, except for its treatment of student loans that had become more pro-creditor because of changes to the federal education law. In 2005, after little analysis or review, Congress made sweeping changes to the provisions concerning consumers, which was known as the Bankruptcy Abuse Prevention and Consumer Protection Act (BAPCPA), which I also write about in Part 3.

Due to the hectoring cries of creditor lobbies, the Bankruptcy Code was amended to return to an erroneous belief that any individual who filed a bankruptcy case was engaged in fraud or other questionable behavior. We should return to the days, under the old bankruptcy law, when student loans were forgiven like any other consumer debt. Student loans have nothing to do with a debtor being a bad actor. Even if the individual did fraudulently obtain a student loan, there are other provisions of the Bankruptcy Code that already provide a remedy for such actions.[2] There is no reason to leave in place onerous provisions that make it nearly impossible to discharge a student loan.

3. Amend/Delete Many of 2005 Consumer Bankruptcy Code Provisions

Change provisions concerning consumer credit card debt.

For at least fifteen years before the Bankruptcy Code was amended in 2005, credit card companies lobbied for changes making it more difficult for consumers to discharge their credit card debt, arguing that there was too much consumer fraud out there. Of all the many studies done on consumer fraud, not one supported the credit card companies' alarmist rhetoric.

Moreover, their claims triggered investigations that found that the credit card companies were offering cards with little or no analysis of the proposed individual's financial situation. And a default? That was just an opportunity for the credit card companies to roll unpaid interest into the principal amount of debt, with the individual to pay interest on interest.

---

2. See Section 523 of the Bankruptcy Code, which does not allow for the discharge, or forgiveness, of certain debts.

At the same time, the company also increased the debt limit or the amount that could be borrowed on the card, making it more unlikely that the individual could ever repay the debt. The companies were also making money from the default fees they were charging. The final straw? The companies encouraged the individual to repay only the minimum monthly payments, which didn't even cover the interest on the debt. That meant that each month, the principal on the debt grew, and the individual would never repay the debt.

Allow individuals to choose to liquidate or pay creditors over time.

Return to the days of old when a consumer debtor could choose liquidation of certain assets and getting forgiveness of their debt or pay creditors over time if the debtor had the financial ability to do so. Now most consumer debtors are forced into proposing plans to pay creditors over five-year periods even when everyone knows they will be unable to make the payments over time.

Moreover, if the consumer debtor does not complete all the payments under the plan, the debtor will not receive forgiveness of any debt unless the individual can show that it would be an "undue hardship" to continue to make any further payments. "Undue hardship" is also used in the test to determine whether student loans should be discharged. It's a test that requires an individual to live in a state of penury for the rest of their life.

Get rid of the means test.

In 1984, Section 707 of the bankruptcy law was amended concerning individuals. Those who had the ability to repay creditors should do so, paying creditors over a three- or five-year period.

To ensure that such policy provisions were enforced, the amendment to Section 707(b) stated that the individual's case would be dismissed "if substantial abuse of the provisions" of the bankruptcy law were found. For the next twenty-one years, almost everyone was satisfied with the change.

Let's look at a case to get a better idea of what was happening from a practical standpoint. In 1988, the Ninth Circuit Court of Appeals considered whether an attorney had substantially abused the bankruptcy law with the filing of his case.[3] He had substantial income, but he refused to pay a $21,000 judgment. Reviewing the statutory language, the Ninth Circuit concluded that if the individual could repay a "meaningful portion" of his debt but chose not to do so, that was substantial abuse, requiring the dismissal of his case. The point is that Section 707(b) was working just fine to curb abuse.

But creditors that had begun to advocate for changes to credit cards and student loans created an impression in the public's psyche that wealthy individuals were also abusing the bankruptcy system by filing cases when they could simply pay creditors. Section 707(b) needed to be changed, they argued, to force individuals into those provisions that required them to pay overtime to receive a fresh start through the forgiveness of their debts.

What emerged was one bankruptcy law subsection that consisted of 2,532 words! The new Section 707(b) was deemed nonsensical, contradictory, and unable to stop abuse. For instance, just before filing a case, an individual could obtain a new loan, in any amount, which was secured by his recently purchased mansion. "Secured" meant that the financial institution that provided the funding to purchase the home would be repaid first as a creditor if the individual didn't repay the loan and the mansion had to be sold. So the individual would stack up the secured debt, with huge monthly payments, *reducing* the amount of money he had to pay in any plan he proposed to creditors.

The individual could also purchase a new car, Jet Skis, and other toys using secured loans, whether the individual could

3. See the decision of In re Kelly, 841 F.2d 908 (9th Cir. 1988).

repay the loans or not. One could create lots of new secured debt, leaving little or no money left to repay those creditors who helped the individual prebankruptcy. The new Section 707(b) only encouraged fraud.

Moreover, those individuals who had substantial monthly income *but no secured debt* were frequently forced into the bankruptcy law's repayment provisions. Attorneys worried about malpractice lawsuits began to advise individuals not to file cases requiring repayment of creditors over five years. Instead, the attorneys encouraged individuals to load up on secured debt before filing, have no extra monthly income to pay creditors, and file a case to liquidate certain assets quickly and get a fresh start. Given Congress's concerns, the amendment to Section 707(b) had an anomalous result.

Section 707(b) was so complex that attorneys' costs immediately increased in amount, becoming unaffordable to many individuals. Forms were created to focus on the income and expenses of the individual. The Internal Revenue Service (IRS) tables were used to simplify the process, allowing the average individual's monthly income and expenses to be used rather than actual expenses. The average expenses also varied depending on where the individual lived in the United States.

Instead of simplifying the process, the IRS tables were considered complex, unrealistic, or wildly inconsistent as to the individual's actual income and expenses. Then Congress stepped in, creating more confusion by adding thirty to forty additional expenses that could be used to reduce an individual's monthly income to pay creditors that were *not* a part of the IRS tables.

Some other problems surfaced. Section 707(b) focused on what an individual earned the six months before filing a bankruptcy case as a part of the analysis in determining whether the individual should be forced into a creditor repayment plan or simply liquidate certain assets. However, how to determine "monthly income" to repay creditors was not the actual individual's income received but an artificial test. The individual added up the last six months of her income and divided it by six. That was great for an individual who received the same salary monthly. But what if an individual received a bonus or was unemployed during the six-month period?

Let's assume Barb received $2,500 in monthly income. She also received a bonus of $5,000 from her employer within the six-month period before filing. Barb received $2,500 times six, or $15,000, for the six-month period. With the bonus, her income was inflated to $20,000 ($15,000 plus $5,000). The sum of $20,000 would then be divided by six to change her monthly income from $2,500 to more than $3,333. Unfortunately, the $3,333 amount would then be used to determine her income, minus her expenses, to pay creditors in any proposed plan. The problem is that there is no certainty that she will continue to receive a bonus of the same amount every year she has to pay creditors, but the artificial income manipulation *assumes that she will* and forces her to make higher monthly payments. If she gets less money, she could miss payments under her plan, have her case dismissed, and never get the fresh start that she deserves.

The same problem arises if the individual is unemployed during the six-month period before filing. Let's assume Barb receives $2,500 per month for three months but then loses her job. For the remaining three months, she receives no income. For the six-month period, Barb receives only $7,500 (3 times $2,500), reducing her artificial monthly income to $1,250 ($7,500 divided by 6). That lower figure would be used to determine her income, minus her expenses, perhaps allowing her to file a liquidation proceeding and obtaining immediate forgiveness of her debt to creditors, even though she subsequently becomes reemployed at a higher monthly wage. In effect, without considering her actual finances over time, she is getting an unfair benefit.

Bottom line? Accurate figures should be used to ensure

that an individual's financial circumstances will be considered, with plan payments increasing or decreasing in amount as necessary. If the individual's circumstances no longer permit a repayment plan, the individual should be allowed to switch to the liquidation provisions to receive a fresh start. Conversely, if the individual makes more money, the overall payment to creditors should be adjusted to accommodate the change.

After 2005, even matters that should have been easily determined have become complex under Section 707(b). For instance, in deciding how much an individual should repay creditors, a court must determine the size of the individual's household. Let's say an individual files a case and has a husband, two biological children, and three stepchildren in her home. The children live with her only half the year. All the children are treated the same as far as expenses are concerned. She may not claim a household of seven.

Rather, her children become "fractionalized" household members, artificially reducing the amount of expenses she may assert monthly. If her expenses are reduced, it means that she must pay more to her creditors monthly in her plan even if she cannot afford it. One idea? Create a presumption in favor of counting all occupants even if stepchildren or unrelated adults who have been living part-time with the individual filing the case as "full" household members. To avoid fraud, the individual would have to show actual expenses paid for the other household members by her over a certain period, such as one year.

The need for reform in this area is clear since there are now at least four ways courts are approaching such households.

a. Count all people who live in the individual's home, like the US Census.
b. Use the IRS tax approach, which allows for people in the home who are supported by the individual

to be deducted as a dependent on the individual's tax return. If deducted for tax purposes, the people living in the home could also be included in the individual's bankruptcy household.

c. The economic support unit. Count only those people who contribute income or have some other financially independent relationship to the household or who are supported by the household.
d. Fractional economic unit. The court focuses on the amount of time minor children spend under the same roof with the individual filing the case and the financial realities of the child custody arrangements. The children are counted as fractional household members. Nontraditional families are penalized.

One individual, I call her Ms. Smith, had the misfortune of having a court apply the fourth way to her household. She resided with her husband, who lived with her full-time; her two children from a prior marriage, who lived there 204 days a year; and her three stepchildren, who resided with her 180 days a year. The court decided that her two children counted as .56 household members each and her three stepchildren counted as .49 household members each, which would be .56 times 2 and .49 times 3, for a total of 2.59 household members.

The court rounded up the fraction to three household members. Instead of seven household members (the actual number in the house), she was reduced to five (she, her husband, and the artificial number three), which dramatically decreased the expenses that she could claim, thereby increasing her monthly payments to creditors.

What about nontraditional families that have unmarried partners, adult children, or adult siblings residing in the individual's home? It is unclear how these households will be treated.

What are the problems with the different approaches as to what constitutes a household? First, there is diminished predictability. There are already four approaches to the problem, and there will probably be more. Second, there is an increased financial burden to the individual who must litigate basic issues. Next, those who have filed bankruptcy cases are listed in the public record, and court opinions are also made available to the public. An individual and her family could be subject to ridicule, or worse, if they are a nontraditional family. Finally, counting children as fractions borders on the absurd. It is the actual expenses that should be the determining factor.[4]

Amend or delete other provisions that assume consumer debtors are bad actors.

For instance, we should amend the provision that assumes an individual has engaged in fraud if they've obtained a cash advance of more than $1,000 on a credit card less than seventy days before filing a bankruptcy petition.[5] This assumption places the burden on the individual to justify the cash advance, rather than forcing the credit card company to show that the debtor has somehow acted improperly. In many cases, consumers use cash advances to pay ongoing medical expenses. The individuals are already dealing with difficult emotional and financial issues, and yet they immediately face an issue as to why they used their credit cards just before filing a bankruptcy petition.

Consumers are now penalized for having previously filed bankruptcy petitions. This is the three-strikes rule in bank-

---

4. For a well-researched article on what constitutes a household for bankruptcy purposes, see "The Modern Family Debacle: Bankruptcy Judges Decide that Some Debtors' Loved Ones Do Not Count as Household Members!" by Creola Johnson.
5. See Section 523(a)(2)(A)(i)(II) of the Bankruptcy Code.

ruptcy: If you file three times within a short period of time, no automatic stay goes into effect. The automatic stay is a bankruptcy court order that forces all creditors and others who have disputes with the individual who has filed a bankruptcy case to stop what they are doing until they get a court order permitting them to take action.

If a creditor wants to telephone the individual to see when he is going to pay up, file a lawsuit against the individual, try to take his car from the parking lot at the mall, or take other *affirmative action*, they need permission from the bankruptcy court judge first. So not having the automatic stay go into effect has a profound negative effect on an individual who may have recently lost a job or may be having medical issues and is struggling to complete the paperwork for a bankruptcy case.

We should amend the Bankruptcy Code to provide more discretion to judges. As of now, creditor lobbyists argue that consumer debtors just file case after case to halt the creditor from being paid or getting property back that it has a security interest or lien on. The thought process is that a consumer has no need to file a case.

Having presided over many trials with consumer debtors who do not have the assistance of counsel, I can attest that they frequently arrive at the trials with cardboard boxes full of papers, eager to show what has happened to them. Most debtors file for bankruptcy because of an immediate crisis. Should we assume that they will have all their financial documents in order so that they can quickly and completely fill out all the official forms that we expect them to file in a mere fourteen days?

Another provision further reflects the mistrust of individuals that creditor lobbies have incorporated into the 2005 Bankruptcy Code amendments. It states that if a consumer debtor has a case dismissed for failure to file or amend certain official forms, the next case that the individual files within a one-year period is presumptively filed in bad faith. [6]

A one-year period is a long time to limit the right of someone to file who has made a mistake on their forms. If the individual should decide to refile, the automatic stay or injunction will only protect the individual for a period of thirty days after the second case has been filed. In the same thirty-day period, the individual must also request a hearing to convince the court to keep the stay in place to protect the individual from their creditors. At the hearing, the individual must show, by clear and convincing evidence, that they filed the petition in good faith.

In most civil proceedings, such as those that occur in the bankruptcy court, the plaintiff must show sufficient facts that would lead the court or a jury to conclude that when the plaintiff's facts are balanced against those of the defendant or other opposing party, the plaintiff should get the relief that they have requested. This lesser evidentiary burden is known as a "preponderance of the evidence."

In contrast, clear and convincing evidence is rarely used in bankruptcy courts and is harder to prove. Clear and convincing evidence requires the plaintiff to produce direct evidence that is clear and explicit and that leaves the court with the firm conviction that the plaintiff's facts have certainly occurred, allowing the plaintiff to have the relief requested. Placing a clear and convincing burden of proof on individuals who have filed another bankruptcy case within a one-year period reflects Congress's belief that such individuals are bad actors.

4. Should Hanging Paragraphs Ever Be Included in Statutes?

6. Section 362 (c)(3) of the Bankruptcy Code.

On November 22, 2024, the Ninth Circuit Court of Appeals issued an opinion that caused me to pause. Most people don't sit around reading statutes or court decisions in their spare time. But sometimes a case can illustrate to everyone what's problematic about the law, not just the bankruptcy area.

The case of *In re Jorden Marie Saldana* focuses on a woman who was a surgical technician earning more than $100,000 a year. The opinion does not state whether she had student loans to repay, a chronic medical condition, or unemployment as a concern. However, she had two issues: she owed $8,549 in taxes and $56,045 to her other creditors.

The opinion does not provide an explanation as to how she found herself in such a financial situation. In many cases, the individual has a rapid increase in income over a relatively short period of time and no one to provide tax advice. The individual does not withhold enough money from her paycheck, and the unpaid taxes (with interest and penalties) soon become a sizable sum. As for the unpaid creditors, they usually surface when an individual frequently uses a credit card for vacations, routine medical examinations, or a trip to the hospital.

Credit card companies are of particular concern. They may advise the individual to pay a minimum amount each month (not the full amount owed), which keeps the individual out of default but also allows her to continue to use the credit card. Unfortunately, paying the minimum amount due never pays the credit card debt in full. Interest accrues on the debt, which is added to the principal balance. The principal balance increases in amount, with interest accruing on that. Now the individual is paying interest on interest. Suddenly the credit card balance balloons in amount. It is not surprising, given how credit card debt is structured, that someone like Jorden may need bankruptcy relief.

Because of 2005 changes to the bankruptcy law, Jorden

had to file a chapter 13 case, which required her, as an above-average wage earner, to pay her creditors over a five-year period. That seemed fair. Wouldn't all creditors at least get something? Not necessarily. In Jorden's case, certain creditors would take priority, or get paid first, over other creditors. Jorden's unpaid taxes, for instance, would get paid before her unsecured creditors.

Federal and state laws also usually protect individual retirement accounts, pensions, and thrift and savings plans from creditors. The idea is to preserve retirement funds so individuals are not destitute when they grow older. So retirement funds held by an employer or in the individual's retirement account are carved out from the assets used to pay creditors.

Jorden had a retirement account and had also taken out a loan against that account. In 2005, amendments to the bankruptcy law protecting retirement plans allowed Congress to garner the necessary support for passage of the Bankruptcy Abuse Prevention and Consumer Protection Act which dramatically and adversely affected consumers. The principal change was permitting an individual, after filing a bankruptcy case, to make payments to a retirement plan without having to direct those funds to creditors. From a policy standpoint, the changes made sense. The individual's retirement account would not be affected by the bankruptcy case.

Unfortunately, some say the 2005 changes were made on an expedited basis. Whatever the reason, clarity of language was not the focus. Jordan soon had an issue as to her retirement account payments that needed to be resolved by the courts.

The Ninth Circuit Panel had to determine what a statutory paragraph meant. Why the confusion? Think of a paper that you're looking at that has paragraphs that are numbered or have alphabetical letters for differentiation. You see Paragraph A, B, and C, then suddenly there is a gap followed by a paragraph that is separated from the others but has no alphabetical letter. You wonder why the inconsistency?

Many experts and courts have also puzzled over formatting differences. The paragraphs have become known, some would say appropriately, as "hanging paragraphs," which leave the reader hanging in every sense of the word. Many would like to amend the bankruptcy law to resolve the ambiguities. In the meantime, the Ninth Circuit and other appellate courts struggle with what Congress intended.

As to the hanging paragraph discussed in Jorden's case, courts have come up with at least four different interpretations of what it means and what should be done. The view of most courts, which was adopted by the Ninth Circuit in Jorden's case, followed the policy of preserving retirement funds and allowing an individual and employer to make contributions to the individual's retirement account even after a bankruptcy case was filed.

In Jorden's case, it meant that she could continue to make contributions to her retirement account even after she filed her bankruptcy case. Those payments would not be considered in an analysis of what she would pay her creditors over time in her plan. The effect was to reduce the amount that she would ultimately pay her unsecured creditors.[7]

Is there any fix? Yes. Rather than using a general provision of bankruptcy law that pertains to individuals and corporations as to what assets will be available to pay creditors in any plan, changes should be made to specify what assets only individuals may use to repay their creditors over time. After all, individuals have retirement accounts that need to be protected. Bottom line: Delete the nonsensical hanging paragraph added to the wrong provision of the bankruptcy law.[8]

---

7. Most courts follow the reasoning in Baxter v. Johnson (In re Johnson), 346 B.R. 256, 263 (Bankr. S.D. Ga. 2006).

8. For those with inquiring minds, delete the hanging paragraph following

Because the hanging paragraph is in the bankruptcy law's consumer area, it is difficult to find advocates who will fight to make changes. Lobbyists consistently only advance what is most beneficial for wealthy corporate creditors with the most power. In the meantime, the hanging paragraph forces those who can least afford it to fight to make the bankruptcy law clear and the system fairer.

5. No Free Passes for the Those Controlling a Company

I described in Chapter 8 the Sackler family's use of the Purdue Pharma reorganization proceedings to release or forgive any liability that they might have to the opioid claimants. Johnson & Johnson was using the bankruptcy system to protect its valuable assets from the talc-based baby products that caused cancer.

Increasingly the bankruptcy system is being used to protect corporate malfeasance. Why should the victims be left waiting to be paid from a fund of money that does not solve the egregious medical issues caused by the company or its leaders or ever make whole those victims for the pain and suffering that they have endured or will endure?

The people that control such entities, that destroy the lives of so many, should not get any free rides from the corporations that they control, and there should be a new provision in the Bankruptcy Code that would make such individuals forever liable on the obligations that have resulted from the misery that they have caused until all victims are paid, in full, for all of their medical costs, attorneys fees, loss of income, and pain and suffering.

The June 2024 United States Supreme Court decision in

Section 541(b)(7)(A) and (B), and add a new Paragraph (C) to Section 1325(b)(2).

Purdue Pharma may have caused corporate lawyers, wrongdoers, and immoralists to rethink their legal strategies. For now, individuals who have caused injury to others and hid behind their corporate, partnership, or entity shell will have to come up with sufficient cash or other personal assets to get the consent of their victims to any plan the individuals propose on behalf of the entities they control.

6. **More Educational Programs**

For high school, community college, trade school, and university students, we should insist on programs providing an understanding of credit card debt, such as how the amount owed by a student on a credit card may balloon dramatically within a short period of time, how to apply for and obtain student loans, and how long the student will be committed to repaying the loans. Also, there should be a basic course in budgeting, including the payment of necessary expenses and providing for fun activities so life is not drudgery without pleasure.

The National Conference of Bankruptcy Judges has a CARE program (Credit Abuse Resistance Education) that presents educational programs, on an ongoing basis, across the nation. Usually, the bankruptcy court website in your area will provide information about your local CARE program.

Adults may find similar programs at local nonprofit organizations that are assisting those with no permanent housing with a path toward employment and a safe place to live.

7. **Providing Hope for Generations Under Forty**

For a decade, I was an adjunct professor at the Sandra Day O'Connor College of Law, Arizona State University. My students were Gen Xers, millennials, and a few Gen Zers.

They shared a pessimistic view of the future. They felt that the baby boomers had the benefits of job security, including pensions and social security as safety nets, consistent wage increases that allowed them to purchase affordable housing, unions that protected workers, and the opportunity to make changes that would have staved off global warming. They are measurably worse off than their parents, and they are bitter. We still have the opportunity through cooperative legal and political action to provide a better future for them.

CONCLUSION

The bankruptcy laws have increasingly become more complex, yet ambiguous, and pro-creditor. No data supports such a change. The bankruptcy system should be fair, which can be ensured with changes to the current law, including the allowance of more discretion to judges.

To make changes, I encourage you to become advocates through local groups. Present your changes to your congressional representative or senator. Contact your local chief bankruptcy judge asking for changes that provide easy access to the court for everyone. Encourage local schools to provide a basic education on finance and budgeting.

Bankruptcy affects everyone. Do you still believe that you or your family members will never be affected by bankruptcy? Be informed about your finances and what is happening in the world around you. Don't wait until you get the bankruptcy court notice to determine what your next steps should be. It may be too late.

ADDITIONAL RESOURCES

For Readers' General Guidance:

The Road Out of Debt: Bankruptcy and Other Solutions to Your Financial Problems by J. N. Feeney and Theodore Connolly

Treatises for Legal Professionals and Students:

Collier on Bankruptcy (LexisNexis)
Norton Bankruptcy Law and Practice (Westlaw)

ACKNOWLEDGMENTS

Almost a decade ago, I first visited Benabbio, a small village at the top of a mountain near Florence, Italy. In the distance, I could see the white-tipped Carrara Mountains. It was marble, not snow, that shone in the sun. It was the marble used by Michelangelo in his statues.

Benabbio has always been a magical place, having hosted pilgrims in the Middle Ages on their way to Rome. It has a castle that includes a Romanesque church dating back to AD 1218. Part of the Villa San Rocco was built in the late Middle Ages, with layer after layer added over the centuries. The chapel across the road from the villa has served as a place of prayer for fourteenth-century pilgrims and as a meeting place for present-day artists.

In modern times, Benabbio has become an inspiration for artists. In 2016, I was staying at the Villa San Rocco to write a short story and create platinum-palladium photographic prints. I had brought some of my writings to discuss with my writing coach. But instead of working on one of those pieces, I created a new work overnight. During that week, I wrote the first chapters of my memoir. Even after I left the village, the memories of that magical time remained with me and helped me craft what is now this book. A heartfelt thank-you to Carol Panaro-Smith and James Hajicek, who had the brilliant idea of creating the Benabbio workshop and who have become good friends as we live the artful life, and to Mary Kay Zeeb, who served as my first writing coach and an invaluable critic over many years.

I also took several writing courses at the Loft Literary Center in Minneapolis, Minnesota, and wish to thank Kate St. Vincent Vogl for her ongoing support. As a result of one of the authors' meetings at the center, I was able to connect with Leigh Stein, author of the current national bestseller *If You're Seeing This, It's Meant for You*, who became my editor and coach. Thank you, Leigh, for all your help over the years.

I wish to thank Lauren Taylor Shute and Brooke Suermann at Intrepid Literary for their able assistance in helping me publish this book and Lauren Embling, who served as one of my editors.

I also wish to thank my mother (who has now passed on) and sister, who listened patiently to my story; other members of my family who encouraged me over the years; my supportive friends in the BBCE, one of my book clubs; my friends at the Arizona Bankruptcy American Inn of Court for their encouragement; and my friends at Soroptimist International of Phoenix for their support. Although not associated with the writing of this book, I also wish to thank members of my chamber's staff who were of invaluable assistance to me as a judge for almost twenty-eight years prior to my retirement.

BIBLIOGRAPHY BY CHAPTER

PART ONE

Chapter One

Allis, Samuel. "Broadway's Fallen 'Angel.'" *The Washington Post*, May 3, 1979. https://www.washingtonpost.com/archive/lifestyle/1979/05/04/broadways-fallen-angel/1b0508d7-26dc-4dc8-9b41-11adeef0d7d7/.

Graeber, David. *Debt: The First 5,000 Years, Updated and Expanded*. New York: Melville House, 2014.

"Z. Albert Joseph; Began Concept of Shoe Salons." *Chicago Tribune*, March 26, 1987. https://www.chicagotribune.com/1987/03/26/z-albert-joseph-began-concept-ofshoe-salons/.

PART TWO

Chapter Four

"The Common Law and Civil Law Traditions." UC Berkeley Law, 2017. https://www.law.berkeley.edu/wp-content/uploads/2017/11/CommonLawCivilLawTraditions.pdf

Duda, Jeremy. "A Massive 2011 Dust Storm Popularized the Word 'Haboob' in Arizona." Axios Phoenix, September 22, 2023. https://www.axios.com/local/phoenix/2023/09/22/dust-storm-haboob-arizona.

Chapter Five

"Stern v. Marshall." Casetext, archived September 18, 2024, at https://web.archive.org/web/20240918132726/https://casetext.com/case/stern-v-marshall-3#p2609.

"Wellness Int'l Network, Ltd. v. Sharif." Casetext, archived December 26, 2024, at https://web.archive.org/web/20241226152707/https://casetext.com/case/wellness-intl-network-ltd-v-sharif-1.

Chapter Seven

Abcarian, Robin. "Charles Keating Scandal Proves Supreme Court Is Dead Wrong on Money." *Los Angeles Times*, April 2, 2014. https://latimes.com/local/abcarian/la-me-ra-charles-keating-scandal-supreme-court-20140402-story.html.

"Five Senators Involved in the Keating Affair." Pima County Public Library, April 25, 2022. https://library.pima.gov/content/five-senators-involved-in-the-keating-affair/.

Furlong, Tom. "Arizona Hotel Exemplifies Lincoln S&L's Extravagance." *Los Angeles Times*, December 28, 1989. https://www.latimes.com/archives/la-xpm-1989-12-28-fi-1513-story.html.

Hardle, Alexandra. "Goodyear's Master-Planned Community of Estrella Is Still Growing. Here's What's Coming." *AZ Central*, November 5, 2023. https://www.azcentral.com/story/news/local/southwest-valley/2023/11/05/goodyear-estrella-community-development/71256743007/.

"The History of the Phoenician." The Phoenician. https://www.thephoenician.com/history/.

Kammer, Jerry. "Keating Profile: Still Riding to the Sound of the Guns." *AZ Central*, April 2, 2014. https://www.azcentral.com/story/news/politics/2014/04/02/charles-keating-profile-archive-still-riding-sound-guns/7213525/.

Purdy, Elizabeth R. "Charles H. Keating." *Encyclopedia Britannica*, November 30, 2025. https://www.britannica.com/biography/Charles-Keating.

Robinson, Kenneth. "Depository Institutions Deregulation and Monetary Control Act of 1980." Federal Reserve History, November 22, 2013. https://www.federalreservehistory.org/essays/monetary-control-act-of-1980.

Robinson, Kenneth. "Savings and Loan Crisis." Federal Reserve History, November 22, 2013. https://www.federalreservehistory.org/essays/savings-and-loan-crisis.

Chapter Eight

"A History of Asbestos and the Manville Trust Fund." *The Washington Post*, November 19, 1990. https://www.washingtonpost.com/archive/business/

1990/11/20/a-history-of-asbestos-and-the-manville-trust-fund/fb60ed34-2a94-4570-9648-9e2efb8167f0/.

"AG Sunday Announces National Settlement with Purdue Pharma and Sackler Family Will Bring Up to $212M to PA. for Substance Abuse Treatment and Recovery Resources." Pennsylvania Office of Attorney General, January 23, 2025. https://www.attorneygeneral.gov/taking-action/ag-sunday-announces-national-settlement-with-purdue-pharma-and-sackler-family-will-bring-up-to-212m-to-pa-for-substance-abuse-treatment-and-recovery-resources/.

Harrington v. Purdue Pharma L. P. No. 23–124. U.S. (2024).

Mann, Brian, and A. Martinez. "Purdue Pharma and Sackler Family Members to Pay $7.4B in National Opioid Settlement." NPR, January 24, 2025. https://www.npr.org/2025/01/24/nx-s1-5272769/purdue-pharma-and-sackler-family-members-to-pay-7-4b-in-national-opioid-settlement.

National Bankruptcy Review Commission. "Treatment of Mass Future Claims in Bankruptcy" In "Bankruptcy: The Next Twenty Years." October 20, 1997. https://govinfo.library.unt.edu/nbrc/report/09bmass.pdf.

Chapter Nine

Bauer, Jon. "Buying Witness Silence: Evidence-Suppressing Settlements and Lawyers' Ethics." *Oregon Law Review* 87, no. 2 (2008): 481–574. https://scholarsbank.uoregon.edu/server/api/core/bitstreams/a24ee9d1-580a-48a4-8cb9-72a48a2bd93a/content.

Chapter Ten

Seely, Taylor. "What's Sun Valley Parkway, the 'Road to Nowhere'? Valley 101 Found Out." The Arizona Republic, September 21, 2020. https://www.azcentral.com/story/news/local/arizona/2020/09/21/whats-story-behind-sun-valley-parkway-road-nowhere/3481272001/.

Chapter Eleven

Curley, Sarah Sharer. "Most Recent Bankruptcy Inventiveness Hurting Local Communities." Substack.com, June 5, 2023. https://sarahsharercurley.substack.com/p/most-recent-bankruptcy-inventiveness.

LoPucki, Lynn M. "Courting Failure." *UF Law Faculty Publications* (2006): 325–41. https://scholarship.law.ufl.edu/cgi/viewcontent.cgi?article=2109&context=facultypub.

Chapter Twelve

Atkins, Scott, and Hannah Alysha. "Enhancements Proposed to Singapore's Corporate Restructuring and Insolvency Regime." Norton Rose Fulbright, 2025. https://www.nortonrosefulbright.com/en-us/knowledge/publications/6c59b7ec/03-enhancements-proposed-to-singapore.

Curley, Sarah Sharer. "Beware--The Money Owed to You May Be Settled in Asia." Substack.com, December 12, 2024. https://sarahsharercurley.substack.com/p/beware-the-money-owed-to-you-may.

Nair, Suresh, Piere Dzakpasu, Bryan Tan, and Noel Chua. "Singapore's Insolvency Law in 2023: Navigating New Frontiers from the SICC to Cryptocurrency." Global Restructuring Review, January 17, 2024. https://globalrestructuringreview.com/review/asia-pacific-restructuring-review-archived/2024/article/singapores-insolvency-law-in-2023-navigating-new-frontiers-the-sicc-cryptocurrency.

United Nations Commission on International Trade Law. "Insolvency." United Nations. https://uncitral.un.org/en/texts/insolvency.

Yang, Kiki. "Hong Kong to Legislate on Inward Re-Domiciliation Regime for Foreign Companies." Citco, November 7, 2024. https://www.citco.com/insights/hong-kong-to-legislate-on-inward-re-domiciliation-regime-for-foreign-companies.

PART THREE

Chapter Fourteen

"A History of America's Credit Cards." The Bottom Line. *Square*, March 11, 2019. https://squareup.com/us/en/the-bottom-line/managing-your-finances/a-history-of-americas-credit-cards.

Albanesi, Stefania, Jaromir Nosal, Zachary Bleemer, and Matthew Ploenzke. "Insolvency after the 2005 Bankruptcy Reform." Liberty Street Economics. *Federal Reserve Bank of New York*, February 23, 2015. https://libertystreeteconomics.newyorkfed.org/2015/02/insolvency-after-the-2005-bankruptcy-reform/.

Curley, Sarah Sharer. "The Chequered History of the Credit Card Industry." Substack.com, February 14, 2024. https://sarahsharercurley.substack.com/p/the-chequered-history-of-the-credit.

Hernandez, Joe. "The Trump Administration Has Stopped Work at the CFPB. Here's What the Agency Does." NPR, February 10, 2025. https://www.npr.org/2025/02/10/nx-s1-5292123/the-trump-administration-has-stopped-work-at-the-cfpb-heres-what-the-agency-does.

Lee, Jinjoo. "Credit Cards Could Swipe Department Stores' Profits." *The Wall Street Journal*, February 7, 2024. https://www.wsj.com/finance/regulation/credit-cards-could-swipe-department-stores-profits-bfccb82f.

"New Regulation Proposed by Biden Administration Would Limit Overdraft Fees at Big Banks to as Low as $3." PBS NewsHour. *PBS.org*, January 17, 2024. https://www.pbs.org/newshour/economy/new-regulation-proposed-by-biden-adminstration-would-limit-overdraft-fees-at-big-banks-to-as-low-as-3.

Stein, Robin. "The Ascendancy of the Credit Card Industry." Frontline. *PBS.org*, November 23, 2004. https://www.pbs.org/wgbh/pages/frontline/shows/credit/more/rise.html.

Chapter Fifteen

Konish, Lorie. "This Is the Real Reason Most Americans File for Bankruptcy." *CNBC.com*, February 11, 2019. https://www.cnbc.com/2019/02/11/this-is-the-real-reason-most-americans-file-for-bankruptcy.html.

Chapter Sixteen

"A Look at the Shocking Student Loan Debt Statistics for 2022." Student Loan Hero, archived December 31, 2022, at https://web.archive.org/web/20221231202241/https://www.studentloanhero.com/student-loan-debt-statistics/.

"An Examination of State Efforts to Oversee the $1.5 Trillion Student Loan Servicing Market." Congress.gov, June 11, 2019. https://www.congress.gov/event/116th-congress/house-event/109631.

Al-Muslim, Aisha. "Upending Bankruptcy 'Myths,' Judge Erases $220,000 Student Loan Debt." *The Wall Street Journal*, January 8, 2020. https://www.wsj.com/articles/upending-bankruptcy-myths-judge-erases-220-000-student-loan-debt-11578523767?reflink=desktopwebshare_permalink.

Cook, Nancy, Jarrell Dillard, and Josh Wingrove. "Biden Drags His Feet on Student Loan Plan as Allies Urge Bold Action." *Bloomberg*, May 12, 2022. https://www.bloomberg.com/news/articles/2022-05-12/biden-drags-feet-on-student-debt-plan-as-allies-urge-bold-action.

Curley, Sarah Sharer. "Don't Cancel Student Loans. Let Bankruptcy Law Forgive Them." *Newsweek*, June 21, 2022. https://www.newsweek.com/dont-cancel-student-loans-let-bankruptcy-law-forgive-them-opinion-1717664.

Grieve, Pete, and Kaitlin Mulhere. "Trump Administration Halts Student Debt Collections for Social Security Recipients." *Money*, June 3, 2025. https://money.com/student-loan-debt-social-security-garnishment/.

Higham, Aliss. "Student Loan Repayments Changed by Trump's Big Beautiful Bill: What to Know." *Newsweek*, July 2, 2025. https://www.newsweek.com/student-loan-repayments-trump-big-beautiful-bill-2093676.

Jiménez, Dalié, and Jonathan D. Glater. "Student Debt Is a Civil Rights Issue: The Case for Debt Relief and Higher Education Reform." *Harvard Civil Rights - Civil Liberties Law Review* 55, no. 1 (2020): 131–98. https://journals.law.harvard.edu/crcl/wp-content/uploads/sites/80/2020/09/Jimenez-Glater.pdf.

Minsky, Adam S. "Unprecedented Student Loan Overhaul in 'Big Beautiful Bill' Passes House, Heads to Trump." *Forbes*, July 3, 2025. https://forbes.com/sites/adamminsky/2025/07/03/unprecedented-student-loan-over haul-in-big-beautiful-bill-passes-house-heads-to-trump.

Scott-Clayton, Judith, and Jing Li. "Black-White Disparity in Student Loan Debt More than Triples after Graduation." Brookings, October 20, 2016. https://www.brookings.edu/articles/black-white-disparity-in-student-loan-debt-more-than-triples-after-graduation/.

"Total Household Debt Increases in Q1 2022, Driven by Mortgage and Auto Balances." Federal Reserve Bank of New York, May 10, 2022. https://www.newyorkfed.org/newsevents/news/research/2022/20220510.

"U.S. Department of Education to Begin Federal Student Loan Collections, Other Actions to Help Borrowers Get Back into Repayment." U. S. Department of Education, April 21, 2025. https://www.ed.gov/about/news/press-release/us-department-of-education-begin-federal-student-loan-collections-other-actions-help-borrowers-get-back-repayment.

Williams, Sean. "A New Social Security Garnishment Is Set to Begin This Summer -- But There Are 2 Legal Ways Most Retirees Can Avoid It." Yahoo! Finance. *Yahoo.com,* June 8, 2025. https://finance.yahoo.com/news/social-security-garnishment-set-begin-074400008.html.

Chapter Eighteen

Clark, Alicia. "Phoenix Neighbors, Camelback Mountain Castle Owner Battle over Property's Condition." AZ Central, April 10, 2016. https://www.azcentral.com/story/news/local/phoenix/2016/04/10/phoenix-neighbors-camelback-mountain-castle-owner-battle-over-propertys-condition/80018102/.

Lowe, Sam. "A Castle Isn't Always a Castle." Arcadia News, November 1, 2021. https://www.arcadianews.com/local_news_and_features/the_lowe_road/a-castle-isn-t-always-a-casthttps://azmemory.azlibrary.gov/nodes/view/144686le/article_3b30185e-3aa5-11ec-95c9-4f9a2aa78068.html.

TOH Clips. "Bob Vila Tours Copenhaver Castle 1987." YouTube. November 12, 2020. https://www.youtube.com/watch?v=VIHyOeJNWuA.

Chapter Nineteen

"Arizona Economic Trends 1992-12." *Arizona Economic Trends* 16, no. 12 (1992). https://azmemory.azlibrary.gov/nodes/view/144686.

"Glendale Garcia's Restaurant Sells for $3.4M." Daily Independent, January 24, 2022. https://www.yourvalley.net/stories/glendale-garcias-restaurant-sells-for-34m,282269.

PART FOUR

Chapter Twenty-Two

Boston, Claire. "DOGE Layoffs Are Starting to Leave Their Mark on D.C.'s Housing Market." Yahoo! Finance. *Yahoo.com,* June 28, 2025. https://finance.yahoo.com/news/doge-layoffs-are-starting-to-leave-their-mark-on-dcs-housing-market-090043990.html.

Curley, Sarah Sharer. "Where Are All the Employees?" Substack.com, February 19, 2023. https://sarahsharercurley.substack.com/p/where-are-all-the-employees.

Drenon, Brandon. "US Government Seeks to Rehire Recently Fired Nuclear Workers." *BBC News*, February 18, 2025. https://www.bbc.com/news/articles/c4g3nrx1dq5o.

Fowler, Stephen, and Shannon Bond. "What Has DOGE Done in Trump's First 100 Days?" NPR, April 28, 2025. https://www.npr.org/2025/04/28/nx-s1-5377445/doge-musk-trump-100-days.

Helmore, Edward. "Trump Administration Backtracks on Firing Nuclear Arsenal Workers." *The Guardian*, February 15, 2025. https://www.theguardian.com/us-news/2025/feb/15/trump-administration-nuclear-arsenal-worker-firings.

"How Much Has the U.S. Government Spent This Year?" Fiscal Data. *U.S. Treasury.gov*. https://fiscaldata.treasury.gov/americas-finance-guide/federal-spending/.

Chapter Twenty-Three

Barber, C. Ryan, and Camila DeChalus. "Alzheimer's Disease, Retirement 'Pacts,' and Serving Until You're 104 Years Old: Inside the Federal Judiciary's Reckoning with Age." *Business Insider*, September 27, 2022. https://www.businessinsider.com/gerontocracy-federal-judges-red-white-and-gray-courts-supreme-2022-8.

Blazina, Carrie, and Drew DeSilver. "House Gets Younger, Senate Gets Older: A Look at the Age and Generation of Lawmakers in the 118th Congress." Pew Research Center, January 30, 2023. https://www.pewresearch.org/short-reads/2023/01/30/house-gets-younger-senate-gets-older-a-look-at-the-age-and-generation-of-lawmakers-in-the-118th-congress/.

Curley, Sarah Sharer. "Is There a More Compassionate Way to Deal with Judicial Disability?" Substack.com, May 19, 2023. https://sarahsharercurley.substack.com/p/is-there-a-more-compassionate-way.

"Judge Biographies." U.S. Court of Appeals for the Federal Circuit, June 12, 2025. https://www.cafc.uscourts.gov/home/the-court/judges/judge-biographies/.

Shatzman, Aliza. "A 95-Year-Old Federal Judge Is Suing to Avoid Taking a Cognitive Test." Slate, May 19, 2023. https://slate.com/news-and-politics/2023/05/judge-pauline-newman-sues-cognitive-test.html.

Weiss, Debra Cassens. "Federal Circuit Judge, 95, Flunked Security Training, Displayed Hacking Paranoia, Exam Order Alleges." ABA Journal, May 18, 2023. https://www.abajournal.com/news/article/federal-circuit-judge-95-needs-competency-exam-after-reports-of-confusion-and-agitation-order-says.

Chapter Twenty-Four

"Code of Conduct for United States Judges." United States Courts, March 12, 2019. https://www.uscourts.gov/judges-judgeships/code-conduct-united-states-judges.

Curley, Sarah Sharer. "Judging Judges' Conduct." Substack.com, December 30, 2022. https://sarahsharercurley.substack.com/p/judging-judges-conduct.

Curley, Sarah Sharer. "Texas Bankruptcy Judge's Conduct Called into Question." Substack.com, October 22, 2023. https://sarahsharercurley.substack.com/p/texas-bankruptcy-judges-conduct-called.

Gladstone, Alexander, Andrew Scurria, and Akiko Matsuda. "Top Bankruptcy Judge's Exit Shakes Houston Hub He Built." *The Wall Street Journal*, October 19, 2023. https://www.wsj.com/articles/houston-judges-sudden-exit-threatens-bankruptcy-hub-he-built-33026f80.

Nani, James. "Bankruptcy Watchdog Probes Jackson Walker Fees after Judge Exit." *Bloomberg Law*, October 27, 2023. https://news.bloomberglaw.com/bankruptcy-law/bankruptcy-watchdog-probes-jackson-walker-fees-after-judge-exit.

Nani, James. "Ex-Bankruptcy Judge Got Combative in Secret Romance Questioning." *Bloomberg Law*, January 8, 2025. https://news.bloomberglaw.com/bankruptcy-law/ex-bankruptcy-judge-got-combative-in-secret-romance-questioning.

Nani, James, and Ronnie Greene. "Bankruptcy Judge Tasked with Scandal Cleanup of 'Adopted Son.'" *Bloomberg Law*, May 31, 2024. https://news.bloomberglaw.com/bankruptcy-law/bankruptcy-judge-tasked-with-scandal-cleanup-of-adopted-son.

Chapter Twenty-Five

Curley, Sarah Sharer. "Will Alternative Dispute Resolution Replace Court

Trials?" Substack.com, January 22, 2023. https://sarahsharercurley.substack.com/p/will-alternative-dispute-resolution.

Chapter Twenty-Six

Curley, Sarah Sharer. "Should Cameras Be Permitted in Federal Courts?" Substack.com, February 4, 2023. https://sarahsharercurley.substack.com/p/should-cameras-be-permitted-in-federal.

Chapter Twenty-Seven

Curley, Sarah Sharer. "The Allure of Online Legal Documents." Substack.com, August 21, 2023. https://sarahsharercurley.substack.com/p/the-allure-of-online-legal-documents.

Chapter Twenty-Eight

Abovyan, Kristina. "Where Are They Now? Updates on People in 'Maui's Deadly Firestorm.'" Frontline. *PBS.org*, January 8, 2025. https://www.pbs.org/wgbh/frontline/article/updates-lahaina-wildfire-documentary/.

Curley, Sarah Sharer. "Living in a Hot, Dry, Fiery World." Substack.com, February 17, 2025. https://sarahsharercurley.substack.com/p/living-in-a-hot-dry-fiery-world.

Roth, Sammy. "Meet the New PG&E. It Looks a Lot Like the Old PG&E." *Los Angeles Times*, June 18, 2020. https://www.latimes.com/environment/story/2020-06-17/pge-bankruptcy-new-pge-looks-like-old-pge.

Westervelt, Eric, and Matthew S. Schwartz. "California Power Provider PG&E Files for Bankruptcy in Wake of Fire Lawsuits." NPR, January 29, 2019. https://www.npr.org/2019/01/29/689591066/california-power-provider-pg-e-files-for-bankruptcy-in-wake-of-fire-lawsuits.

Chapter Twenty-Nine

"FAQs." National Register of Historic Places. *National Park Service*, September 5, 2024. https://www.nps.gov/subjects/nationalregister/faqs.htm.

"National Register of Historic Places." Arizona State Parks & Trails. https://azstateparks.com/national-register-of-historic-places.

Chapter Thirty-One

Jacoby, Melissa B. *Unjust Debts: How Our Bankruptcy System Makes America More Unequal.* New York: The New Press, 2024.

PART FIVE

Chapter Thirty-Two

Curley, Sarah Sharer. "Should Hanging Paragraphs Ever Be Included in Statutes?" Substack.com, December 18, 2024. https://sarahsharercurley.substack.com/p/should-hanging-paragraphs-ever-be.

Harrington v. Purdue Pharma L. P. No. 23–124. U.S. (2024).

Hayes, M. Jonathan. "Congress, It's about Time to Get Rid of That Stupid Means Test." Daily Journal, April 30, 2020. https://www.dailyjournal.com/articles/357461.

Johnson, Creola. "The Modern Family Debacle: Bankruptcy Judges Decide That Some Debtors' Loved Ones Do Not Count as Household Members!" California Law Review, August 2023. https://www.californialawreview.org/print/the-modern-family-debacle.

Thomas, Sidney R., and Consuelo M. Callahan. In re: Saldana v. Bronitsky. (9th Cir. 2024).

ABOUT THE AUTHOR

Photo by Everardo Keeme, Photo Fusion Studio

Sarah Sharer Curley served nearly three decades as a U.S. bankruptcy judge in Arizona, becoming the first woman appointed to the court and its first female chief judge. A nationally recognized expert, she later taught bankruptcy law at Arizona State University and received the American Inns of Court's Bankruptcy Distinguished Service Award in 2023. Her career has focused on expanding access to justice for those without representation. She lives in Scottsdale, Arizona.

www.ingramcontent.com/pod-product-compliance
Lightning Source LLC
Chambersburg PA
CBHW031338230926
51848CB00002B/288
9781972992050